81 chev.

3/4 ton.

THE SODBUSTERS

THE
RED
RIVER
CARTS

From Original presented to City of Winnipeg 1947

Courtesy of O'Keefe's Brewing Co., Limited

The Sodbusters

by

GRANT MacEWAN

THOMAS NELSON & SONS LIMITED
EDINBURGH TORONTO NEW YORK

Printed and Bound in Canada by
Press of The Hunter-Rose Co. Limited
Toronto, Ont.

To my 90-year-old pal,

Charlie Sampson of Saskatoon,

who for as many years

has been spreading

cheer and good will,

this effort is respectfully dedicated.

Books by the Same Author

The Feeding of Farm Animals

The Breeds of Farm Livestock in Canada

The Science and Practice of Canadian
Animal Husbandry
In collaboration with A. H. Ewen

Preface

Piecing together these stories about pioneers in Western Agriculture, some of which were included in Canadian Broadcasting Corporation programmes, has been fun and it has been profitable. It is always fun to know interesting and entertaining people and it can be intensely profitable, particularly for agrarian folk, to study the experiences, the mistakes and triumphs, of those who went before and planted the first seeds.

The pioneers were not uniform like MacIntosh Red apples packed in an Okanagan box. Rather, like the bronchos in a range band, they were outwardly very different, yet with many inconspicuous qualities in common. The frontier attracted men with imagination; fearless men; men with a longing in their souls for adventure. And certainly only those with initiative and a bit of bulldog determination remained through those testing years. Thus there was a common denominator.

The pioneers were practical; they had to be. There wasn't much time for romancing when a prairie fire was bearing down upon the homestead or when a horse was dying from swamp fever. But when the fire was out and the horse was either better or buried, a man's imagination might very well go to work. Certainly anyone studying the lives of Western Canada's first farmers will conclude that there was no lack of humour, no lack of sentiment, and mischief was not wholly absent.

In addition to the benefit of their experiences, in an experimental period, those heroes of the great adventure left traditions of priceless worth. They would never admit defeat; they took pride in "getting things done", and best of all, they left traditions of good will. Example is a good teacher, and the nation-builders of today may benefit.

Western Canada's Agriculture has inherited a personality, rich and attractive. Obviously there were hardships and suffering in pioneer years but there were colour and excitment and fun too. We may have better farmers when we pause to recognize and enjoy the personality of our agricultural industry which, indeed, is the essence of the personalities of the men who made it.

Grant MacEwan

Contents

Captain John Palliser, Sodbuster No. 1 13
Adam MacKenzie, The First Bonanza Farmer . . . 20
Angus MacKay, The Scientific Sodbuster 27
Pat Burns, Sodbuster and Cattle King 34
George Lane, Foothills Sodbuster 41
Joe Greaves, Inter-Mountain Sodbuster 47
Rutherford, The Farm Teacher 53
The Unknown Sodbuster 60
McGregor of Glencarnock 66
Fred Kanouse, The Trader 73
Sir John of the "76" 79
Samuel Larcombe, Manitoba Wheat King 85
Alex Galbraith, The Horseman 91
John Ware, Alberta's Black Sodbuster 97
Okanagan Ellis 103
A Barr Colonist Sodbuster 108
The First Homesteader 115
Norman Lee, Chilcotin Pioneer 121
Another Unknown 127
My Friend Ole 134
Pioneer at the Prairie Gateway 140
Clement Cornwall, Ashcroft Pioneer 146
"Twelve Foot" Davis 153
Motherwell, Statesman in Overalls 159
Sheridan Lawrence, Emperor of the Peace 166
Seager Wheeler, Searcher for Seeds 173
Sinton of Regina. 179
"Dreadnought Joe" Wylie 185
Old Doc Shadd. 190
Cross of the "a7" 196
Walter Lynch of Westbourne 202
Charlie Rear, Horseman Extraordinary 208
Frank Collicutt, The One and Only 215
Kootenai Brown 221
The Man Murray 226
The Horticulturist of Dropmore 232
Manitoba Cattle Barron 237

Illustrations

The Red River Carts . . . . *Frontispiece*
Angus MacKay 29
Pat Burns 40
Dean Rutherford 55
J. D. McGregor 72
Sam Larcombe 87
Alexander Galbraith 92
Barr Colonists 112-113
John Sanderson 120
The Big Outfit, Brandon 1899 128
Mr. Friend "Ole" 138
Archibald Wright 145
The "Twelve Foot" Davis Stone 158
Mr. Motherwell 161
The One and Only Frank Collicutt 218
Kootenai Brown 225

Captain John Palliser

Sodbuster No. 1

I choose Captain John Palliser as Sodbuster No. 1. I believe he deserves that honour in spite of the fact that he never lived on a homestead. I'm sure he never drove oxen and I doubt if he could even milk a cow. But I like to think of him as the great agricultural explorer, and as most people know, his report about the farming possibilities of this country is almost classical.

We must go back in our thoughts to the middle of last century. Farming was established at Red River but westward over a vast country reaching to the Rockies, "fur was king". About the farming possibilities in that area, there was nothing but ignorance, and a little fear. Some folk had expected that the Hudson's Bay Company, overlord of the land, would investigate farming. But that great organization was concerned with furs and trading and had an indifferent interest in agriculture and colonization. But in Canada and also in the mother country, questions were being asked about farming and settlement "out there" in the limitless hinterland. Opinions were as contradictory as those about the effect of eating fresh buns and at least it became clearly necessary to make a systematic study.

The Imperial Government appointed Captain John Palliser to examine that portion of the British North-West lying south of the North Saskatchewan River and between the Red River and the Rocky Mountains. He was to observe the physical features of the country, the forest resources, coal and other minerals, the quality of the soil and the suitability of the area for farming. Full instructions came from Downing Street in London; and with them came caution about the hidden dangers in Indian country and the need for economy. That was in 1857. That was less than 100 years ago; it was 32 years before my father came west. Let's pause to consider that so recently this west country which is today a food reservoir of world importance, was a vast buffalo pasture, little known to any except traders. Imagine the extent of national development in that part of a century. But that is another story.

There is no more important link in the chain of agricultural adventure in the new land than this man Palliser and his investigations. His party was well qualified, packed with scientists of various varieties, astronomers, geographers, geologists, engineers, as well as untrained men. In an unscientific moment he classified his men as, gentlemen, Scotch half-breeds, French half-breeds, Americans, Canadians and one coloured man called Dan Williams. Where they found black Dan, isn't clear.

After a long journey by Lake Superior, the party arrived at Fort Garry on the 11th of July. The next day was the Sabbath and according to the journal, Palliser and his men rode four miles to attend Church. Before leaving Fort Garry, final arrangements had to be made. More men were hired because of the hazards attached to an expedition along the South Saskatchewan where the gathering of white scalps was a popular hobby with the Indians. Well, the equipment was finally loaded on two small American wagons and five Red River Carts, and the little cavalcade set out.

At Fort Ellice, close to the confluence of Assiniboine and Qu'Appelle, the travellers encountered a suggestion of farming; there was a patch of ground growing potatoes. And a few cattle owned by the Hudson's Bay Company, were thriving on the fine native pasture. It was recorded that the soil was well suited to wheat and barley as well as vegetables.

Sunday, September 13th, found our trailblazers at Fort Qu'Appelle. They conferred with Mr. Pratt, a full blood Cree from Red River who was serving as Church of England missionary. He too had been successful in growing wheat and corn near the fort, but only in garden-sized patches.

Palliser, apparently, could hold his own in either a fight or a horse deal. It seems that he had a flair for that ancient pastime of horse trading. Before he left Fort Qu'Appelle, he got a "very fine mare" from Mr. Pratt, in exchange for what he describes as "two wretched horses, one of which is not likely to live long". Horse trading may become chronic, incurable like leprosy, and four days later Palliser was again trading horses. This time it was with a band of Cree Indians between Moose Jaw Creek and the Elbow. But he doesn't say what advantage he gained in this deal; the Indians may have had more cunning than the minister.

The explorers were now in the heart of the buffalo country. Some idea of the herds is given in an entry in the journal which reads,

> "the whole region as far as the eye could reach was covered with buffalo, in bands varying from hundreds to thousands."

And by the way, there must have been grasshoppers as well as pronounced drought that season because Palliser says,

> "the grass in this arid soil . . . . was now actually swept away by the buffalo who assisted by the locusts, had left the country as bare as if it had been overrun by fire."

The records give some idea of other game animals on the prairies at that time. Somewhere not far from the Elbow, they saw a grizzly bear and for September 30, there is this record,

> "During the last three days, ... enjoyed excellent shooting . . . . elk, black tail deer, common deer and antelope."

The events of that day must have taken place a short distance south-west of where Saskatoon now stands.

Here is a tall tale about shooting, under date of October 1st,

> "Our Indian ran buffalo also that morning, killed a good cow but complained of having lost his ramrod, went back some distance to look for it. At length he abandoned his search and returned to cut up his animal, in the body of which he subsequently found the remains of his ramrod. He called to Mr. McKay and said, 'I have been looking for my ramrod and see where it was all the time'. He had loaded (his muzzle loader) with the ramrod and forgotten to withdraw it before firing."

At the Elbow of the Saskatchewan River, our party tasted the thrill of discovery. Attention was arrested by a tributary flowing in from the East and investigation showed it to connect with the chain of Qu'Appelle lakes. Here they supposed was a water communication between the South Saskatchewan and Red River. Others who came later had similar hopes of a water route across the prairies but it never gave sufficient promise to invite development.

The Captain was for penetrating south-westerly from the Elbow but his men had a wholesome and fashionable fear of Blackfeet Indians and the party did not go far in that direction. Instead, they turned their course toward Fort Carlton on the North Saskatchewan, where they were to winter. As they approached Fort Carlton on October 6th, some of the men donned good clothes in preparation for their entry to the post which they were sure was only a short distance away. But Palliser's instruments told quite a different tale, another 30 or 40 miles; but the native helpers only laughed, that anyone who had never been there would dare to venture determined opinions. "How can you know, when you have never been there?", they questioned, all the while contending that another hour of travel would bring them in. Next morning they were still sure they could be at the fort for breakfast. They discovered their mistake however, discovered it on an empty stomach, and formed a new appreciation for Palliser's sextant.

Palliser saw his party located in winter quarters and then struck off for Montreal. The first lap of the journey was by horseback and he was at Fort Garry 21 days after leaving Carlton. Not bad time, I would say. Going south from Fort Garry, his horse was killed and he was obliged to walk 450 miles before reaching the stage coach.

The party that remained at Carlton reconnoitred in various directions. Dr. Hector was at Fort Edmonton in January. There he found 150 people living within the fort but not much interested in farming, although 30 acres had been cultivated. A few potatoes were rationed but buffalo meat continued to be the main item of diet as is shown by the fact that the daily allowance for adults was six pounds. Yes, six pounds which works out to 2190 pounds per year.

Palliser was back at Fort Carlton on June 4th, following. During that second season, the expedition was working between the north and south Saskatchewan Rivers, mainly in that area marked now by the Province of Alberta. Sorties were made into the foothills and mountains, partly for purposes of finding a pass that would be suitable for horses and carts.

Then, in the next winter, they made headquarters at Fort Edmonton and in the spring of the third season the party moved southward into the Bow River country and eastward to Cypress Hills. The Hills in which there is a delightful summer resort today, must have been a pleasant surprise. Palliser wrote,

> "These hills are a perfect oasis in the desert we have travelled . . . . We are now well supplied with wood, water and grass, a rare combination of happy circumstances in . . . . this season's explorations."

West of the hills in our short grass ranching area, the country was said to be desolate and without grass and water. More evidence that Palliser was here in one of the very dry periods certainly not restricted to recent years.

Late in the season, the party was split and one group under the leadership of the Captain went over the mountains to Vancouver. From there Palliser sailed for England, thankful I am sure that he still had his scalp. It was there that much of his report was prepared and in the conclusions which he reached, we must find much of interest.

He had made many contacts with the Indians and considered their accommodation as an essential prerequisite to settlement. He was one of the first to suggest reservations where the Indians would indulge in agriculture. It may be that he had more faith in the conversion of the Indians to agriculturists than the experiences of intervening years would warrant. Indian schools, rigid liquor laws and the establishment of a mounted police force were other conditions which he considered vital to agricultural development. And he was convinced that the Hudson's Bay Company could never provide government that would be satisfactory in an agricultural country.

No matter what may be said to the contrary, Palliser did envision a great agriculture in this land but he was a conservative soul and cautious. He recognized the variations in soil and climate and the need for special treatment. Unfortunately, many others who came failed to recognize these and settlers paid a big toll. About the northern part, or park belt, he was particularly hopeful and optimistic. It was his "Fertile Belt." In the prairie section, where he observed short grass and lack of wood and water, he was pessimistic about cropping. He wrote,

> "Whenever we struck out on the broad prairie, we generally found the soil worthless, except here and there . . . ."

But what is sometimes overlooked, Palliser had no previous experience with prairie land and must have been guilty of underrating it.

The "Palliser Triangle" about which we hear a good deal every time we enter a drought period, enclosed the prairie region which Palliser thought might be unsuited to cropping. The base of the triangle was along the International Boundary and the sides extended to a point not far south and west of Lloydminster. Indeed the area so defined has coincided remarkably closely with the drought areas of some recent years.

Anyway, he visualized settlement on a growing scale, first on the fertile soil around Lakes Manitoba and Winnipeg and then along the Assiniboine, westward along the Saskatchewan and finally onto the prairies. Of grain growing on the whole, this was his estimate;

> "The capabilities of this country and its climate for the success of the cereals have hardly been sufficiently tested. But I have seen first rate specimens of barley and oats grown at many of the forts. Wheat has not been so successful . . . ."

And as for live stock, he foresaw large herds of cattle and sheep grazing on the prairie grass in spite of his complaints about its mean growth. His statement shows that he recognized the fine nutritional value of that grass. Here it is;

> "The richness of the natural pasture in many places on the prairies . . . . can hardly be exaggerated. Its value does not consist in its being rank or great in quantity, but from its fine quality, comprising nutritious species . . . . which remain throughout the winter sound, juicy and fit for the nourishment of stock."

In another part is the statement that,

> "the only objection to raising sheep and pigs would

> arise from the number of their natural enemies, the wolves."

Then in conclusion, he says,

> "This large belt of country embraces districts, some of which are valuable for the purposes of agriculturists, while others will for ever be comparatively useless."

Palliser made mistakes but in many respects, time has shown the wisdom of his judgments. I don't know of any early explorer whose guesses were quite so good. Indeed he offered advice which if studied would have saved time and money, and I choose to classify him as one of the foremost of our agricultural trail-blazers; I would name him Sodbuster No. 1.

Adam MacKenzie

The First Bonanza Farmer

Show me a boy who hasn't heard tales about Paul Bunyan and his "Big Blue Ox". The big ox, according to the yarns told me, was "42 pick-handles and a plug of tobacco" from horn to horn. Well, Minnesota had its Paul Bunyan but Manitoba had Adam MacKenzie. There was one very notable difference however; volumes have been written about the mythical Minnesota woodsman while the realistic Scotch-Canadian almost escaped the records. You may search a modern library without finding reference to this exciting pioneer, first among Canada's bonanza farmers.

Many of the Manitoba pioneers living today knew him or knew something of his exploits. In the Manitoba community in which I was reared, the name of Adam Mackenzie was a household term. It was a name linked with big undertakings, agricultural achievement and powerful determination. Indeed, Adam MacKenzie must have been the hero of countless farm boys who listened, as I did, to tales about his success.

The MacKenzies have been trail-blazers in distant parts of empire and it is not surprising that members of the illustrious clan were in the agricultural vanguard on these prairies. Adam's father, Kenneth MacKenzie, was a product of Inverness-shire, Scotland, from whence have come many good things. As a young man he migrated to Canada and was at Puslinch, Ontario for a time; but the Ontario community did not afford him the elbow room he wanted and in 1868, the year after confederation, two years before the province of Manitoba was created and more than ten years before there was a railroad west of the Great Lakes, this MacKenzie turned his face toward Fort Garry. He arrived late in the spring. And among the belongings which he unloaded from the river-boat on the Red River, was a Shorthorn bull; they called it Baron Solway and it was the first pure bred representative of the breed in the West.

From Fort Garry, the elder MacKenzie trekked westward

along the Assiniboine to the "Prairie Portage" and then another ten miles to claim land at Rat Creek, now Burnside. There was no survey but using a pocket compass, Kenneth MacKenzie laid out an 1800 acre farm and ploughed a furrow around it to establish his claim. This MacKenzie was a leader of men; the first school west of Portage la Prairie was erected in his district; he started an agricultural society, a co-operative mill, and dozens of progressive institutions. He represented his constituency in the Manitoba Legislature for several terms. And on Burn's Night, Kenny Mackenzie was right there in his tartan trousers and Glengarry.

Kenneth and Adam MacKenzie must constitute the most fascinating father-son combination in our agricultural history. When Adam came West to join his father in 1871, he brought more cattle with him and drove them from St. Paul in Minnesota. A fair sized job for a lad of 23 who did not know the country. But he knew it later. After three years at Burnside, Adam got married and the young couple set out to make their own way; they spent the first night of their honeymoon under their democrat. They went to Arden and there young MacKenzie set in motion the biggest farming enterprise that Manitoba had known. I have heard it said that in going to Arden, Adam MacKenzie outran a government courier who was dispatched to Minnedosa for the purpose of abolishing certain applications of scrip and that Adam's large holdings on the White Mud River were obtained by trading shot-guns with half-breeds. Then a furrow ploughed around the land would rivet the claim.

Down on the flats, he had 800 acres of hay land and he could put up enough hay to winter 200 cattle and horses, enough to supply settlers or travellers who wanted to buy. For some years, the business of making and selling hay was a sideline. Robert Gordon, who operated a livery barn at Arden for a time, made hay on that MacKenzie land on a share basis. He told me of MacKenzie, on one occasion, sending a green team of bronchos to the hay-meadow and going along to see them started. He insisted upon hitching them to a mower directly and he did it without mishap. But he was no sooner on the mower seat than the terror stricken broncs were away. The mower was in gear; Bob said, "it sounded like a freight train on a bad track" and one could see nothing but flying hay. But Adam stayed with the outfit and after he had cut a swath around a quarter section, he handed the reins to his man and said "the horses are broken". He fancied wild horses,—said they were tougher.

Another time, Bob Gordon arranged to buy hay from MacKenzie. "Alright," said Adam, "but take it away clean so there'll be no waste." Gordon often made supper late at night for MacKenzie and sometimes he would make him a bed at the Livery Stable. Anyway, Gordon got about 20 tons of hay and asked how much his debt was. "To be sure, how much did you get?" asked MacKenzie, and the answer was "about 20 loads". Of course he hated waste but he had a great sense of justice and generosity and his response on this occasion was, "you've been a good body to me and you don't owe me anything". And so the matter stood.

At one time MacKenzie's nearest neighbour to the west was Archie MacDonald at Fort Ellis, 156 miles away. Adam, as a matter of fact did not fancy having neighbours too close. He continued to buy land as opportunity arose and with each new purchase, he said it was "to stop some meanish neighbour from coming too near". At tax sales, he was always present and usually buying. At one such sale, he was buying as usual and after the title for one of the quarters he bought was examined, lo and behold, he had bought one of his own properties. He had forgotten that he owned it.

It was the practice in some municipalities, in those days, for land owners to be permitted one day of road-work for every quarter section in order to help defray taxes. Somebody estimated that at one time, Adam MacKenzie had nearly enough land to warrant keeping a man at roadwork steadily the year around.

He was well established when the settlers began to flock into the country and he sold them horses, oxen, cows, pigs, cured meat, seed grain, hay and a multitude of other commodities. Similarly, he would undertake to do any job that offered fair reward; there was no stream that he could not ford or swim with his ponies and buckboard and there was no freight that he would not contract to haul. When he was at Arden, he took 25 carts of flour to Edmonton, nearly 800 miles.

Of course flour at that distant point was worth $25.00 per 100 pounds, which explained a lot.

It must have taken tremendous amounts of equipment to maintain the MacKenzie operations. Pete Mitchell, a blacksmith, had just arrived in the district and had never seen Adam MacKenzie, but his slumbers were disturbed before the hour of four one morning, by a huge and powerful man, who wanted some work done. "My wee bit body, what would you charge to make me a few clevises?" The yawning smithy wanted to know how many and the answer was "not over fifty". The number startled this newcomer and he enquired for a reason. "To be sure," said the MacKenzie, "the damn coyotes have chewed or eaten all we had." It seems that he had previously used raw-hide clevises and the coyotes chewed any that had been left in the fields.

They said there was harness on the farm to hitch an artillery unit. But there was lack of order in the way the harness was apportioned. The last man to the barn in the morning took the harness that was left for him, often not much. Wire figured prominently in harness repairs. And incidentally, it was by the use of barbed wire that an Englishman working on the farm, cured a balky mule, all very much to Adam's satisfaction.

Jenny had a habit of watching the load being built behind her and when it exceeded a certain size she refused to draw. The Englishman was trying to haul sheaves and was properly exasperated by the mule's antics. He fastened a barbed wire to the neck-yoke and passed it back between the mule's hind legs. When the mule balked the Englishman gave the wire a pull and the load came in from the field at a speed that astonished everybody. Adam MacKenzie asked, "What happened to the Jenny Mule?" and when he learned the secret he laughed and said, "Boy, that's a good idea; I'd like to try it on some of my men".

In 1881, Adam MacKenzie, without reducing his holdings at Arden went to the Carberry Plains and bought about five sections. This proved to be wonderful land for wheat, except when August frosts resulted in a product that had to be sold at 25 cents a bushel. When wheat was being hauled out in the late fall or early winter, 30 or 40 of MacKenzie's wagons might be seen together on the road. Sometimes the return trip to the farm would shape into a race; all the teamsters would take to the fields or open prairies, and from the noise and dust, settlers knew that MacKenzie's men were on their way home. The master was not one to object to such conduct because after all, the boys were saving time. Let no one suppose, however, that the MacKenzie horses were not wild. Wild horses held no terror for the boss and he often bought the kind that nobody else would take a chance on. Dan Hamilton of Neepawa handled a lot of bronchos and knew that he could always find a home for the "bad ones" over at MacKenzie's, if the price were right.

Frozen wheat or no, the MacKenzie enterprises continued to turn to profit and although he talked poverty continuously, there was always money in his big purse. The purse he carried for many years was given to him by his father; it was a leather shot-bag of a type used with a muzzle-loading gun. Nobody ever saw directly into that bag because when it was opened Adam would turn his back upon his company. One of the tragedies of his life occurred when he went to the Winnipeg Exhibition for the purpose of buying a threshing machine one year and was robbed of bag and several hundred dollars. But he seemed to have more regret about the loss of his "wee bit baggie" than of the contents. He did buy a separator on that Winnipeg trip, bought one that had a good deal of plate glass in it so that one could observe the internal operations.

When larger sums of money were to be transported to or from the bank, perhaps prior to pay day on the farm, the purse would be replaced by a grain sack. When Adam MacKenzie drove his team into the livery barn at Carberry on one occasion and hung a bag tied with binder twine on the harness-hook, the stable hand, supposed that the bag contained a couple of gallons of oats for the horses and proceeded to untie it and empty its contents into the oat boxes. But he was quickly checked by MacKenzie's words, "Halt you fool, it's no oats, just a wee pouckle of money". Seems it was banking day and Adam brought some accumulated savings to town.

Adam MacKenzie was a big man, 6 feet 2 inches and built in proportion. He was not given to bragging; in fact he was a man of few words but there was one respect in which he claimed absolute superiority. "There is not in all of Manitoba," said he, "a bigger pair of feet than my own." When he placed them end to end, no spectator was likely to dispute the claim. He was not only big; he was powerful. And there were those who had the unpleasant experience of being caught by the lobe of one ear and lifted clear off the ground, by him. And nobody about the MacKenzie farms did as much work or kept such long hours as the master. During a busy season, the team which hauled his democrat was harnessed continuously. Sometimes he had a boy to drive him, in which case MacKenzie would sleep during the trips from one farm to another and the boy could take a sleep at the end of the road.

On the home farm, he was the first to arise in the morning and he would then awaken the head horseman or stableman by ringing a cowbell that hung by the man's bedroom door. During one of his many absences, the MacKenzie home was favoured by a visit from the minister and because "distances were great" in those years, Mrs. MacKenzie prevailed upon the reverend gentleman to remain for the night. She gave him the horseman's room and the horseman agreed to sleep in the hay. MacKenzie was driving all night and arrived home unannounced at 4:00 a.m. He decided he might as well call the stableman. He rang the cowbell but there was no response; impatiently, he entered the still-dark room and turning the occupant face down in the bed, he proceeded to chastize him with the palm of his powerful hand. Naturally, such a violent spanking in an appropriate region should be adequate and MacKenzie went immediately to the barn. But there, to his surprise and embarrassment he found the stableman feeding the horses. When the hired hand had explained that he had been up for some time and that the minister had occupied his bed, Adam MacKenzie reharnessed his team and announced that he was not stopping for breakfast. Several days elapsed before the minister could sit or walk normally and it was just as long before MacKenzie returned home.

Thousands of pigs were grown on the MacKenzie farms. Pat Burns bought some of the first pigs that were shipped from Western Canada to the East, from Adam MacKenzie. Those were the pigs which Burns shipped experimentally over the C.P.R. with the understanding that he would be entitled to a rebate on freight if the venture was unprofitable; he never asked for the rebate but kept on shipping pigs.

It was about 1908 that Adam MacKenzie disposed of a lot of his land and moved to Victoria with the idea of making his home there. But he grew restless and moved to Cuba to embark upon more large undertakings, plantations and live stock. His dynamic spirit would not accept retirement and at one time his Cuban herds comprised 3000 head of stock. Eventually, however, he returned to Manitoba, the province he loved and the province he did so much to develop. His colourful and immensely constructive life came to an end in 1926. He was one of the pioneers to whom the untried was a challenge. He was one whom the rising generations should not forget.

Angus MacKay

The Scientific Sodbuster

When Grant MacEwan writes about Angus MacKay, at least the members of the Caledonia Society should be expected to give attention. But however much I am attracted by the Scottish name of Angus MacKay, there are other and better reasons for including him with the heroes of our farm history. He was the most distinguished "trial and error" man of the pioneer years; he was the number one teacher so far as better farming methods were concerned. And in extending the prairie wheat fields westward toward the Rockies and northward into the higher rows of townships, his influence was unsurpassed.

The district of Pickering in Ontario, where he was born and reared, couldn't hold him. He had inherited the restless, Highland spirit of a Caithness-shire father. New country, untried and unsurveyed, away beyond Fort Garry, was inviting hardy and brave men. Young MacKay would go West. In '82 he and three kindred spirits from that Ontario Community decided upon a four-man company, to farm cooperatively. Incidently, it was one of the early farm co-ops that worked. A car of settlers effects was loaded and billed to Winnipeg. But there were big floods in Minnesota and Manitoba that spring and freights were held up. Four weeks it took, for the car to reach Winnipeg. Already the season for seeding was well advanced and the bridge across the Assiniboine at Brandon was out. So in spite of intentions to push farther west that spring, MacKay advised that they rent a farm near the booming metropolis of Winnipeg for the year and go west after seeding.

They found a piece of high land which was for rent. Much of the valley land was still under flood water. When the newcomers went to visit a neighbour called Lumsden, presumably to ring in on a decent meal, prepared by feminine hands, they rowed their boat right into the house at the front door and disembarked on the stairway; the Lumsdens were living upstairs.

After they had seeded 20 acres of Red Fife wheat and 80 acres of oats, they were ready to push westward in search of a permanent location. Folk said there was good land in Assiniboia, for homesteaders who didn't mind going far back and beyond the rim of civilization. MacKay was for Assiniboia. The C.P.R. extended a little way west from Brandon and it was at the westward end of the steel that MacKay and his friends took to the trail with their horse and ox-drawn outfits. How far they would go and exactly where, they did not know; but they were determined to have good land and to go until they found it. The outfit had two teams of oxen, those sullen brutes which did the spade work in a lot of homestead districts and encouraged the pioneers in the use of bad language. MacKay became a driver of oxen and set out over the winding trail at about 10 miles a day.

They got stuck in the mud and got out again; they lost the trail and found it; they ran out of meat and shot rabbits; they met people who said they were crazy; but they pushed on. They were nearing Fort Qu'Appelle. Evidently there were hitch-hikers in those days too, because it is recorded that MacKay picked up a stranger, an engineer, and gave him a ride on the ox-drawn wagon. The engineer could not have been in much of a hurry or perhaps he was a judge of good company. Anyway, in recognition of MacKay's kindness, the engineer tipped him off about some "awfully good" land and MacKay headed his oxen toward it and his friends followed.

It was good land. But it was a dry country. The survey was not complete but the township corners, six miles apart, were marked and Angus MacKay and his companions secured farm sites, 2000 acres altogether, for which they paid $2.00 an acre.

Just a short distance away, in the same district, was the famous Bell Farm, started at the same time as MacKay's enterprise. Before the Ontario men reached their destination, that spring of '82, they were overtaken by a large outfit of men, teams and equipment. They supposed it was a railroad gang but it was discovered later that it was Bell's outfit. Major Bell's company had secured 60,000 acres in one block, except for one or two small parcels in the centre, occupied by ornery squatters. The government had given Bell the homestead sections and the other land was bought from the C.P.R. Anyway, when MacKay arrived at his destination, Bell's teams were breaking on the very section which later became the Dominion Experimental Farm at Indian Head. It was probably the first breaking west of the Manitoba boundary. Bell did things the big way; he even made his mistakes the big way. As many as 45 binders were sometimes sent to operate in a single field. And some of the furrows on the Bell land were so long that teamsters made only one round in a day; they would have their noon-day meal at the far end of the furrow and be back near home at night.

MacKay broke 30 acres in his first season in Assiniboia. The sod was tough; but so was MacKay. And he was stubborn too, as are all good Scots. The first crop, harvested in '83 was fair. He broke 300 more acres and the second crop, a bumper one, was frozen. There was no sale for frozen wheat; but during the summer a grist mill had been built on the Bell Farm and MacKay decided to try selling his frozen wheat as flour. A car-load of flour was sent to Winnipeg but it failed to sell; it was sent to Toronto with the same result and finally, at Montreal, it sold to yield a net loss of $8.00 to MacKay.

Many of the settlers were discouraged. Some said the effort was in vain; the country was too dry and the frosts came too early. Should MacKay give up? He didn't; he broke more land. And in the spring of '85 his plans were for a big seeding.

ANGUS MACKAY

The Scientific Sodbuster

The spring opened early and seeding operations were going fine when bang, hostile half-breeds up the way of Duck Lake became terribly careless about where they were shooting and before the settlers realized the dangers, rebellion had broken out. A little army is rushed from the East and men and wagons and teams along the C.P.R. are recruited to freight equipment and supplies to the scene of battle. The need is great. Major Bell sent 100 men and 100 teams to the north and got $10.00 a day for each team and driver. More profitable than producing frozen wheat, of course it was. MacKay had seen active service back in the East at the time of the Fenian Raids, but this time he sends his teams and men and is left with a fraction of his crew, not nearly enough horses to complete spring operations on time.

About half the cultivated land was left unseeded. MacKay concluded, however, that if he could not seed all his land early enough to give the crop a fair chance of escaping fall frosts, he would at least keep the weeds from growing, and a large area was left fallow.

Well, the Rebellion was smothered in the middle of May and the men and teams returned to farm. It was too late to seed but not too late to cultivate and kill weeds, and cultivate they did. The crop seeded in that year was good but in the next year, 1886, it was a different story. It was a hot summer and dry; hot winds wilted the thirsty vegetation and most crops were not harvested. But lo a miracle; MacKay's land, fallow the year before, yielded 35 bushels to the acre. The lesson was plain; in dry country one cannot count on getting a crop every year from the same land but allowing the land to be idle or fallow for a season, gives it a reserve of moisture. In very truth, MacKay's was an experimental farm, even in those days. And settlers came for miles to see the good crop and the drought-beaten, side by side. That was the begining of the prairie practice of "summer-fallowing".

It was the very same year that the Canadian Government delegated to William Saunders, the big job of studying the Experimental Stations in the United States and organizing the Dominion Experimental Farms. He reported in April, 1886, and in less than two months an act was passed giving authority to establish five experimental farms. The Ottawa or

Central Farm was first and then Saunders went west. He travelled by train, by wagon and by democrat over the southern belt of the prairies. By good fortune he met up with Angus MacKay and learned about the summer-fallow experiment. The result was that Indian Head was the choice for one of the farms. By this time, 1887, the Pickering men had decided to dissolve their partnership and Angus MacKay was appointed superintendent of the proposed experimental farm. He was called to Ottawa to assist with organization; and then he and Saunders began a search for a site. Their final choice was a section of the Bell Farm which they could buy at $12.50 an acre. In '88 the Experimental Farm was in operation. Trees were planted; buildings were erected; most important of all, grains and potatoes and roots and small fruits were put to the test.

As the years went by and settlement was continuing, good and promising crops continued to fall victims to early autumn frosts. MacKay lost no opportunity to remind Ottawa of the need for earlier varieties of wheat. Red Fife was the "wheat" in those years. Certainly it was better than wheats which had preceded it in Manitoba but it wasn't good enough. It was the wheat that had its origin down east, near Peterboro, where lived that Scottish settler, David Fife. Fife sent home to Scotland for seed wheat but he got no better than the kinds he saw about him. He tried again; he wrote to a friend who was a grain clerk at Glasgow; and as the story goes, the friend took a handful of wheat from a cargo just in from Poland and hid it in the lining of his cap. From this sample, one seed produced superior heads, five of them. Then Fife's hungry and fence-breaking oxen reduced the number of good heads to three; and from these, Red Fife originated and spread over the spring wheat belts of Canada and United States.

But it wasn't good enough for MacKay and it wasn't good enough for the new west. William Saunders and his two sons had been playing about with plants; they seemed to have a complex for cross-breeding. At Agassiz in British Columbia, a cross had been made between a Red Fife dad and a Hard Red Calcutta mother and from the resulting lines, one head selected in 1903 was to be the progenitor of Marquis, the new variety which was to sweep across the West like a prairie fire. Evidently, the first sample of the new wheat sent to William Saunders got lost in the Ottawa offices. But it was found and in 1906, all the Marquis wheat in the world amounted to 40 pounds. Of this amount, 23 pounds were sent to MacKay; Indian Head was to be the proving ground and MacKay, the judge. Ottawa recognized that if MacKay placed his O.K. on it, it must be good. Nineteen hundred and seven was a tough year; there was a late spring; and then an early autumn frost provided the "knock-out" blow for all but the quick-maturing sorts. It was a case of "survival of the fittest" and Marquis was clearly the fittest. It was a Saunders-MacKay victory and in 1909, the distribution of Marquis was started. Nearly everybody knows the result.

And speaking of "knock-out" blows, MacKay told about a Mounted Policeman who went down for the count of ten, right on his barn floor. When he came to the country Angus MacKay and his friends brought a small thresher and a "horse-power" to drive it. He also brought a flail, one of those terrible hand implements used by pioneer Ontario farmers to thresh the grain. The flail, in the hands of one who wasn't too cautious, had a habit of "back firing". Well, when MacKay was using it at his Indian Head farm on one occasion, there happened along a Mounted Policeman who posed as an expert with flail. The smart visitor was granted permission to show his skill but it was a brief demonstration because the short end of the flail hit the policeman on the side of the head and the victim went down. It was a self-inflicted knock-out.

A tale perhaps never placed in the records was told about a particular variety of grain that was being developed at Indian Head; it was a variety that gave great promise and filled Angus MacKay with hope. All the seed in Christendom, about 30 pounds, was in a bag in the storehouse. It disappeared. MacKay was worried. He suspected theft; probably somebody about the farm had visions of multiplying it and making a handsome profit. MacKay was not so much interested in punishment on account of the loathsome deed, but he did want his seed back. He made it clear that the store house in which the seeds were kept would be left unlocked and unguarded on a certain night, and if the man who had the seed would return half of it, during the hours of darkness, there would be no investigation. The next morning all of the seed was back in its place and the work and study of years were not lost. He had a way of gaining his purpose.

In 1910 he was appointed inspector of the western Experimental Farms, a nice tribute to his good judgment and clear vision. And then when he retired, he chose to remain right at Indian Head where he became known as the "Grand Old Man of Indian Head". I can see him yet, tall, erect, square-jawed and stern. He displayed the dignity of his calling, the dignity of agriculture. Yes, rising generations should remember Angus MacKay as the advocate of better farming in a pioneer land.

Pat Burns

Sodbuster and Cattle King

I can't recall many Canadians who managed to pack so much action and achievement into the space of half a century as Pat Burns. I've called him "Cattle King", but actually I think of a lot of appellations which would be equally fitting. He was just plain "Pat Burns the homesteader" when my father came to Manitoba and his land was only about 30 miles north of where the MacEwans settled. Then he was "Burns the cattle trader", "Burns the meat contractor" and "Burns the rancher". And after a span of years, he was "Burns the millionaire" and "Burns the Senator". But always he was "Burns the Business Man" and "Burns with the Big Heart".

When he was 22 years of age he announced to the members of his family, farming folk at Kirkfield in Ontario, that he was going west to take advantage of the free homesteads. In that conservative Ontario community, it had all the ear-marks of a reckless decision; because the West was still associated with ferocious Indians and whiskey traders weighted down with cocked guns. But young Burns was going west and before the day of departure his elder brother, John, decided to go too.

The Winnipeg which the Burns boys saw when they arrived one spring day in 1878, was a bustling little city of 7000 people. It was still without a direct rail connection with the East although the rails reached Winnipeg from St. Paul that year. But to the west, canoe and bull-team constituted the established means of travel.

Most land seekers flocking into Winnipeg were being attracted to Souris Plain and Grand Valley just at that time but Burns had a hunch that by going farther back, there would be more good land from which to choose. The boys struck off on foot. And it wasn't even good walking because it was early spring and the trails were wet. But they possessed the buoyant energy of youth and walked 35 miles the first day. When they bedded down to spend that cool May night, they had nothing over them but the starry skies. Five days after leaving Winnipeg, the foot-sore lads relaxed at Grand Valley, two miles east of the present city of Brandon. It was whispered that there was good land at Tanner's Crossing. Tanner's Crossing, by the way, became Minnedosa and for that point the Burns boys set out. When they reached it they had walked 160 miles. They found homesteads that suited them but they were now penniless; and instead of remaining to develop their farms, they walked back to Winnipeg to get jobs. They weren't fussy about the kind of work and quickly found employment blasting rock on the new C.P.R. grade away east of Winnipeg. The job paid $25 a month and board; and after a few months young Pat figured he had saved enough to buy a yoke of oxen and a plough and wagon, for the homestead.

A few years ago, I drove north from Brandon on the road over which Pat Burns often hauled hay. And then I stood on the quarter section which he homesteaded, right beside the village of Clanwilliam, north of Minnedosa. It was there that he built a log cabin; it was there he upset the first sods and there that he started his live stock activities. The first years were exceedingly difficult and the young Irishman worked hard.

Oh, to be sure, he took time out for a little social digression. He attended the occasional dance but somebody in that district said he was a "rotten dancer". But he was a perfectly natural young man, and liked the girls, especially the pretty ones. I talked with one charming old lady who remembers that Burns in those days could be "an awful tease". She and Pat, as young folk, sometimes met in the Sewell and Proven butcher shop in Minnedosa and Pat would threaten to kiss her. She would make a hasty retreat by door or window and be pursued playfully by the young Irishman with the black mustache. She never told how often she was overtaken but she did confess to me that if she had known he was going to be a millionaire, she wouldn't have been so hard to catch.

Burns the homesteader, had no capital to speak of, and his trading in cattle was along modest lines at first. One of his first purchases was a single cow which he got from Walter Lynch, a pioneer stockman who lived over at Westbourne.

On that cow he made a profit of four dollars and in later years he said they were the biggest dollars he ever made and still had them. The next time he went to visit Lynch, he bought two cows.

The settlers needed breeding stock and it was never very difficult to find a home in the district for a good cow or promising heifer. Pat Burns acquired a two-year-old heifer in one of his deals and had her only a few days when a homesteader wanted her and bought her. The new owner led his prize home and tied her in the log stable to await the day when she would freshen and supply the family with milk. The good women of the neighbourhood assembled there to knit, or pass judgment upon the affairs of the community, and took the opportunity to inspect the new cow. The comment was complimentary until one lady observed a total lack of teeth on the forward part of the upper jaw, and the conclusion was drawn forthwith that this was no heifer, but rather an aged cow, already in decline; and that the man who sold her for a heifer must be a rogue indeed. Burns' reputation was dangerously at stake, at least until he could prove to the female satisfaction that the upper incisors were not part of a cow's natural equipment.

Mr. Harry Mullins, later Senator Mullins, knew the Burns family at Kirkfield, and bought sheep from Michael Burns, Pat's father. When Harry Mullins and Pat Burns chanced to meet on a lonely country trail between Rapid City and Minnedosa, there was a pleasant reunion. Burns was driving a team of oxen and leading a small red steer. Mullins was almost as much interested in the steer as was its owner, and conversation shifted to values. Burns said the steer would net him $30. Mullins was not quite so optimistic and could see just $29 in it. There was $1 of difference between the two appraisals. It is doubtful if the West has had two better judges of cattle values than the pair which met on the prairie trail and which in years later sat together in the Canadian Senate.

In a reminiscent mood, a few years ago, Senator Mullins mentioned that he sold Pat Burns the 5000 head of cattle on the Waldrond Ranch in shorter order than they took to settle the value of the little red steer when they met on the trail that day more than 50 years ago.

Keith MacDonald was a son of Auld Scotia. He had been reared on haggis and whiskey and he farmed down toward Westbourne. When MacDonald and Burns traded in cattle, it was as though the honour of Scotland and Ireland was in the balance. In the course of one lengthy struggle over a 3-year-old steer, there was more than the usual argument about the bullock's weight. The deal was finally concluded with a side-bet; if the steer when delivered to Burns, exceeded 1300 pounds, Ireland would buy Scotland a new hat and if the weight was less, MacDonald would buy the hat for Burns. The steer was delivered and paid for at 3 cents a pound, but it weighed only 1270 pounds. In due course MacDonald bought a hat and delivered it to the Irish drover; but it did not fit satisfactorily. Burns protested that the hat was too small and the Scot replied, "So was the price for my steer".

Having attained some success and profit in cattle, Burns thought he would try pigs. Pigs, however, could not be driven overland like cattle. He bought a car load of pigs and billed them to Toronto, but he had an understanding with the railroad company that the undertaking must be considered an experiment. And in the event of a loss, he would recover part of the freight costs. Three weeks later, Burns visted the freight office, not to collect a refund but to ship more pigs. His was the first shipment of Western pigs to the Toronto market.

One business activity led to another and pretty soon Burns was doing freighting and custom work over a large area. He bought more oxen and took a contract to break land for Sir Clifford Sifton's father, just south of Brandon. And then the "meat contracts". Mackenzie and Mann, railroad builders, took their first contract in the State of Maine and when they needed someone to keep the hungry workers in meat, William Mackenzie remembered his friend of Kirkfield school days and Pat Burns got the contract. The undertaking proved profitable and when it was completed he got the call to furnish beef for the crews building the Qu'Appelle, Long Lake and Saskatchewan Railroad, which was to link Regina, Saskatoon and Prince Albert.

The chubby and good natured young Irishman who bought

cattle here and there, became well known to the settlers. They liked him. He had a big camp at Boggy Creek, north of Regina and he bought a lot of cattle around Dundurn. I know he bought 35 cattle from George Wilson of Dundurn; on account of rapidly expanding business, Burns had difficulty in paying Wilson at once. Wilson did not press for settlement and two months elapsed before payment was completed. Burns appreciated Wilson's help and when Christmas came, Wilson received an unusual Christmas present, certainly one that would create quite a stir if it were found at my fireplace on Christmas morning; it was a pure bred Shorthorn bull, "with best wishes from Pat Burns".

The Calgary-Edmonton Railway was next and again Pat Burns was keeping the workers in beef. It marked the beginning of a long and mutual admiration between Pat Burns and his adopted province of Alberta. He grew to love Alberta and Alberta was good to him. There he laid the foundations for a multiplicity of enterprises, farming, ranching, mining, retailing and meat packing.

It was when Burns was working on the Calgary-Edmonton meat contract that Mr. Dan Riley, now Senator Riley of High River, first met him. Mr. Riley was operating a livery stable, a hotel and a ferry at High River. Burns drove in late one night. At best he kept terrible hours. But this time he enquired if an old man riding a good horse had stopped there. Riley answered "yes" and added that he bought the horse and gave the old man a bed for the night. "Well", said Burns, "it's my horse; the old man stole it." A lantern was lighted and the two future senators strolled to the barn to inspect the horse and decide its ownership. Sure enough, it was Burns' horse; it had Burns' brand as plain as day. The culprit, "Old John" they called him, had been working on a meat job. But liquor was his weakness and when he failed to get more money for drink, he made off with a Burns horse and sold it to Mr. Riley for $70.

What was to be done? Old John was awakened and questioned. He admitted everything. He had spent $5 but the balance of the $70 was turned back to Mr. Riley and Burns made up the shortage. It was not in Burns' thoughts to turn Old John over to the police; instead, and it was typical of the man, he said, "John, you're coming back with me and going to work". The scene closed with Burns and John seated side by side in Burns' democrat, driving back to the meat camp and leading the stolen horse.

Burns experienced every stage in the development of the meat industry. He was producer, processor and retailer. Industrial growth from the building of a lowly slaughtering and processing plant in East Calgary in 1890, to the operation of an abattoir business with interests extending around the world, is a story by itself. It is a story that marked Burns as a man of tremendous business capacity.

But for my part, I am more interested in his ranching activities than his meat processing. I believe that ranching was his first love; he delighted to be associated with ranchers. His extensive ranch interests and huge herds won for him a place along side of George Lane, A. E. Cross and Archie MacLean, as the "Big Four" in Canadian ranchland. It was the "Big Four" who sponsored and backed the first Calgary Stampede; that was in 1912 and the Calgary Stampede has become a national institution. Any worthy organization could count on the whole hearted support of those big ranchers.

And while speaking of Alberta's "Big Four", I recall that one of them may well have saved the life of another. Burns and George Lane had a meat contract on the Blood Reserve. Burns drove from Macleod to see how his partner was getting along dressing beef on the reserve. When he arrived at the corral where they were slaughtering, Burns noticed that Lane was having trouble with the last steer. This big fellow, with long horns, had become infuriated and had broken away taking Lane's lariat with him. There was an Indian on a pony, watching the competition between man and steer and Burns said to him, "you hold my team and lend me your pony while I help with that steer". Burns was a good rider; he seemed to be built for a saddle, but there was trouble ahead this time. According to his own telling, he was closing in on the longhorn when the animal looked up at the newcomer wearing a hard hat and said to himself "this is my victim". The steer charged and with the best of aim because he completely upset the horse and rider. He lost no time in getting organized for the next charge but Burns was on his feet and heading for the corral fence. But he was leading a losing race when George Lane saw the seriousness of it all and drew his "six-shooter" and dropped the steer. It was Senator Riley's comment that Burns' record for 100 yards dash on the Blood Reserve, still stands.

It will always be one of my regrets that I missed his 75th birthday party in the Palliser Hotel in Calgary in 1931, and a piece of the two-ton birthday cake that was later cut into about 15,000 pieces. The 700 people who congregated on that occasion represented agriculture, industry, church, and state; it was there that Mr. Burns' appointment to the Canadian Senate was announced. It was one of the finest tributes that could be paid to "a grand pioneer, a true Canadian gentleman, a philanthropist and a prince of good fellows".

PAT BURNS—*Sodbuster and Cattle King*

George Lane

Foothills Sodbuster

He was a lean and rather awkward looking cowboy; and not very handsome. If he had dropped off an incoming freight in 1936, looking as he did most commonly in those early years, the authorities would merely have said, "another 'bo' in town". But he was no "bo"; he was George Lane, cowboy extraordinary; he was a friend of the Prince of Wales and owner of the biggest Percheron ranch in the world. He was one of the "Big Four" in Canadian Ranchland.

The story begins with the North West Cattle Company, later known as the "Bar U". Honourable H. M. Cochrane was the first Canadian bold enough to conduct the ranching experiment on a big scale on the western range; he was the first Canadian who dared to trail 3000 cattle from Montana and turn them loose just west of Calgary; that was 1881. But the North West Cattle Company which had been organized by the Allens of the Allen Steamship Company, was next and drove 3000 Montana cattle to range along the Highwood River.

Now, when the mighty Cochrane herd was breaking trail northward to its new Canadian range, among interested spectators was the young Montana cowboy, George Lane. Born in Iowa, (in 1856), he had come to the Montana range at the age of 16, expressly to ride horses and drive cattle. He was filled with curiosity about the grass farther north and ventured as far as Fort Kipp to spy out the land and see what British cow-country was like. His chance to "get the feel" of the Canadian range came in '84 when the North West Cattle Company placed an order with the Sun River Stock Association in Montana for the best cattleman procurable. George Lane was the answer to that order and he was hired as foreman at the munificent salary of $35.00 per month.

It was the period of extraordinary expansion in ranching. Men with money had visions of becoming ranchers and boys without money longed to be cowboys. It was the period of open range and big round-ups. There was no phase of early ranch life more exciting than the round-up, when the annual inventory was taken. June was the month and all the ranchers took part in a genuinely co-operative way. It meant hard riding and long hours but it was fun. The biggest round-up in the history of the Canadian range was conducted the year after George Lane's arrival; 100 cowboys took part; there were 16 chuck wagons in service and 500 saddle horses. Jim Dunlop directed the combing process up Pincher Creek that year and George Lane was captain of the operations in the Willow Creek country. Over 60,000 cattle were gathered and sorted and started off in the direction of their respective home ranges. George Lane's success as a round-up captain, his agility and resourcefulness, made him the best known man in all the Canadian Kingdom of Cattle. He could sleep anywhere and could eat anything that came from a chuck wagon; wild duck eggs in any of several stages of incubation were quite all right with him. And there wasn't a horse in all that country that could wear him out or shake him off. "Nigger John Ware", one of the top riders of all time, and George Lane were with the North West Cattle Company at the same time; and between them they must have made it awfully discouraging for any horses who thought themselves smart at bucking.

But this Lane was a business man as well as a cowboy. He soon had his own cattle and horses and after seven years with the Bar U ranch, he resigned to ranch for himself on the Little Bow River. "Birds of a feather" soon find each other you know, and Lane and Pat Burns were running cattle together and furnishing beef as a buffalo-meat substitute for the Indians on the Blood Reserve, for whom the buffalo came no more. Then Lane bought the Flying E Ranch in the Porcupine Hills (in 1893).

Just after the close of the century, Lane entered into a partnership with Gordon, Ironside and Fares, meat packers and cattle exporters in Winnipeg and Moose Jaw, and bought the "Bar U" ranch for roughly a quarter of a million dollars. It included 1000 horses and 5000 cattle then on the ranch; and in the years which followed as many as 25,000 cattle were carried for short periods.

Like other ranchers, George Lane had his ups and downs.

The severe winter of 1906-07 dealt a knock-out blow to a lot of cattlemen between the Red Deer River and the State of Texas, and Alberta operators did not escape. It was reported that on the "Bar U" about half of the 24,000 cattle counted the previous fall, did not survive to see the spring. Indeed a 50% cattle loss was estimated in much of the ranch country.

To students of agriculture, the name of George Lane suggests Percherons. He imported his first Percheron horses from Montana in 1888, drove 30 mares and two stallions overland. His enthusiasm for horses mounted. He increased his breeding stock; made more importations from the States. Was he afraid of what the bicycle and steam tractor would do to horses? Not Lane; he bred more Percherons. He was determined to have the best blood; brought 72 mares and three stallions from the home of his favourite breed in France in 1909. The average cost of those horses in France was said to be $1,000.00 and he had transportation costs on top of that. But the "Bar U" was gaining world wide recognition for its Percherons and in 1918, the tables were reversed and the Lane ranch made the first recorded shipment of Percherons from North America to Europe; 26 mares and one stallion were sent to England. Those Alberta Percherons must have been well received in England because a bigger shipment went over a short time later to give the Percheron a foothold in the land of Shires and Clydesdales. Prior to Mr. Lane's death in 1925, there were 700 pure bred horses on the ranch, the biggest stud of pedigreed Percherons in the world; and indeed, one of the best.

If anybody were to question the extent of the operations of the quiet cowboy who came to Alberta at $35.00 a month, I would just say that in 1920, he and his associates held 50,000 acres of deeded land, 9000 cattle, 500 pure bred horses and about 1000 other horses; they were paying $14,000 a year in taxes and $50,000 in wages. That really represents big business whether a man were manufacturing horse power or horse medicine.

Yes, the Prince of Wales was among his particular friends. When the Prince was about to tour Canada in 1920, he was anxious to see all shades of Canadian life and industry. He specifically asked to see a Western ranch. The "Bar U" was chosen and George Lane was to be host to His Royal Highness. Entertaining royalty wasn't just in Lane's line; he was confident that he could make a better showing in a steer decorating contest; but he was game. Likewise, it was a new experience for the Prince but he fell completely in love with the foothills and with his new friend, the rancher. It had been feared, and naturally enough, that the rancher and the Royal visitor would find little in common, and that they might become bored with each other. But they found each other fascinatingly novel and they discovered one "common denominator", horses. On that subject they could talk as "man to man". George Lane was never very conventional; ranchers generally are not; and in addressing his guest he was inclined to dispense with formalities such as the long salutation, "Your Royal Highness". He would just call him "Prince".

Of course ranching folk are generous and nothing is too good for a visitor. The Prince of Wales remained for several days and before leaving he expressed his love for that ranch setting, a combination of hills, good grass, running water and mountain scenery. Somehow it reminded him of the Scottish country around Balmoral Castle. George Lane had a hunch; his hunches were usually good. "Prince should own a ranch here in the Foothills." There was the Beddingfield Ranch adjoining the "Bar U" and it could be bought. "Just in case," said George Lane to himself, "I'll get an option on that property;" and he did. The Prince of Wales was for it; a message was sent to London; His Majesty the King gave approval and when the Prince was returning through Winnipeg, the deal was completed and the ranch of George Lane's choosing became the personal property of the Prince of Wales. George Lane went farther; he released Professor W. L. Carlyle, that gentleman who had been Dean of Agriculture in Oklahoma before coming to direct the "Bar U" horse breeding operations. And Professor Carlyle was manager of the "E.P." ranch for over twenty years.

I heard a fellow rancher say that George Lane was the most awkward thing he ever saw at the steering wheel of an automobile. It brought to mind the fact that Lane was particularly slow to admit his need for one of those "rubber-tired horses". He said, "My old saddle horse and I understand each other pretty fair and that's more than I can hope for when I start riding one of those things". When a salesman went out from Calgary or High River, hoping to interest the rancher in a modern and comfortable automobile, he invited George Lane to get in and have a ride. But Lane saw no particular point in that; he could tell that it was comfortable without riding in it. However, he was not averse to a demonstration and said, "If you want to show me the car, you get in and drive it around in a circle and I'll watch from here". That didn't make sense to the salesman; but orders are orders and the new car was driven around and around while George Lane watched the performance, just as he might have done if buying a horse. Finally he said to the agent, "If you can follow everywhere I go on my saddle horse tomorrow, I'll buy". That wasn't what a salesman would call encouraging, especially if he knew the trails on the "Bar U".

I'm sure George Lane could never have won a beauty competition; but he had a big heart; he was the understanding soul and I think this will illustrate. There was good fishing up Pekisko Creek. A young chap over the way of High River, who was working as "trouble man" for the telephone company had been regretting that his work would not permit him even a day's fishing up in the hills. Next time Lane was in High River, he notified the telephone office that a line in the hills needed immediate attention. The young man who longed to try for trout, was delegated to go out the way of the "Bar U", prepared to make the repairs which George Lane considered necessary. The young fellow reported to Lane but the likeable old rancher was too much occupied with something or other to give instructions; he said, "Sorry, I'm too busy today to give you directions; you might as well take my fishing pole for the afternoon. You can sleep in the bunkhouse tonight and tomorrow morning I'll tell you where to look for that telephone trouble".

And was the young man happy to accept such orders? It was like an answer to prayer. He fished to his heart's content and checked in at the bunk-house that night with an elegant string of fish. Next morning, refreshed in body and spirit, he enquired again from the old rancher where he should look for that telephone trouble. Lane just told him that he could go back to town and report the line now in good order. Truth was, there had been no trouble with the lines, but through the mischievous generosity of George Lane, the younger man had satisfied a longing to fish "up creek". It was like the master of "Bar U".

He saw the ranch country in the years of open range; he saw the settlers flocking in with their terrible barbed wire and encroaching upon the ranchers; he saw the Province of the Foothills taking shape and becoming a leader in Canadian agriculture. And High River was "the best little ol' town this side of Rio Grande". It was a gay little ol' town if you ask me; it's still a gay town and they still play polo there. But I agree with George Lane and I hope they always play polo at High River. If other towns can't support polo, that's their misfortune.

George Lane had a healthy philosophy. He was an outdoor man and I know he could commune to the full with nature. He had his share of disappointments, yes, but he discovered that when he had a horse between his knees, and got back in the foothills, it all looked like God's country once again. Fact is, a lot of folk have discovered that this old world looks a little better from the top of a good horse.

Will Rogers said he was sure there would be a good horse and saddle awaiting him in Heaven. Somehow, I think there was a horse and saddle there for George Lane.

Joe Greaves

Inter-Mountain Sodbuster

When I visit the Fat Stock Shows at Kamloops from year to year, and enjoy the good cattle from the Inter-Mountain ranges, I feel pleasantly haunted; I don't believe in ghosts although sometimes I wish I could. The haunting reminders which surround me there are those of the daring and heroic cattlemen who founded that Kingdom of Cattle. I think of Jerome and Thaddeus Harper, of Thomas Ellis, and the two Joes, Joseph Guichon and Joseph B. Greaves. Bold men they were and courageous. And I'm not sure that Christopher Columbus could have navigated their ships of destiny over the uncharted courses with any more success. But old Chris was lucky and bumping into a new continent had much more publicity value than producing beef in a remote wilderness.

To have driven cattle to that inter-mountain wilderness, years before there was a railroad, does seem a bit preposterous. But I reject the theory that those men were just mad adventurers; I choose to conclude that they had unusual vision. Because their dreams came true, and some of the biggest cattle ranches of the present day rest upon the early efforts of those pioneers.

Most Canadians have heard of the Douglas Lake Cattle Company. Besides being one of the best known ranches, it has long been one of Canada's biggest. And it was Joe Greaves who planted the seed from which that mighty enterprise grew. He was a Yorkshireman by birth and Yorkshiremen are made to roam. At fourteen years of age he was a stowaway on a sailing vessel, the *Patrick Henry*, bound for New York. The stowaway was discovered but it was too late to send him ashore and the Captain said he wouldn't feed the lad to the sharks; he would give him the job of feeding the ship's pigs. It wasn't uncommon for ships to carry pigs because they would consume waste food and convert it into fresh pork for the crew. Little Joe Greaves knew nothing about pigs but before the sixty day voyage was completed, he knew a lot.

He even discovered that he could like pigs. Arriving at New York, he posed as an "expert" and hired with a New York farmer.

Pigs were all right for a time but Joe Greaves was an ambitious youth and the urge to do big things was welling up within him. A strike had been made in California. It is a mysterious effect that the word "gold" has upon people; it can mesmerize them. Joe Greaves joined an emigrant train going clean across the continent, to the "gold diggings" in California. Five hundred horses, one thousand cattle and oxen and a large number of prairie schooners made up the train. There was the customary hardship but with 65 able-bodied men in the expedition, they got through without being molested except by a few Indian snipers who weren't very good shots.

Well, according to my friend, Thomas Stewart who worked for him in after years, Greaves went to British Columbia in 1859 and took cattle and sheep and turkeys. His live stock were for the purpose of sale or trade at the mines up the Fraser, where gamblers and peddlers and parasites and all who called themselves gold miners, had to eat. His venture proved profitable and he went back to Oregon for more stock but on the third trip north, in 1863, he found the market failing so turned the cattle loose on the Thompson River about Walachin. The cattle had practically no value so he abandoned them, temporarily at least, and went to Soda Creek to be a butcher. But before leaving the cattle he had the good judgment to place his brand upon them and when he returned to that range three years later, he was pleasantly surprised to find his cattle in good condition. The cows had not been wasting their time and the herd was enlarged by the addition of calves and yearlings and two-year-olds. Wise man, this Greaves; friends told him the cattle were not worth owning but he rounded them up and branded the young stock. After 1868, he actually took a few cuts of surplus beef stock to the coast, shipping from Yale to Victoria or New Westminster by boat. Still those semi-wild cattle were increasing faster than sales could be made.

Sooner or later something would have to be done to move cattle out to a better market however that might be accomplished. The Harper Brothers, Jerome and Thaddeus were worried about the same problem and well they might be. They had turned cattle on the open ranges of the interior about the same time as Greaves had done it. The ranch site they selected was a few miles east of Kamloops and their brand "J.H." is still in use as the oldest registered brand in British Columbia. But what interested Greaves was the fact that Thaddeus Harper in 1876 performed a daring experiment in marketing. He found the limited markets in New Westminster and Victoria flooded with beef from the south and had the colossal nerve to start overland in the general direction of Chicago, with cattle. Eight hundred steers from three to eight years of age were assembled and moved south along the Okanagan trail. Before reaching the State of Washington, more steers were bought and a herd of 1200 cattle swung south and east to winter in Northern Utah. During the winter Harper learned that beef was in strong demand in California and when spring came the herd was headed westward instead of eastward and arrived at San Francisco a year and a half after leaving the home range in British Columbia. It was the year of the Custer Massacre but Sitting Bull and his beef-hungry Sioux were sitting in the wrong place to benefit from Harper's big herd which they might very well have intercepted.

If Harper could do that, the Yorkshireman Greaves could do it and would do it. Eighteen-eighty was the year. Harper started with 600 cattle; Greaves rounded up 4000; they were mostly his own but there was an occasional cattleman about who would risk adding a few head. They were headed for Chicago; 4000 dollars may not seem much when cabinet ministers talk about appropriations, but 4000 cattle make a mighty herd to be driven overland through mountainous country. The drive was conducted as far as the boundary between Oregon and California during the summer and after the snow fell, it was headed eastward through country which could not be travelled in summer on account of lack of water. Greaves had planned that drive with care, you see. He knew nothing about highway maps and radio beams but he did know the country. He hadn't been travelling about looking for gold and grass and dodging scalping knives with his eyes shut.

The eastward movement continued all winter and until rails were reached at Cheyenne in the south east corner of Wyoming. It was a bustling cow town which had received a Union Pacific rail link in 1867. The cattle had crossed the States of Washington, Oregon, Idaho and most of Wyoming and so did the Greaves' cowboys. The exact mileage will never be established but it is safe to say that the cattle were driven between 1500 and 2000 miles before being loaded on cars and sent to Chicago. If the same distance were travelled on a straight course eastward from Calgary, it would have taken the herd to about North Bay in Ontario. It occupied the best part of a year because such a large herd could not be expected to average more than eight or at most ten miles per day. It was one of the epics in North American history and while it is not recorded, I fancy that Greaves' men hung up some new world records for cowboy celebrations after the last big steer was chased up the chute at Cheyenne.

Tom Stewart tells me that the big herd was delivered at Chicago without any losses except those which might be attributed to natural causes. That's a marvellous record. But Greaves did reget that he hadn't taken another three months in making the trip and thus reached the market at a season of better prices. We sometimes think we have all the marketing problems but compared to those that Greaves surmounted, ours are not so terrible.

Well, he returned to the interior, his pockets bulging with good American money. Raising cattle was good business. He met up one day with an Oregon cattleman, Charles Beak, who wanted to become established in British Columbia. This man had bought the holdings of Thomas Douglas for whom Douglas Lake was named; and then he persuaded Joe Greaves to join forces with him. Sooner or later there would be a railroad linking the east and west of Canada and that would open new markets. Greaves and Beak needed more capital with which to expand. Greaves went to Victoria and interested his friend C. W. R. Thomson, and Thomson interested Wm. C. Ward, a young banker who had come to the Bank of British Columbia in Victoria in 1865. A four-man partnership was formed and the Douglas Lake Cattle Company was incorporated in 1886.

Just as soon as the partners felt assured that the transcontinental railroad was more than a pipe dream, Greaves went out buying cattle. He bought freely in many parts of the interior but left the cattle on the farms for delivery later; said Greaves to his colleagues, "This gigantic job of rail construction through the mountains will mean many workers and big appetites; and a new demand for beef." It was a good guess; beef values soared and so did company profits.

The Douglas Lake Company was out in front in many respects. After the C.P.R. was completed, Beak went to the Old Country and when at the Glasgow Stallion Show he bought the 1st prize two-year-old, a stallion called "The Boss" for $5000.00. The stallion was sent across the water and to the mountains in the care of John Blackwell who became very well known. Then Clydesdale mares were bought in Ontario and the breeding stud was built up in the course of time to 300 pedigreed animals. Horses represented a hobby with Greaves but it was the type of hobby that should be particularly popular with people of my own race, a profitable hobby. Douglas Lake horses were in strong demand and many stallions were actually sold before they were born.

Then came a bad winter; 1886-87 was the winter of disaster on the Great Plains but in between the mountain ranges, it was 1893-94. I asked one old timer from up Chilcotin way for something about that winter; he said, "I'll tell you MacEwan, it wasn't exactly the kind of winter the Florida Real Estate men brag about; why, we found jack rabbits frozen in mid air that winter and in the spring we still had snow when we should have had flowers". Anyway, the market in the preceding season was off, with the result that more cattle were left on the range. The Douglas Lake had 20,000 head when the snow fell and it was reported that about 8000 were lost before the count was made after a big storm in the following April. But the lessons of that winter brought a change of ranch policy with more attention being given to oats and hay and other winter feeds. The new plans called for more help on the ranch and the decision was made, rather reluctantly I take it, to try some Canadians from Ontario. The easterners gave a good account of themselves; they were good horsemen, good axe-men and they could construct log buildings. Greaves concluded that they were the best men the ranch had employed up to that time. And what makes one smile is that, evidently it came as a bit of a surprise to him.

The Klondyke Gold Rush produced the next big rise in beef values and some of the cattle from the interior were actually driven north to Teslin Lake, where they were slaughtered and their carcasses sent by raft to Dawson City.

Beak withdrew from the Douglas Lake Cattle Co. about 1890; and in 1910, Mr. Ward bought out the other partners and Greaves retired. For more than 30 years, Manager Joe Greaves had been going to his ranch bed at 8:30 in the evening and arising with his helpers or before them, at 4:30. He was now retiring from the management. He was going to live in Victoria. If ever a man earned relaxation in the evening of his life, it was Joseph Greaves. I never actually saw him but I think I know that pioneer type. They said he looked like King Edward VII and was built along similar lines. I know he was a quiet man, and modest; he had a kindly word for everybody, employees and others. He liked to have friends and guests come to the ranch and he made them very welcome, just as long as they did not keep him from his bed when it came 8:30. I rejoice that my father was not the only one whose sociability ceased with brutal suddenness at what he considered bed-time. I know too that Greaves had a quick wit; how else could he have carried that burden of management in a big cattle company until his 80th year, yes 80th year.

The stowaway who had to feed the pigs on the *Patrick Henry*, retired a wealthy man but his wealth was employed most generously. When he died in 1915, much of what he had accumulated went to the aid of hospitals. And he did not forget the little hospital in California which had brought him back to health, nearly half a century earlier. Big men don't forget.

Rutherford

The Farm Teacher

Here is another sodbuster who never fought prairie fires and never actually broke western sod. But Rutherford of Saskatchewan was a great farm teacher and a great leader. When Saskatchewan laid the foundation for higher education, the Agricultural College was established as an integral part. It was the first Agricultural College in Canada to be organized as a part of the Provincial University, occupying the same campus and buildings as Arts and Law and other faculties. It was a bold decision; but time was to confirm the good judgment of those who made it. And then the Agricultural College had the honour of having the first dean appointed in the prairie University and that dean was William John Rutherford whose leadership served to make the college a most happy link between the Provincial University and the rapidly expanding farming industry.

I saw the dean for the first time when as a half-grown and exceedingly green farm lad, I attended the Farm Boys' Camp at Regina Exhibition. On the programme arranged for us was a visit to the Parliament Buildings and we boys were graciously granted permission to sit in the "seats of the mighty", the seats of the members of the Legislature. I proudly sought out the seat of the "Honourable Member for Melfort", G. B. Johnston, and sat there to listen to an address by Dean Rutherford. And I recall very well that there were two surprises in store for me that day; I expected to see a big and husky dean and I expected to hear him talk about farming. He wasn't big and husky and he didn't say anything about farming. This is what he took for his subject, "The boy increased in wisdom and stature and in favour with God and man". I've managed to forget nearly everything contained in at least a thousand lectures to which I've been exposed in the intervening years but Dean Rutherford on that occasion about which I write, delivered a message which thirty years have failed to erase from my memory.

But I want to say something about his early life. He was born in New York State, (in 1868) from a Scottish father, and a mother of Canadian birth. But William John's childhood was saddened by misfortune. As he romped through the fields one day, watching the birds and animals which were always his friends, a thorn pierced his knee. Complications left him permanently crippled and comparatively frail in body. But a devoted mother undertook to direct her son's education; while he was convalescing, she taught him to use his hands by knitting and then she instructed him in reading. The second tragedy in his life was the death of that Godly mother when he was eight years old. It was said of her that "reverence for God, respect for fellow men, love of children and kindness to beasts formed her code of conduct". And anyone who knew the dean will agree that he certainly inherited or acquired these qualities.

When he was ten years old the family moved to Ontario and took a farm in Dundas County. After Collegiate, he taught school. At one school he took care of the fires and did the janitor work and on the strength of that asked for a salary increase of $5.00 but it was refused. He confessed that it was the only time in his life that he asked for a raise in pay. He had an urge to study agriculture and place himself in a position to help make farming a brighter occupation. He enrolled at the Ontario Agricultural College (in the fall of 1901). With him at Guelph incidently were two others who were to become Deans of Agriculture in Western Canada, A. E. Howes of Alberta, and L. S. Klinck of British Columbia; both were his life-long friends.

Upon graduation, Rutherford took a teaching position at the Iowa State College. From there (in 1906) he went to Manitoba and after another short period, (1908) he was named Deputy Minister of Agriculture in the recently created Province of Saskatchewan. It was then that he adopted Saskatchewan and Saskatchewan adopted Rutherford.

They were making plans for a Provincial University. The Honourable W. R. Motherwell was Minister of Agriculture and he was as anxious as the newly appointed University President, Dr. Walter C. Murray, to give the new province a good system of agricultural education. There were those who argued that the Agro College should not be too close to the University; sure, the college at Guelph was a "safe distance" from the University of Toronto and Saskatchewan should follow the example. Anyway, one of the first jobs delegated to Mr. Motherwell's new Deputy was to proceed to the United States and Eastern Canada to study agricultural education. The report which Mr. Rutherford brought back was strongly in support of an agricultural college linked as closely as possible to the University. He recognized you see, that the University could help the Agricultural College and the College could help the University; and both could best serve a farming province by functioning together. It was a hope for a "people's University in a farming province". That settled it because President Murray had already declared himself for the plan, even though there was no precedent for it in Canada. Then when plans for the college were completed, Mr. Motherwell gave his Deputy Minister to be the Dean; he gave his Superintendent of Fairs and Institutes, John Bracken, to be Professor of Field Husbandry and another of his lieutenants, F. H. Auld, to be Director of Extension.

Somebody said Rutherford was a dreamer. Of course he was and so were Abraham Lincoln, and Robert Burns and Sir John A. Macdonald. He came to Saskatchewan with a vision of farming that included more than big fields and wheat; he foresaw trees and flowers and fruits; he envisioned farms with comfortable homes, and good live stock; and com-

DEAN RUTHERFORD

munities enriched through good organization. He said he hoped to see apple blossoms growing on the prairies; he did.

A farm without live stock was beyond his comprehension. Farm help was a scarce article in 1916 and the dean was looking for someone to help with the milking. He appealed to some young chaps who were working on the experimental plots and living in the Farm Boarding House. The first lad encountered was from Ontario,—said he couldn't milk. "What, you raised on an Ontario farm and can't milk a cow?" And as the dean indicated how utterly preposterous it all seemed, the end of his cane hit the ground with such angry force that it penetrated about six inches.

Agricultural education was a great challenge. He saw the seed of a planned educational system planted in good Saskatchewan soil; he tended the seedling well and saw it grow into a noble tree bearing harvest of trained students and scientific workers to help in the improvement of agriculture. He liked to tell of the achievements of science, especially as they affected the farmer. Progress in the fight against rust and drought and frost, brought him justifiable pride and satisfaction. For many years, it was almost expected that "wheat and other grains would freeze in the northern parts of the prairie provinces or be killed from drought in the south . . . . but science came to the help of the farmer . . . ." And then he added, "The young man of the future who purposes making agriculture his life work, should be an educated man in order that he may co-operate in the most cordial and sympathetic way with Science his leader, his teacher and friend". I like that.

The college was a matter of great pride to him and especially close to his heart was the Associate Course, practical training for the boys returning to the farms. It was a constant wish that they would enjoy the same opportunities in classroom and on the playing fields as those in degree classes. He knew his students and followed them in rugby and hockey and so on. And although he had been denied the opportunity of participating in many of the field sports, he was an enthusiastic curler and lawn bowler; the Rutherford Bowling Green and the Rutherford Rink in Saskatoon are memorials to his enthusiastic interest in healthful sport.

He was closely in touch with progress in the various departments. He was absent on a Royal Commission when the Barred Rock hen, Lady Victorine, was heading for a world record with 358 eggs in a single year and more than once, Professor Baker of the Poultry Department received a long distance phone call from the Dean to enquire how the lady was progressing.

If he was an educator first, he was a horseman second. He loved flowers and birds and all things living; but nearest his heart was a good horse. One of the rewards of living was to see "colts growing into horses". He was a familiar figure in all the major show rings. He judged at the International Show at Chicago; associating with the master breeders and herdsmen at that great show afforded special satisfaction; while to "sit for a time in the gallery of the hall of fame of the Saddle and Sirloin Club and feel its magic spell" was a supreme opportunity.

The late Alexander Galbraith said, "I would rather take Rutherford's judgment on my horses than that of any man I have ever known". And he was a fearless judge; judging at Winnipeg on one occasion, a big class of stallions came before him and after he had examined them, he announced to the clerk that they were all disqualified and all could be "given the gate"; he was satisfied that there wasn't a sound horse in the ring. It certainly wasn't the work of a judge who was looking for popularity. I saw him judging driving horses; one of the exhibitors was not getting along very well and the dean stopped him and said, very kindly, "you're afraid of your horses and they know it. Somehow your nervousness travels down those reins". The driver accepted the judge's advice; he braced himself and drove off with new confidence which evidently brought better results. As a matter of fact, he had a pretty fair opinion of his own ability to handle a pair of lines and usually when out riding, he was in the driver's seat. When he took the reins behind the Hackney-bred horse, Scotty, the performance would be one to make folk stand and look.

I can see him as he was about to judge a class or treat himself to an inspection on a good horse. His gaze would be riveted first of all upon the feet, then the hoof-heads, the pasterns, and the hocks, all in the best Scottish fashion. He was escorting a group of visiting Homemakers through the barns one day and stopped to examine Craigie's Meral, a mare that was a particular favourite with him. But one of the visiting ladies showed such bad taste as to say she didn't like "that funny coloured one; she's the colour of an Ayrshire cow". It was the equivalent of heresy and the reply was short, "Madam, look at those legs".

Yes, so far as horses were concerned, Clydesdales were his weakness. A man who enjoyed his company in Scotland told of the Dean standing alone for a full hour, leaning on his cane, at the end of the brig across the Clyde at Glasgow; he was watching the massive Clydesdale geldings, perfect in feet and hock and true in movement, hauling the big lorries. And while he was confined to his residence with illness that produced his death, just a few weeks before the end, he asked that some of his favourites be brought from the barn, that he might see them. Accordingly, Jimmie Slessor, the horseman whom the Dean brought from Scotland to care for the University horses, groomed and dressed some of the good ones, Craigie Fyvie, Kinleith Footprint and others. And the Dean from an open window watched and enjoyed. They were his friends; he knew their parents and their pedigrees; he knew their weaknesses and merits.

He loved Scotland and Scotland's live stock. Oh, he was at home with good stock of all kinds. He would wax eloquent in his description of the Scots' achievements in animal improvement, ever contending that the animal breeder is an artist of the first order. He favoured the Scottish method of growing the colts before making them fat. It was with evident satisfaction that he told about the farmer who was buying a young stallion from Davie Riddell, the man who was so successful with the noted horses Darnley and Prince of Wales. Riddell asked £80 and the farmer said, "Too much for this horse". Riddell replied bluntly, "I'm not selling you a horse,—just a frame. You will make the horse with proper feeding".

In 1920, the Dean went to Scotland as a member of a commission to purchase two Clydesdale stallions for Saskatchewan. Two of the most promising young stallions of the year were secured and landed safely at Saskatoon but misfortune was in store. Craigie Enchanter died shortly after arriving and Bonnie Fyvie developed trouble that justified his destruction. The loss was partly offset by later events. As a result of judging at Chicago, the Dean knew George B. Cluett who had assembled some of the best Clydesdales available in Scotland. Cluett was obliged to sell and quietly indicated that if Dean Rutherford would take his horses and keep them together, he could have them for the amount of the insurance on Craigie Enchanter, a fraction of their appraised value. The purchase was made and such aristocrats as Rosalind, a Cawdor Cup winner in Scotland, Eva Footprint, Langwater Jessica, Craigie Sylvia and the $10,000 Kinleith Footprint, came to the University. Dean Rutherford once confessed to John Gardhouse as they sat on the lawn at Saskatoon, that it was his ambition to raise a stallion that would be Grand Champion at Chicago. Green Meadow Footstep was Grand at the International in 1925, and a dream came true.

As the years went by, there were increasing public demands upon the Dean's time; he was chairman of the Royal Agricultural Commission in Saskatchewan in 1920; he was a member of a Royal Grain Commission appointed in 1923 to study wheat marketing and again in 1928. He was back at the University only a short time in the fall of 1929 when he suffered a throat infection which became steadily worse and resulted in his death in June 1930.

As one examines agricultural progress and organization of this day, it is not difficult to recognize the hand of Dean Rutherford. But best of all I like that zeal which was his, a determination to see the position of the farmer made better. And as a concluding note, I offer his own words,

> "We must see to it", said he, "that more of the lads from the farms are given an opportunity to attend school and college; and that the girls who will be the homemakers of the future will be given equal chances with those who live in the urban centres. . . . We are looking forward to the time when our farmers will be so educated and trained for their life work that they cannot be distinguished by dress or speech or manner, from their brothers and sisters engaged in other respectable work."

The Unknown Sodbuster

He passed on just the other day. What his name was, doesn't matter at this time because he wasn't known except to a small circle of friends. I suppose his name didn't appear in the public press a dozen times in that many years. He never sought publicity; indeed he didn't even think about it. But his record is so nearly the equivalent to that of thousands of unsung heroes of the frontier, that I don't have to name him. I'll just call him the "Unknown Sodbuster"; I can recount some of his experiences and pay him some of the honour due him and to that noble army of pioneers who came to this land as he did and about whom nothing has been recorded.

If I refer to him as Will, it is for convenience only. As a lad of nine years, he arrived in Manitoba with his family. That was in 1883. In the next year they were again on the move, pushing farther west. This time they went almost to the foothills; they settled beside the Red Deer River right on the old Calgary-Edmonton trail. There they built a stopping house where many a weary traveller took his rest. But this was no ordinary house with a sod roof; this house had a shingle roof and was the first of its kind on all the 200 miles of trail between Calgary and Edmonton. It was not that these newcomers from Michigan were proud; they were progressive and they came determined to stay.

They were just nicely established, with a few acres of prairie land ready for crop when word came of rebellion on the Saskatchewan. Hell had boiled over among the half-breeds at Duck Lake. There was no assurance that this conflagration would not extend clear to the mountains; that the Indians, out of sympathy for the half-breeds, might not attempt a complete extermination of the scattered whites. And certainly the Indians considered it. Anxious weeks they were for the settlers. Nobody relished the idea of an "Indian hair cut", cutting as close to the skull bones as they liked to do. The family living under the shingled roof permitted a Montreal battalion to take over the new house and use it for a fort.

They built a stockade; then a moat and drawbridge as typical as any that greeted Cromwell and his Ironsides when they were on their castle wrecking expeditions; it was all to ward off possible attack by the Blackfeet. No more savage red men roamed the plains than those of the Blackfoot confederacy in the South-west. The whiskey traders had discovered that they could dilute imported rum, one part to four of water for Crees; but one to six was the limit of safety where Blackfeet were involved.

The women folk were sent to Calgary but young Will, of the age of eleven tender years, took a gun and announced to his elders that he was a member of the "home guard". If there was any shooting, he was going to see it. Well, there was no shooting at that point but plenty of manoeuvring and when the embers of rebellion had cooled, the lad held right onto his gun; it could be awfully useful on the frontier. The Red Deer River was his plaything; he knew the best crossings and when the water was high he was often required to carry mail and messages across, swimming a pony which became expert. "Only once", said my old friend, "was that pony drowned, and that was on the last trip we made." The fatal crossing was in the spring and a big piece of ice hit the horse and knocked the young rider into the icy water and he had to swim for his life.

The lad became virtually indigenous to the frontier. He could ride a bronc; he could chew tobacco; he could take care of himself; he had to. When he was 14 years of age he was ready for anything and his step-father gave him a horse and saddle, a lariat and a shotgun and said, "Now Will, you're on your own. Get out and make your own way in the world". And he did. The life of the cow puncher was the life. It held a spell over him and he rode the range in a vast empire of grass and cattle south of the Red Deer River.

He saw the mighty bull teams belonging to I. G. Baker & Company which did much of the freighting between Calgary and Fort Benton on the Missouri; he knew the rare specimens who drove the bull teams and employed a language which the bulls understood. The drivers were known as bull-whackers or skinners. On one occasion, our young cowboy slept with an I. G. Baker bull wrangler and as the episode was described to me, the skinner didn't stop driving and swearing all night.

Will said if he had to make his choice again, he would have slept with the bulls rather than with the sleep-swearing skinner. He told of the bull-whacker who had a parson as a passenger along with a load of freight. The big wagons stuck in the mud and the driver, exercising unprecedented restraint, spoke gently to the oxen but gentle words meant nothing to them and nothing happened. In desperation, the driver turned to the reverend gentleman and said, "Parson, you've got to put your thumbs in your ears for a few minutes or we'll be in the mud all night". The passenger stopped his ears and the bull-whacker went into action, addressing the oxen in the manner best known to them and the big wagons were slowly but surely eased onto firm ground.

But few folk have any conception of those colossal bull teams which hauled that pioneer freight; team units consisted of from six to twelve pairs of oxen hitched to a trio of wagons built for that purpose. Up to twenty tons of freight could be carried on three wagons. What became known as the "bull train" consisted of from four to ten of these units, perhaps 100 oxen or more.

Then he hired with Pat Burns when Burns was doing a meat contract on the Calgary-Edmonton railroad. Will's job was to bring cattle up to the construction camps for grazing until such time as they would be drafted for slaughter to feed the hungry workers. Some of the cattle drives were long and a rider who was on the drag of a big herd for a 100 mile drive inevitably ate a lot of Alberta soil. The drives were usually northward. One herd of 150 head delivered for holding at the scene of construction, disappeared. Either the cattle strayed or were driven off; in any case they were lost. The camp could not be without beef and more cattle must be rushed in. Our cowboy was about where the present Bowden is situated, working his way to Calgary for more cattle when Pat Burns riding a sweaty horse caught up with him. Burns told about the loss of the beef herd and said, "You may kill your horse but you've got to get to Calgary this afternoon and be on your way back with cattle tonight". Calgary was 85 miles, but the young rider made the journey as ordered, changed horses at Calgary, restocked with chewing tobacco and was on his way north with 200 head that night.

The chewing tobacco helped to counteract the dust when driving cattle and he was sure he had chewed enough plugs of his favourite brand to pave Portage Avenue. But he wasn't like the chewers I've known; he had done some freighting with an old uncle who held all local records for long-distance spitting; "he could split a shingle at ten feet" and in the same field of endeavour, young Will was an utter failure. The old uncle would laugh at the feeble showing and the young fellow resolved to hide his limitations. From then on it was eating tobacco, not just chewing tobacco. And I know of at least one dollar that he won in a bet by devouring a five cent plug of chewing tobacco in less time than his opposition could consume a dry soda biscuit. My own view is that gold medals have been awarded for less.

One of his pastimes in those range days was braiding lariats from rawhide. He would do the braiding when the leather was wet, tie the braided article to a fence to stretch for a few days and then oil it with neat's-foot oil. Finally, he would catch a broncho, tie the leather lariat to the animal's tail and release the frightened brute for a few days, when the lariat would be worked as pliable as chamois.

My friend became an expert horseman. He liked them tough, said, "the wildest colts make the best horses". Well, horses on the open ranges of Alberta increased rapidly and hundreds of those undomesticated animals were unbranded and unclaimed. But farther east, in Assiniboia and Manitoba, the settlers needed horses. In 1895, Will and three others rounded up 400 head of wild bronchos and headed them toward Beaver Lake and on to the Edmonton-Winnipeg trail. As the band was driven eastward, horses were sold to the settlers at $15.00 per head, the buyer taking his choice. To facilitate finding the horses when they strayed, the drivers placed bells about the necks of a few of them. It was soon observed that when settlers were buying a horse, they always took one with a bell, thinking of course, that the horse had been handled. The resourceful horsemen soon began belling the poorer horses and when they reached Winnipeg, they had 30 "pretty good·beasts" which they soon sold for C.P.R. construction work. The venture was profitable.

In a barren and unsettled part, somewhere between Edmonton and Battleford, they came upon a family of American land-seekers, stranded, pathetically stranded. The four mules upon which they depended for transportation had strayed away one night and been lost for two weeks, leaving them on the cold and friendless prairie with a cow, some chickens and a wagon loaded with equipment. The immigrants were despondent; their food was exhausted and they were obliged to eat the chickens with which they had hoped to stock their homestead. But horsemen have big hearts; the four horsemen took compassion on the ill-fated travellers and gave them a piece of bacon, half a bag of flour and four bronchos. How the man from Missouri got along with four undomesticated cayuses, nobody ever knew.

The old timer told of another incident from that journey. They halted in the Qu'Appelle Valley to rest up for the last lap of the trip to Winnipeg. No sooner had they made camp than two Indians took up a position on a nearby ridge and remained until relieved by two others. They seemed to be doing a "guard herd", but for what reason? The Indians refused to talk and no reason was offered until the Indian agent happened along and explained that there was a "tree burial" just beyond the Indian sentries. A year earlier, two medical students had gone through and taken an Indian corpse to get the skeleton. The natives were taking no chance on a repetition, even after the agent tried to explain that these horsemen were totally disinterested in the carcasses of red men.

Back in Alberta, our "Unknown Sodbuster" again took to the range. He was riding south around about Innisfail one day when he encountered a strange monster on the trail. It was a steam tractor, the first he had ever seen. He got down from his terror-stricken horse and watched the iron giant move slowly past him. It was a wonderful sight and in his awe, he said to himself, "I wonder if I could learn to drive one of those things". Next time in Calgary he hung up his boots and spurs and accepted a job in a machine shop where he could learn steam. Three years went by; they were not what you would call happy years because he yearned for the "cow country". Then one morning when he went to work, he found the machine shop burned down; the boss told him there was no more work. But there were no tears shed; all the boss heard was, "That's fine, that's what I've been waiting for; I'm climbing aboard the first horse and saddle I see".

He went to Major Walker, one of the exciting characters in the early history of Canadian ranchland, and asked for work. The major was a graduate from Mounted Police ranks, having come west to Fort Macleod with the famous force of 1874. He was a "two-fisted" sort who achieved fame at the very time he struck the West. A severe storm broke over the Police camp at Dufferin, Manitoba, as the original force was about to trek overland to establish law and order in the south-west. Police horses became frantic and went into a frenzied stampede. Walker, it was, who grabbed a horse and followed the frantic animals through the storm for 60 miles of darkness that night. With the aid of police officers who followed him, all the men and horses were safely back in camp thirty hours after the storm broke.

In response to the enquiry for work, Major Walker said, "Sure, I'll fix you up. First I want you to take a saddle horse and a stallion to my ranch". Then came the question, "Where is your ranch?" and the reply was, "130 miles about in that direction: you'll find it all right". Sure he would find it. He saddled a stout gelding and started out "about in that direction", leading the stallion. But the stallion wanted to fight the saddle horse and the only way to prevent trouble was to ride at a fast clip. That was exactly what he did and on the second evening, after two days of riding, he overtook a mounted cowboy and enquired for Major Walker's ranch. It was one of the pleasant shocks of his life that he was just over a ridge from the ranch gate he wanted. But it was hard to know which was most tired that night, man, gelding or stallion.

Like many others of the agricultural pioneers, this one tried various occupations. Besides being farmer and rancher and cowboy, he was machinist and engineer. He had his fingers in flour milling and mining, but he was never very far from agriculture, and his heart was the heart of the sodbuster. He was one of those who witnessed a great and exciting drama in the opening of the West; he was active and generous; he was a rank individualist; he was just one of the pioneers; but he was a treat to know.

McGregor of Glencarnock

I'm fascinated by the history of Clan MacGregor. Scotland's fighting MacGregors wanted no Crown Charter for their lands; they resented South Country interference and they were among the last of the Highlandmen to yield to the new order. So stubborn was their resistance and so annoying, that a Royal Decree went forth to totally abolish the name of MacGregor. But there is no hope of draining the Atlantic Ocean or growing figs at Port Churchill, and there was no hope of abolishing the name of MacGregor or crushing the stout spirit that went with it. Rob Roy MacGregor proved that in Scotland and J. D. McGregor of the same fighting clan might have done it in Manitoba.

"J.D.'s" Grandfather McGregor came to Canada in 1832. One generation later, David McGregor who was "J.D.'s" father left his Ontario farm and brought his growing family to Winnipeg. That was 1877, one year before Winnipeg had a railroad. The McGregors had come in by St. Paul and made the last of the long journey by river boat and stage coach. You see it wasn't a small matter to get around in the Great Lone Land at that time. Indeed I'm not sure that many people wanted to get around more than necessary. Life insurance hadn't become standard equipment and men realized that there would be fewer widows and orphans if they didn't venture farther than they had to. And speaking of travel in the new land, when Col. Macleod of the Mounted Police fame travelled from Fort Macleod to attend the first meeting of the Council of the North West Territories, at Fort Livingstone that year in which the McGregors arrived, this is the way he made the journey: he travelled into Montana by wagon, thence to St. Paul in Minnesota by rail, to Moorehead by river boat, then to Winnipeg by stage and from Winnipeg to Fort Livingstone on the south side of Swan River by dog team.

Things were primitive; of course they were and there was hardship and some risk but the McGregors said it was their country; they knew it from the beginning, and a good place for vigorous people. But what they didn't know was that they had a great nation builder in the family; he was just Jimmy McGregor in his 17th year. I was going to say wee Jimmy McGregor but I'm not so sure that he was ever very wee. His school days were over and he had to help dad who was bringing in horses and cattle for sale to the settlers. The flow of landseekers was increasing and most of them outfitted at Winnipeg to push on over westward trails in search of homesteads. Horses and oxen and cows for the settlers represented big business and Jimmy was his father's right hand man.

Then to Brandon and there the famous Glencarnock Farms took shape. Live stock were always J. D. McGregor's choice but after he sold frozen wheat for 15 cents a bushel and oats at 10 cents, live stock were more than ever to the fore. His interests were expanding. He was attracted by ranching in the south west; he acquired some large ranch holdings and was one of the first to release young Manitoba steers, "dogies" as they were known, on the Alberta ranges. So attractive was the ranching that Manitoba nearly lost him. An important government appointment about that time took him into the north and changed many of his dreams; he was appointed Gold Commissioner in the Yukon in that memorable year of gold rush, 1898. Again he travelled over primitive trails. There was no alternative; the Gold Commissioner had to go in to Dawson City the same as the lowliest gold seeker, over rocky passes and up the treacherous Yukon River.

For six years he was at wonderful and terrible Dawson City and when he came out he was ready for new adventures. He embarked shortly upon a large scale farming and settlement scheme in Southern Alberta. It was organized in 1909 with English capital. They called it the Southern Alberta Land Co.; J. D. McGregor was Managing Director. And let nobody suppose they didn't do things the big way. "Big Jim" McGregor had to do things the big way because he didn't know any other. A large tract of land west of Medicine Hat was secured from the Dominion Government at a low figure upon condition that a certain acreage would be irrigated. A gigantic irrigation project was planned, the cost to exceed 10 million dollars; water was taken from the Bow River near

Gleichen and Snake Valley was dammed to create an artificial lake called Lake McGregor. Then in 1911, another company organized in England, Canadian Wheat Lands Ltd., bought 64,000 acres from the original company, it being understood that water for irrigation would be delivered not later than 1914. Mr. McGregor hastened his plans for development; 12,000 acres were broken in that spring of 1911 and 13,000 acres the next year. That was the scale on which work was carried forward. War in 1914 put a temporary stop to development but water was delivered to the irrigation ditches in the Vauxhall block about 1917. True the plan did not develop according to blueprint and some ditches never got the water but it represented an exceedingly interesting and worthy pioneer effort.

But for all his interests, live stock on his Glencarnock farms, Aberdeen Angus cattle especially, gave him the finest satisfaction. J. D. McGregor it was who put the Aberdeen Angus breed "on the map" in the West. Hon. Walter Gordon-Cummings in 1889 imported about 40 Aberdeen Angus females and three bulls from Scotland and placed them on the Quorn Ranch in Alberta. "J.D." was interested in those cattle from the beginning and shortly took them over to found his Glencarnock herd. Perhaps the chief reason for his success with cattle was in the selection of sires; he showed almost uncanny judgment. There was no distance too great nor price too long if he could get the bull he wanted. He imported some of the best he could buy in Scotland from time to time and after 1906 he was out at the shows piling up ribbons and medals for Glencarnock.

For a herd from the young province of Manitoba where corn wasn't grown and the winters were severe, to venture into international competition at Chicago in 1912 seemed a bit overambitious. But was it? This is what Glencarnock did; the herd entry won first, a seemingly nervy thing for a new herd to do in that old beef stronghold; Leroy 3rd of Meadowbrook won the grand championship for bulls of the breed; Violet 3rd of Congash was first prize cow; Queen Rosie of Cullen won 1st for two-year-olds and Glencarnock Victor won the most coveted honour of the show, the grand championship for steers. "Wouldn't happen again in a hundred years", said the wise men who stand around every show ring, as the Brandon steer got the championship. But it did happen again; very next year, to demonstrate that Victor 1st was not an accident, "J.D." fitted another steer, Glencarnock Victor 2nd, and won the Grand Championship at Chicago. It was the first and only time in the history of the International Fat Stock Show that an exhibitor has won two successive championships for steers.

Then there was the famous Blackcap Revolution. Mr. McGregor said he was lucky with that bull but it is more than luck when a man selects great sires rather consistently. "J.D." saw this bull when shown as a calf at Chicago. He liked him, liked him better than the judge who placed him third. He tried to buy him but the little black bull was not for sale. In 1921, however, the bull was entered in the sale of his American breeders, Escher and Ryan, and Mr. McGregor went south; told the herdsman before he left to have a box stall ready for "the best bull in the United States". Sure he had talked it over with the boys; the bull should be bought for $500.00 because cattle values had dropped and dropped. The boys reminded dad that it took a lot of bull to bring $150.00 in Manitoba at that time. But J. D. McGregor dealt in "futures". He did nearly always. I can visualize the scene at that American sale ring; as I got the story, J. D. McGregor had a ringside seat; he appeared a bit restless; the bull he had dreamed about is before the auctioneer, low set, compact block of beef with breed character written all over him. "J.D." adjusts his glasses; his hat gets a backward tilt; something is brewing. As the bids are advancing through the lower brackets, he tries to appear disinterested and says nothing except to mutter something like "nice bull". Then about the time some other bidders were dropping out, J. D. McGregor began and he didn't stop bidding until he owned this great son of Earl Marshal, at $4000. But what would they say at home with cattle prices so terrible? Well, I don't know what the family said but I do know that neighbours did a share of whispering and some of the Canadian breeders sarcastically said they wished they could be as optimistic. But the proof of the pudding is in the eating and Mr. McGregor was able to say a few years later that he had sold over $100,000 worth of cattle from Blackcap Revolution. And that was not all; the bull was fitted for Chicago in 1923; he won the grand championship and then sold by auction to H. O. Harrison of San Francisco for $15,000. And $15,000 of American money at that time was worth a bit over $16,000 in Canada. Blackcap Revolution became known as the "King of Angus Sires" on this continent and Glencarnock earned the title of "Ballindalloch of America"; that meant premier herd of Aberdeen Angus on this continent, just as Ballindalloch was long the premier herd in Scotland.

But let there be no mistake about it; "J.D." liked a good horse as well as a good bullock. All the best people do. He had a special fancy for trotters and usually had one which would clear the first mile out of Brandon faster than any on the road. A fast horse and a shiny buggy with rubber tires represented a goal in human achievement in those days. Back about 1905, his brother John McGregor and a neighbour had a matched race with two trotters, right on Victoria Avenue in Brandon, for a $25.00 bet which the McGregor won. But no horseman is satisfied to accept defeat and the neighbour bought another horse, one called Waneta, and boasted that he could beat any horse in Manitoba. "J.D." could not resist the urge to be in on the show-down which had to come; so along with C. W. Speers, he bought a speed horse called Dalton McCarthy. The race was to be run at Brandon Fair. It had all the promise of a "Battle of Giants" and it was the talk of the community. Folk who met on Rosser Avenue or at Forrest Post Office were spared the necessity of discussing weather; they could talk about the race.

Each owner posted a $500.00 bet, the winner to take all. So mighty a contest called for the best drivers and Charlie Simmonds a famous coloured horseman drove the McGregor horse. The race was one of the track classics in Manitoba and the McGregor horse lost. But I'm glad that J. D. McGregor lost that famous race because it was one of the few times he suffered defeat in public competition and it was sufficient to prove that he was a good loser.

He had quite a few racing horses at one time or another, and some were outstanding in their performance. There was the horse Canuck, raised on his Alberta ranch which made a fine record in the United States and Canada about 1913. And of course he had some that were not outstanding, for example, the fashionably bred horse he brought from California when he was operating a livery stable on 13th Street and Rosser (McGregor & Munn Stable). A darky called Sam had the care of that horse and Mr. McGregor chuckled at Sam's disgust that a horse with such royal blood lines should be neither beautiful nor energetic, worst of all that he should have to be coaxed to take exercise. One of Sam's classical observations was, "Boss, dat hoss has lots of speed in his pedigree, but he hasn't enough in his old legs to win a race".

Mr. McGregor had many honours thrust upon him. He was president of the Canadian Aberdeen Angus Association from 1911 to 1921. He might have been Manitoba's Minister of Agriculture in 1915 but he had no special ambitions for politics. Just two years later, during the period of the Great War, he was named Food Controller for the Western Provinces. He was behind the organization of the Brandon Winter Fair and to his everlasting credit he started the Baby Beef Shows for Boys and Girls. In 1928, he was the recipient of the highest honour which the Live Stock Fraternity can confer upon one of its members; a life-sized painting of Mr. McGregor was hung in the Hall of Fame of the Saddle & Sirloin Club in Chicago. And a life-sized picture of J. D. McGregor was not a small thing. There his portrait will hang with those of the Masters in Live Stock Improvement, McCombie of Aberdeenshire, the bewhiskered old Quaker, Amos Cruickshank of Shorthorn fame, and others. It was a fitting tribute. Then on January 25, 1929, he was appointed Lieutenant Governor of his adopted province and Manitoba did itself honour in honouring one of its pioneers. But though he held that high office, he was still "J.D." to his friends and he was always more at home with cattlemen and horsemen than with civil servants and politicians. Indeed the Lieutenant Governor liked nothing better than to stroll into the livery barn operated by his nephew William L. McGregor on 10th Street in Brandon and seat himself on a bench or a bale of hay and talk to the old timers and farming folk who were coming and going. He talked their language.

He died after a short illness on March 15, 1935. He had

lived for three quarters of a century and seen the miracle of the West; he arrived the year after the first wheat, less than 900 bushels, was shipped out and 52 years later he saw a 500 million bushel wheat crop. That was the miracle in which he had a part.

Sir Walter Scott had it about right:

> "While there's leaves in the forest and foam on the river,
> MacGregor, despite them, shall flourish for ever."

J. D. McGREGOR

Courtesy of Mrs. Miriam Green Ellis

Fred Kanouse

The Trader

I can offer two good reasons for giving Fred Kanouse a membership in the noble Fraternity of Sodbusters; he was a frontiersman of the most devastating kind; and he was one of the brave souls who performed the first ranching experiments on the plains. Yet very few people of the present generation have heard the name of Fred Kanouse and still fewer have encountered anything about him in the records. Were it not for the tales perpetuated by a few pioneers in the south-west, there would be no story about Fred Kanouse on this occasion.

He came to the Canadian Foothills in 1871. Although I have enquired diligently for information about Kanouse's career prior to that date, I can find nothing. Perhaps it is better. Those on the frontier at that time didn't ask personal questions about "the past", and didn't tell much. Actually a man was more likely to achieve old age if his interests in history were not too highly developed. This we do know, however, Kanouse came in from Fort Benton on the Missouri, and travelled by way of the notorious Fort Whoop-Up, and then to a point on the Elbow River, a little west of where Calgary was located later. There he built a fort. He came as a free-trader; and I'm sure he was well supplied with guns and trading stock in barrels. He didn't come alone; evidently four white men and one squaw made up the party. Only bold men ventured into Blackfoot Indian country in those years. The Mounted Police hadn't arrived; men made their own laws from day to day, made them to fit their convenience. The Manitoba metropolis of Fort Garry which later adopted the name Winnipeg, had a population of 271; and westward to the Mountains, the plains were occupied by buffalos and Indians; white men were about as common as grizzly bears.

But just as long as a trader retained his scalp, there was profit in the Indian business and Kanouse knew the precautions one must take. He never turned his back upon a customer and his gun belt was as vital a part of his clothing as his pants and boots. Traders were just beginning to visualize a big business in buffalo hides. And a keg of rum could secure a lot of those robes. The wholesale slaughter that resulted in practical extinction of the prairie buffalo was about to begin.

Anyone dealing in firewater in Blackfoot territory was indeed playing with fire and Kanouse had his full share of thrills. Shortly after the fort was established on the Elbow, one of his colleagues figured in an Indian quarrel and the Indians, it seems, plotted to annihilate the little nest of whites. The Indians were advancing upon the fort; Kanouse and two of his friends went out to meet them in the hope of appeasement. But Kanouse miscalculated that time; his visitors were decorated with more shades of cosmetics than he had seen before; they did not come to talk; they came for slaughter and an Indian bullet dropped one of Kanouse's pals. In the next instant a ball from Kanouse's gun eliminated the chief who was leading the braves. Kanouse was then the target for the next volley and though his arm was injured, he managed to get back to his fort. The little group consisting now of three men and the squaw, organized to withstand attack. The squaw loaded the guns and the males fired them and for three days the Indians were unable to crack the Kanouse defences. Then the Indians retired, presumably to get reinforcements; but they must have found some less hazardous adventure because they didn't come again.

It is not easy to secure exact data about some of those pioneer episodes. But I have satisfied myself that "Kootenai" Brown, another famous frontiersman was associated with Kanouse in that little party which took up trading on the Elbow, and that they stood together that day when Kanouse's arm got in the path of an Indian bullet, prior to the siege. This John George Brown or "Kootenai" Brown had quite a bit in common with Kanouse; both were the fearless, outdoor men, two-gun men when necessary; and while Kanouse was one of the first to turn cattle on the range, Brown had the distinction of being the first or one of the first to actually settle to do some farming in what is now Alberta. A man on the frontier found himself with strange bunk-mates at times and this partner of Kanouse's was said to be a graduate of Eton and Oxford. But I take it that "old school ties" didn't mean much to "Kootenai" Brown. He had belonged to the Queen's Lifeguards. Story has it that he became too friendly with Queen Victoria or some other ladies of the court and was sent to India. But he had troubles there too; somebody got shot and Brown took passage to South America. Still he wasn't satisfied; he turned north; crossed Panama; didn't stop until he reached the Cariboo Gold Diggings in 1863. Two years there and he crossed the prairies to spend a winter trading with half-breeds at Duck Lake. He arrived at Waterton Lakes in 1868 and there he and his Cree wife squatted and built a home.

But the question for which I cannot find an answer is this, "Was 'Kootenai' Brown's Cree wife the squaw who accompanied Kanouse and his party to the Elbow and who loaded the guns when the Indians attacked?" I suppose it doesn't matter but I have an idea that Brown's wife went where he went. Anyway, we shouldn't forget that this "Kootenai" Brown retired from trading to be the first tiller of the soil in what is now Southern Alberta; then he was a rancher and between 1910 and 1914 he was superintendent of the Waterton National Park. He and Fred Kanouse were two of a kind, even if one was an Oxford graduate and the other didn't know for sure if Oxford was the name of a University or a Shorthorn bull. That was the way they came to Alberta, educated and uneducated, cultured and uncultured, saints and sinners. If I have judged correctly, however, the sinners were not at that time in danger of being outvoted by the saints.

The North West Mounted Police trekked westward across the prairies in 1874 and built Fort Macleod. They changed many things; no morality squad ever changed the social life of a community more than did the Mounted Police. The whiskey traders developed something related to a persecution complex and quit; the Fort Whoop-Up racketeers became jittery and went out of business; and Kanouse decided to adopt a more healthful and more dignified livelihood. He tried buffalo hunting; he was on hand with buffalo meat for the celebration when Blackfoot Treaty was signed at Blackfoot Crossing. The meat business suggested cattle; if nobody else would put cattle to the test on the Alberta range, he would.

He went to Montana and returned driving 21 cows and a

bull ahead of his pony. At Fort Macleod he promptly gave his cattle their freedom. Would they survive? There were two or three good reasons why they wouldn't. In the first place the Indians refused to differentiate between cattle and buffalo and would shoot cows with no more hesitation than they would buffalo. In the second place, cattle were likely to become assimilated and swept away by the gigantic herds of migrating buffalo. Then there was the North-West winter to be considered.

The people in Macleod were interested spectators. Some said Kanouse must be crazy; "he'll never find hide or tail of those cattle". Came spring of '78 and Kanouse astride a saddle went out to reconnoitre. Wonders will never cease; he found his cattle, all of them; and they were in good condition. The onlookers were surprised but Kanouse wasn't surprised. He believed that part was just as good for cattle as Montana. The next spring found more cattle on the range and what is now southern Alberta had its first organized round-up; one wagon and sixteen men including Kanouse took part. It was a small round-up outfit compared with those of later years, but the cowboys worked over a lot of country. There was no barbed wire to restrict the cattle and a man could ride 500 miles in any direction without opening a gate. Kanouse cut his cattle out and drove them to Waterton Lakes where his old friend "Kootenai" Brown had more or less settled down. Brown by that time had a few head of his own. Kanouse and Brown agreed that they were in a good cattle country; "anywhere that buffalo lived, cattle will do well". That was what "Kootenai" Brown told Senator Cochrane when they chanced to meet on the prairies, a while before Mr. Cochrane drove the first big herd of 3000 head to graze on Canadian soil.

It was just about that time that Kanouse started the big prairie fire. He just had to be trading, and Indians and horses offered an outlet. He got an Indian pony in a deal and discovered that the poor brute was supporting a large population of horse lice. He decided upon a kerosene treatment. Then too there was precedent for a white man getting a horse from an Indian by sale or trade, only to have the Indian come and steal the horse away. Kanouse knew all the tricks and was taking no chances. He would place his brand on the horse. But he made the mistake of applying the hot branding iron before the kerosene on the hair was dry and the horse's hair took fire. The frantic animal made a dash for freedom, spreading fire as it went; and story has it that the prairie fire which resulted, didn't stop until it reached the Missouri River.

Some Blood Indians who didn't know Kanouse too well, did steal a horse from him on one occasion but they didn't have it long. Learning where the horse was, Kanouse went to the Indian encampment single handed and came away with his horse; and it is told that to assert himself he took an Indian bridle along with his horse, while the surprised red men looked and wondered at what manner of man this was anyway.

But Kanouse was in trouble with Indians from time to time. Evidently he became involved in a dispute with some Kootenay Indians and one of their braves vowed to kill him. Kanouse wasn't one to run away from danger and he wasn't much worried. The Mounted Police thought sufficiently of it all to warn Kanouse to stay away from the inter mountain region where the Indians lived. That was all very well, but Kanouse had business to attend to in that area and would go. He got permission to carry his trusted six-shooter and went in. Did he remain under cover? Not Kanouse; he wasn't that kind of a frontiersman. They tell of him giving an Indian a tip to tell the avowed killer that Fred Kanouse was about. But the boasting red man either decided to take a philosophical view of it all, or else he just lost his enthusiasm.

I know of at least one occasion when the name of Fred Kanouse appeared publicly in print. The journals show that in the year following the first meeting of the Council of the North West Territories, Kanouse was charged by the Mounted Police with gambling and that the accused contributed a fine of one dollar to the public treasury. The cost of government wasn't so high in those days and police fines weren't such a luxury as they are today. But Kanouse was a gambler in the broader sense. Anybody who would bet whiskey against buffalo skins with Blackfeet in those early years was an inherent gambler and anyone who would turn cattle on the open range while the buffalo were still in possession, wasn't to be frightened by "long shots".

That was Fred Kanouse and anyone who visits Pincher Creek or Macleod, provided he makes contact with the right old timers, may hear a lot more about Fred Kanouse and "Kootenai" Brown and another of similar kind "Kamoose" Taylor. Sure they were rough but they were the "he-men" who broke trail in the south-west; they were the links between the old and the "not so old"; links between trader days and pastoral agriculture in southern Alberta. 'Twould be misfortune to forget Fred Kanouse and his ilk.

Sir John of the "76"

Admittedly there weren't many peers and knights among the western sodbusters. But at least there were "sample specimens" of nearly every rank known to society and there were times when the tramp or hobo had no choice but to share a bed with knighthood. And you couldn't always tell from a man's clothes or by the length of his whiskers which category he was in. Certainly Sir John Lester Kaye's clothes never betrayed his rank. And one would have reason to conclude that he felt even more at home on the Canadian frontier which was then the thin edge of civilization, than in the Court of St. James.

The unoccupied farming land of Western Canada was inviting fearless people. Sir John was fearless; he had the spirit that would become an Arctic explorer. To him fertile soil was the thing; with good soil he believed he could overcome the obstacles to prairie farming about which folk cautioned him. His optimism became a maxim. Actually his agricultural undertakings, considered as a whole, were not very successful, but somebody had to perform the experiments and make the mistakes. Those mistakes were sometimes quite entertaining but they did serve a useful purpose in the new country.

Sir John was one of those Englishmen with means, who was more attracted by the romance of the frontier than the comforts of home. There we find him at Balgonie, just east of Regina, in 1885. In this instance he is associated with Lord Queensbury in a 7000 acre farm. I suppose it is just an experiment or a feeler, as it were. Horses were shipped in from Ontario and good buildings were erected. In the spring of '87, Sir John equipped 30 ploughs to turn the prairie grass upside down. Eleven hundred acres were broken and in the next year there was a bumper crop and Sir John's enthusiasm knew no bounds. In stature Sir John was a little man but in business he was a giant and he was not satisfied with a mere 7000 acres. In the same year that he was breaking sod at Balgonie, he formed the Canadian Agricultural, Coal and Colonization

Company and secured 100,000 acres of land in ten blocks of 10,000 acres each. Half of the land was secured from the Canadian Government and half from the C.P.R. and the tracts were at points along the main line of the C.P.R., as far west as Langdon, near Calgary. These blocks of land, fortunately, were free from squatters or homesteaders and Sir John's plan included both farming and ranching. He would develop the land and sell it as small farms to settlers from England. Each small farming unit to be sold to an immigrant would be fenced and stocked with farm animals; and it would have 20 acres under cultivation. That was the plan.

But it was not clear sailing; in much of that area where the ten big farms were located, precipitation was normally light and no amount of optimism would make it rain. Then to make matters worse, the West was wrapped in a period of particularly dry years; indeed the "eighties" of last century may have been quite as dry as the "thirties" of the present century. Sir John had been warned that some of that prairie land while good for grazing, would never be suitable for wheat. "Joe" Wylie of Maple Creek was one who cautioned him but the warnings were not heeded; Sir John would grow wheat or find out for himself why he shouldn't grow it. He was that variety of Englishman.

He ordered 500 Clydesdale horses from Ontario, 50 for each of the big farms. The breaking ploughs were put to work; the grass sod was wrecked and the land made ready for wheat. But it was too dry and there was no harvest in 1889. Sir John would correct that; if the rains wouldn't come at the right time, he would haul water to the fields and spill it on the wheat land. He placed an order in Winnipeg for sprinkling tanks, 44 of them for a trial. The tanks were made of pine, 11 feet long, two feet high and carried on carts. The idea was that when the rains failed, a fleet of these sprinklers would be sent into the fields and thus the wheat would be watered. The tanks were used but needless to say they made no perceptible impression upon the thirsty plants in the big fields. Of course the idea was ridiculously impracticable; even one inch of rainfall or water on a single acre of land would weigh more than 110 tons and to haul that amount for large areas of wheat land must seem a bit fantastic. The idea was abandoned but not forgotten. The policy of growing wheat on some of the farms was also abandoned very soon and Sir John revised his plans so as to feature live stock and ranching more and wheat and colonization less.

The original plans had called for improved types of live stock to be brought from Ontario or the Old Country, Clydesdales, Shropshire sheep, Aberdeen Angus cattle and Yorkshire pigs. But the blueprint for stock production was changed when the difficulties of grain farming were recognized. Large scale stock raising in this land called for hardy animals which were good rustlers and which were also acclimatized. An Englishman D. H. Andrews who became the local manager with headquarters at Crane Lake, came into the picture with the live stock. He had gained ranching experience in the United States; he knew all about organizing a round-up; he knew how to handle a stampeding herd and he knew how to deal with cattle rustlers. He knew "Cattle Kate" that notorious woman of the American range to whom the cowboys and frontiersmen paid their debts by placing her brand on some unmarked calves. It was in this way that Cattle Kate built up a big and valuable herd.

Sir John's first cattle were bought in '88; they were from the Powder River Ranch Co. of Wyoming and carried the brand "76". The brand was purchased with the cattle and hence the name "76" by which the English company became most widely known. The cattle were not far removed from their Texas Longhorn ancestry and were conspicuous by length of horn and length of leg. Five hundred were to be placed as a foundation herd on each of the ten farming units but the first winter was severe and losses were heavy. It was decided in 1890 to consolidate the herds and all the cattle were brought to Swift Current Creek.

From the very beginning, Sir John had some ambitious ideas about dairying. He proposed a very large creamery at Swift Current but there were practical difficulties. But when wheat production failed and the English shareholders were faced with loss, there was a new demand for dairying. It is told that very shortly after the Powder River Ranch cattle came, an order went out from England to milk the cows and make butter. That order must have given Andrews some sleepless nights. And the wild, long-horned critters didn't enter into the spirit of the head-office order any better than did Andrews. I can imagine a mounted cowboy dropping his lariat over the head of an old longhorn matron and snubbing her up or throwing her on the ground so that he could extract the milk. And for receiving the milk from that hostile old cow after she was made helpless with ropes, a platter would probably have been as suitable as a pail. But they devised a better plan; Mr. Wm. Alexander of Swift Current who was hired to erect buildings on the Kincorth place when "Joe" Wylie was the cattle foreman in 1888, was one of the spectators and he described to me long chutes into which some of the cows were driven at milking time. In accord with this arrangement the animal's head was drawn down to a ring in the floor and while two cowboys handled the ropes, a third tried to remove a little milk from the terrified and humiliated old cow. If it takes a contented cow to produce good milk, the milk from Sir John's longhorns should have poisoned the cook. I fancy the cowboys liked the general scheme of things about as well as the cows liked it. But it wasn't for long because that plan too was quickly abandoned and sound ranch policies were adopted.

With sheep, Sir John's company was rather more successful. Ten thousand was a favourite figure with him and when he bought sheep in Montana and Idaho to stock his 10,000 acre farms, he bought 10,000 head. The sheep were driven overland by James Ross and William Riddle. It was a difficult undertaking but they followed the course of streams to Maple Creek and there turned the flocks over to William Rutherford whom Sir John had named sheep manager. And then the sheep were loaded on freight cars and distributed to the various locations for foundation purposes. But in the next year the bands were brought together again and headed-up at Swift Current, Kincorth and Gull Lake. When John Oman, a Scot who came to Canada to "have his own land", entered the services of Sir John's company as an experienced sheep man in 1892, there were 30,000 sheep of all ages including wethers. They were divided among 15 camps with 2000 head at each and the camps extended for about 50 miles. The first sheep were predominantly Merino but Cheviot rams were imported from the

Old Country and the general appearance of the flocks was soon changed.

The market of that day called for big cattle and big sheep. Big joints of meat had lost nothing in favour and surplus sheep were not sold as lambs as they are today. Yet prices were not very encouraging, especially after 1893 when the "Great Sheep Depression" set in and good wethers were sold at Winnipeg at 2½ cents a pound. The "76" sent many sheep across the Atlantic, probably not less than 25,000 head. I know of one particular shipment of 2000 which went to England in 1895. The long journey from Swift Current to London, England, was made with the loss of only one sheep.

Sir John's shepherds were paid $30.00 a month with a board allowance of $12.00 Twelve dollars will buy a lot of oatmeal. At Christmas time, each shepherd received two bottles of Hudson's Bay whiskey. The head shepherd who delivered the Christmas cheer made it a point to remain around the camp for a few days to see that the sheep were not neglected until normal conditions prevailed once again. At least that was the reason he gave for remaining around until the whiskey was done. One of the shepherds who said he would keep the Christmas gift in case of sickness, had to confess later, "Mon it was a queer thing that I was sick every day until the bottle was empty".

Well, Sir John's company experienced one difficulty after another. Many of the early policies were clearly impracticable. Farm implements shipped from England were not as suitable as machinery which could have been obtained in Canada. Likewise, many of the farm and ranch hands were severely handicapped by lack of experience and had to learn by costly mistakes made at the expense of the company. For example, Hon. Hubert Pelham Clinton who was a director sent James L. Smart to Canada with 110 inexperienced men in one group; they had been hired at $10.00 per month with board. It would take a robust organization to carry such a burden. About the time the men might have been useful, many concluded that Canadian life did not suit them and returned to England. On the other hand, I could name some very well known citizens of the West, and especially of the Canadian range, who got their start with the old "76".

With accumulating mistakes, the company was faced with failure and Sir John retired. Manager D. H. Andrews went to England in 1895 and the Canadian Land and Ranch Company was formed and took over the holdings of the failing organization. Andrews continued as manager and the new company met with a good measure of success. Andrews died in 1906 and three years later the Crane Lake ranch and the "76" brand were sold to the well known firm of Gordon, Ironside and Fares.

Now a concluding word about Sir John Lester Kaye; his stay in the West was not a long one; but his few years on the frontier were packed with activity; he made some bad guesses. But still I insist that this dynamic little Englishman made it easier for some of those who followed and that he was one of the trail blazers whom agricultural people should not forget.

Samuel Larcombe

Manitoba Wheat King

I want to turn the Sodbuster spotlight upon a pioneer in whom Manitoba has justifiable pride. He had no university degrees; no initials after his name; and he could never be famous for his wealth for he didn't have it. But Samuel Larcombe had more enduring assets; he had the love of those who knew him and he had the respect of thousands who did not know him.

He was the typical John Bull, short, chubby and jovial; he was John Bull even to the "mutton chop" whiskers. Why no one had ever called him a "two faced old Englishman", he couldn't say; he expected it. Because, as he would good naturedly explain, the fringe of hair about his face was only a little different than the fringe about his bald head, and he "looked about the same coming and going".

I attended the International Fat Stock Show at Chicago in 1925 and Samuel Larcombe was there. I talked to him in the rotunda of the New Southern Hotel where we were staying and he was humorously castigating the Chicago reporters who would not leave him alone. Really though, it wasn't much wonder that they followed him because they had made a discovery; they had found "John Bull"; and Chicago was about the last place one would expect to find John Bull at that time. He had to tell them his life story, and retell it. They took his picture standing beside King of the Fairies, that well-known Shorthorn bull from the Alberta ranch of the Prince of Wales. The white bull was Grand Champion there that year while the Manitoba John Bull was an outstanding winner in the Grain Show. I remember him telling that it was the first time he ever had his picture taken with Royalty and he was pleased how graciously the King of the Fairies had accepted. And then he added, "Broad minded old bull, wouldn't you say".

Of course he was born in England; where else could a John Bull come from? He was a product of beautiful old Devonshire and his people for generations were farm servants;

they were the people who arose early, toiled hard, drank their ale as a matter of course and lived long lives without ever going far from home. Theirs was a humble home. But then most of the world's great come from humble homes. Boys began working as soon as they were able, sometimes before. Young Samuel at the age of eight was doing a "guard herd" on nearby grain fields, scaring birds away. At eleven he was "on his own", working on a farm about a mile from home. That mile can be a long way for a chappie of tender years, especially about bed time, when boys do their serious thinking. There was this about it, however; his salary had advanced and he was getting his keep and sixpence a week, mind you. He was growing up fast because in the next year he went seven miles from home and took a job at a shilling a week; and now that he had increased his earning power to a shilling a week, his father admonished him not to be reckless with his money. Seems to me a MacEwan boy heard that advice every time he was released at Brandon Summer Fair, with anywhere between four and nine cents in his pocket.

Well, the years slid by without much opportunity for schooling and at 16 years of age the Larcombe boy could not read and he could not write. He was doing a man's work and busy earning the farthings he needed for his own support. But an opportunity to attend Night School presented itself and he seized upon it. That was the way he got his schooling but his education he got the still harder way.

And then the thing he dreamed about, happened; a trip to London Town. What bigger reward could a boy wish for? It was as though the Devonshire chappie had been transported to another world, droves of people, pretty shops, funny noises, pretty girls. The two-weeks stay in London passed all too soon. He returned to the farm but the bright lights and the big city had unsettled him and he grew restless. He took a job as a gardener near London; he took a job at Croydon; he got married; he heard tales about Canada, strange tales and contradictory tales. But common to all the tales was something about free land in Manitoba. Some folk said Manitoba was a good place, a land of promise; others considered it unfit for human habitation and that those people who survived the attacks of Indian savages and wild animals, would most certainly be frozen in winter. Sam Larcombe heard both sides of the story; somebody was wrong; he was 37 years of age and would see and judge for himself.

He arrived in Manitoba in 1889, same year as my father came. Settlers were flocking westward, but there was still a lot of God's country that hadn't been converted to real estate. Larcombe got a job on a farm at Birtle. He was the "green Englishman"; he said so himself and "a bright green at that". He put the horse collars on upside down and every time he hitched a team, either the horses ran away or the harness broke or he drove into a gate-post. In any case the result was roughly the same; something got broken and the boss became sufficiently violent to do a small scale massacre. He was the "green Englishman" all right, but not for long because every mistake served as a lesson and I judge he had quite a few lessons.

After a year at Birtle, he rented a farm and then bought that land which was later described as the best cultivated steading in Manitoba. He admitted ignorance in handling some of Manitoba's crazy broncho horses, but in growing plants he was no greenhorn. He had gained valuable knowledge from his father and came to Manitoba better equipped than most people. With vegetables he had uncanny success. Pork and beans were all right if Manitobans liked the dish; indeed the same pork and beans stood between many a homesteader and starvation, "but," argued Larcombe, "with good

SAM LARCOMBE

Courtesy of Mrs. Miriam Green Ellis

Manitoba soil, there is no need for restricted diets, even on the homesteads . . . . any vegetable that grows in England can be made to grow in Manitoba". He grew carrots that looked like mangels and he grew red tomatoes that made neighbours stare. He grew varieties of his own making.

The improvement of garden and field crops for this new land appeared as a challenge; selection of better strains became a hobby. Selection work, so far as the grains were concerned, began in the field and very often Sam Larcombe would literally disappear for half a day or more in one of his fields. "Best place in the world to hide from creditors", he said and I take it he saw a fair share of them; he experienced almost all the varieties of pests known to agriculture, true enough. Being short of stature, he sometimes got lost in a heavy crop; just once was he worried about being lost; he was still in the field pursuing the eternal search for superior heads, when darkness settled down upon Manitoba. As was sometimes his practice, he continued his search by means of a flash-light but with the generous crop towering over his head, all sense of direction had left him. He walked and walked, probably in a circle. He was lost. And then he wasn't lost because he heard the familiar voice of the family cow as she bellowed a message of love or boastfulness or something, and he knew the direction of the barnyard. His humour never failed; said when folk got lost on the prairies they usually had a horse and cutter for company, but when he was lost in a field of oats, there was nothing but an occasional night-hawk with which to share his trouble.

One of his major triumphs was the production of a new variety of wheat, Axminster, a variety which possessed some rust resistant qualities. He stood one day with his two sons and surveyed a 60-acre field of rank-growing Marquis wheat, ruined by rust. He said, "Boys, I'm going to take this thing in hand and I think I can defeat it". Well, he didn't defeat rust but he did some valuable spade work that resulted in ultimate defeat. As he combed a field one night in a rust year, the rays from his flash-light fell upon a single head of wheat that had withstood the attack better than its fellows. Next season, the seed from that head was planted beside other selections; the most promising lines were used in crossing and

Axminster, named after the old home town in Devonshire, was the result. We have Samuel Larcombe's testimony that he would rather produce a new and useful variety of grain for his adopted land than be the "discoverer of the North Pole and winner of the English Derby in the same year".

His success with seeds in National and International competition had few parallels. Chief among his winnings was the world's wheat championship with an entry at the International Grain Exposition at Peoria, Illinois, in 1917. Winning the sweepstakes for wheat with close to 500 entries competing, was not all; he won 32 other prizes, 26 of which were firsts, at that same show. He had a second for oats, second for barley, second for rye and championship for potatoes. And his entries were all from good Manitoba earth.

Actually he was exhibiting grains and vegetables from the first year he was in the country. For three years he prepared large exhibits of vegetables, grains and grasses for the C.P.R. to display in Toronto and other eastern cities. Then the Dominion Government recognized the value of Sam Larcombe's show-window material as an aid in immigration work and bought his products to be sent overseas to Britain and European countries. Indeed, Sam Larcombe was himself sent overseas by the Canadian Government and C.P.R. to tell prospective settlers what they might expect to find "out there". It must have been quite a thrill to go back to the old home district in Devonshire, travelling on a Government Expense Account and visiting with those who knew him when he herded sheep there for a shilling a week. "Look what Canada-West did by Sammy; must be a topping place"; and a good few followed him back to Manitoba.

Somebody figured it up and it seems that Samuel Larcombe won 3000 prizes for his Manitoba-grown products during his 43 years of farming. One must think of the long hours he spent hand picking his seeds, doing much of the work by lamplight. Indeed it would require the patience of Job as well as the judgment of a Solomon. Well might the Manitoba Legislature pass a resolution extending greetings to this man who had brought so much of international honour and publicity to the province; that was on the occasion of his 85th birthday.

One might have expected that reasonable financial reward

would be the team-mate of such outstanding achievement. Evidently it wasn't; and one of my Winnipeg friends could tell about coming to his aid with a subscription, raised expressly to erase some annoying debts. I dare say that his own generosity was one reason for his financial troubles but his kindly acts probably gave him far more pleasure than wealth could have done. He was indeed one who would part with the shirt from his back if a friend needed it. Too often, I fear, the less people have the more ready they are to give it.

But some of the bread he cast upon the water came back after many days. He said that three thrills stood out above all others in his life; the first was his visit to London when 20 years of age; the second was winning the world's sweepstakes for wheat in 1917 and the third came in 1929, after his farm home was burned; in true Western spirit, friends came to his assistance; funds were raised; lumber was delivered; a new house was erected. And that was not all; furniture was provided and the home made comfortable for the big hearted pioneer and his family.

He died on October 2, 1937, at the age of 86. But that smiling face, upon which his whiskers had played the trick of encirclement, will not soon be forgotten. He died as he had lived, poor in this world's goods but rich in agricultural achievement and fabulously rich in accumulated friendship. I consider it appropriate to close this sketch with the words of one who knew Sam Larcombe well, one who helped the old gentleman over stony ground, my friend James Evans;

> "The little town of Birtle was the scene of a final tribute to Sam Larcombe, such as is accorded few men. It was not a tribute to a 'wheat king' but rather a tribute to a lovable Manitoba character."

Alex Galbraith

The Horseman

The name of Alex Galbraith is about as familiar to the older horsemen as that of Joe Louis to the people who buy ringside seats at boxing matches. For many years it suggested good horses; it represented the "supreme court" among men in the horse business; and it stood for the finest agricultural traditions of Bonnie Scotland. Alex Galbraith was the true horseman; if there wasn't a curry comb peeking from his hip pocket, it was a safe bet that there were some horseshoe nails and a harness buckle or two hidden there or perhaps a few horsemen's lien notes. Nobody knew better than Alex Galbraith how lean some of those notes really were. But he was pretty game and was ready to buy or sell or trade horses at any time.

He was born in Sterlingshire, Scotland (1853), not far from Loch Lomond. His father was a cattleman of unusual calibre, and a horseman who won with Clydesdales at some of Glasgow's earliest stallion shows. All in all, I'll bet he was a good farmer. Young Alex grew up around the byre and show-ring. But as sometimes happens, the farm lad turned his back on his father's profession, at least for a time. At the age of 16, he went to work in a shop in Glasgow. He learned a great deal about textiles and dyes and the East Indian Trade. Terribly different from horses! For a while he liked it and then he hated it. He yearned for the smell of a good horse. After fourteen years in the trade, he threw it up, determined to forget it all. He sailed for Montreal. But didn't stop there. He had brothers in the United States and when Alex joined them, the four brothers formed a partnership to import horses of the British breeds, Clydesdales, Suffolks and Shires. For ten years their headquarters were at Janesville, Wisconsin and at least 1000 pure bred stallions were distributed.

You see, he did not have the violent breed preferences that characterized many of the horsemen. As far as he was concerned, "all good horses have good enough pedigrees". And as for breed associations, he served in most of them. In the American Clydesdale Association he was one of the first secretaries, then vice-president and president. He was secretary of the American Suffolk Horse Association for eighteen years. He was president of the American Shire Association for six years and he was prominent in the American Hackney Horse Society. The fact was, a good horse of any colour could make Alex Galbraith forget what he was supposed to bring home for dinner.

Then came the financial panic of 1893 which brought disaster to many. When the crash came, the Galbraiths had two boat-loads of horses on the Atlantic and Alex said, "I leave it to you to guess what we lost". The brothers dissolved partnership and Alex moved to the shelter of a Wisconsin farm. But he was well known and people wouldn't let him go into retirement. His services were sought by the University of Wisconsin for lecturing and judging. And by the way, it was that University which singled Mr. Galbraith out for an elaborate testimonial in 1911 in recognition of his great services to Agriculture.

The financial panic dealt a knock-out but Alex Galbraith wouldn't stay down and at the turn of the century he was back in the business of importing horses. This time his son Graeme was associated with him and the firm name was Alex Galbraith & Son. The next year, 1901, they opened a branch stable in Brandon and it was then that Western Canadians made the acquaintance of this Scot who was one of the giants in the business of supplying farm power.

ALEXANDER GALBRAITH

Courtesy of Mrs. Miriam Green Ellis

At Brandon the Galbraith Barn became a busy place. It was beside the Beaubier Hotel and it was an important meeting place for farmers who had an hour to waste while wives completed the exacting business of shopping. Alex Galbraith was a kindly soul; he never discouraged the city boys who nursed a fancy for horses and his barn was the first place the truant officer went when looking for boys who were "playing hookey". I guess I can speak with authority on that point; I'm not boasting but on at least one occasion I was carefully hidden under a forkful of hay in a manger while the officer decided to take a look for the culprit over at the stable of Trotter & Trotter.

I well remember that over the door of Alex Galbraith's barn at Brandon there hung a fascinating array of horseshoes, perfectly graduated from a miniature shoe for a wee Shetland pony, to a huge specimen for a giant Clydesdale foot. I don't know if Alex Galbraith knew the legend about horseshoes and the origin of "horseshoe luck", but he did have the shoes tacked up the right way. The story is, you see, that Satan once wanted a shoe fitted on one foot and came to get the job done by St. Dunstane, a wise old smithy. St. Dunstane recognized his evil customer and seized the opportunity to inflict punishment by driving a nail into his foot. When the devil cried out with pain, St. Dunstane bargained that he would finish the job painlessly when he had a promise that the evil one would never again come near a person displaying a horseshoe. Anyway, Alex Galbraith was right and the heel ends of the shoes must be up and the toe part down.

But to return to more serious matters, Alex Galbraith did not give all his time to horses. In 1912, his services were secured in connection with a Better Farming Train operating in Alberta. Early in the next year he opened a branch barn in Edmonton and in 1915 when Hon. Duncan Marshall was Alberta's Minister of Agriculture, Alex Galbraith was appointed Superintendent of Fairs and Lecturer at the Schools of Agriculture. He lectured at farm meetings and at short courses; he was very popular in rural districts; he was in a front line position wherever agricultural work was being carried on.

Still his heart was with horses. He reflected so much

earnest enthusiasm about good horses that he made people want to do business with him. An out-of-town visitor stepped into Galbraith's barn in Edmonton, to get out of the rain one day, and before the shower was over, the visitor had bought a Percheron stallion and two pure bred mares. That was Alex Galbraith. Of course horses weren't so hard to sell in those days when settlers needed power most urgently. Horses were more popular than oxen, and tractors weren't offering much serious competition. The tractors of that day had the aggravating habit of "quitting" at the farthermost point in the field while the oxen chose to do their stopping at the centre of the biggest slough.

Alex Galbraith was probably the most noted horse judge of his generation. He would be a bold horseman who would dispute Galbraith's decision in the show-ring. At Chicago International and Madison Square Gardens in New York, he either judged or exhibited consistently for a record number of years. He judged horses at the Chicago World's Fair in 1893; he judged at the St. Louis World's Fair in 1904, and at the Panama-Pacific International Show at San Francisco in 1915. There was just one thing wrong with Alex Galbraith as a judge; he knew nearly all the pedigreed horses in the country and could call them by their first names. And if horses could talk, I'm sure he would have heard "Hello, Alex" from some members of every class ever brought before him.

He knew the ways of the show-ring in Scotland, in Canada and United States as few people did. He was a judge who could not be bribed and could not be influenced, but in years gone by, zealous exhibitors sometimes attempted to "work" the judge on behalf of a stallion or mare or other exhibit. Prior to judging at one show, he received a collection of gifts including a box of cigars, a threatening letter and a bottle of whiskey. If I recall the balance of that story correctly, the exhibitor who sent the threatening letter stood with his horse at the bottom of the class and the man who so thoughtfully supplied a bottle of whiskey didn't fare much better.

He told of the Scotchman who was about to show a colt and saw fit to "prepare" the judge through the gift of a smoked ham. But on show day, the colt got nothing better than fourth prize. The disgruntled owner sought the judge for an explanation; "See here, Mr. Judge, I thought youw'd hae given me better than fourth for yon cult; deed ye no get the ham?" The judge was ready with his defence; "Yes, I got your ham but that fellow who won first prize sent me a whole side of pork".

I choose to think that the modern show-ring is on a higher moral plane. However that may be, the only way to win in a competition where Alex Galbraith was judging was to bring out a sound horse, heavily muscled, hard and clean cut in feet and legs, with true and snappy action, and full of quality. My friend Pete Taylor was telling about the time Alex Galbraith attended the Sask. Horse Breeders' Meeting in 1925. They were talking about quality and Mr. Taylor said, "Just how do you define quality Mr. Galbraith?" The reply was, "Pete, my man, I'll tell you; quality is what makes you and me stop and look,—stop and look at either a horse or a flower or a lady".

One had to be pretty careful what he said about a horse when in the presence of Alex Galbraith, because it might be that Galbraith would know more about that animal than even its owner would know. I heard of one man who tried to sell Alex Galbraith a work horse and said most convincingly that the animal was eight years old. Galbraith's reply must have been a trifle embarrassing; he said, "I sold that horse four years ago and he was eight years old then; you'd think he would be more than that now". He never forgot a horse. Of course the age of a horse cannot be determined accurately from the teeth after the animal is eight years old and it is generally known that many horses which are bought and sold seem never to get beyond eight years of age. Alex Galbraith used to remark that "all mares in Canada must have had twins eight years ago". To be sure, some girls never have birthdays after 22; it's the same principle.

Yes, horses were his first love; but they could not claim all the sentiment in his Presbyterian constitution. He was proud of his Scottish ancestry and it was Alex Galbraith who organized a Caledonia Society at Janesville in 1886, the first in the State of Wisconsin. Of course, where two or more Scots are gathered together, a St. Andrews Society or Caledonia Society must be a foregone conclusion. The records don't state whether or not he introduced haggis or mealy puddings into Wisconsin but he did introduce golf to that state; whether that was to his glory or not I refuse to give an opinion. But he set out an 18-hole course on his own farm and was the first president of one of Wisconsin's oldest golf clubs.

The agricultural leaders in both Canada and United States were proud to call Alex Galbraith a friend. Dean Rutherford of Saskatchewan was a close friend. They had a lot in common. They liked the same kind of a horse; they agreed that tractors would become popular but that good horses would always be needed and that western farmers might find their horses to be one of the best links with security. Another lifelong friend was Robert Ogilvie, one of those who conceived the idea of the International Show at Chicago and in whose exceedingly fertile brain the idea of the Saddle & Sirloin Club with its famous portrait gallery and shrine originated. Just how much Alex Galbraith had to do with the blue prints from which those famous international institutions sprang, no one can tell. I fancy it was considerable.

Yes, Alex Galbraith and his horses constituted a tremendous factor in the real business of sodbusting in this Western Canada. There is no record of how many thousands of head actually passed through his hands. But he did help to ease the pioneer burden. And in spirit he walked with the masters in agricultural improvement.

John Ware

Alberta's Black Sodbuster

According to himself, John Ware's main claim to distinction was in being the first "Smoked Irishman" to raise cattle in the South West. But he had more of distinction than that, a good deal; and his colour was not all in his hide. This darky who had spent his early years in slavery in the south, became one of the best stockmen of his time. More than that he was an exceedingly friendly soul and sympathetic; and he had a fine sense of justice. If the Little Black Sambo story of nursery fame has anything resembling a counterpart in the history of the range, here it is.

The North-West Cattle Company which was later known as the "Bar U", was organized in 1881 and was the second of the big outfits to bring cattle to graze on the foothills grass. Fred Stimson was the first manager and in the spring of 1882, he sent Tom Lynch to Idaho to buy a herd. Three thousand head were bought and driven north. They arrived on the new range in September, to be greeted by a terrific eight-day storm which created hardship and loss. But Lynch brought more than cattle to the Canadian Chinook Belt on that occasion. He brought some helpers, among them that big and powerful negro, John Ware, who was destined to become one of the most highly respected and loved of pioneers and one of the greatest riders in the history of the range.

Negroes have never been noted for horsemanship and certainly nobody expected this dapper young buck with the shiny button boots and the huge polka-dot bow tie, to be a rider. But Lynch in the drive northward needed another rider. He wasn't struck on the idea of taking on any but a seasoned horseman. However, there wasn't much choice, and this son of the far south who asked for work, without making any special claims for himself, was told that he could have a job for a spell; no guarantee for how long. Lynch quite naturally suspected the worst in Ware's horsemanship, and produced an ancient and dilapidated saddle and a feeble old horse. The darky was disappointed. He wanted a horse with some life and even some fight. But he accepted his lot with good nature and spent most of his time in the thick dust that hung over "the drag" end of the big herd.

Before the drive was completed, however, "Nigger John" mustered enough courage to speak to the boss and what he said has been told many times in the South West; "Ah was jus wunderin boss if you w'd give me a little betta saddle and a little wuss hoss, ah somehow think ah can ride um". Well, John Ware got a "worse" horse all right because the cowboys were looking for some fun and they conspired to get this green blackman on the worst horse in the band. The stage was set and "Nigger John" was heard to say, "What will ah do if he bucks?" The cowboys chuckled; they were there to see this tenderfoot from Carolina make a "crash landing". Then he said, "Which side does a nigga get on from?" It looked like suicide. "Nigger John" climbed on board, as clumsily as you like, and the bad horse went into action. He bucked; he kicked; he pitched; he made some "U turns" in mid air and a few "corkscrews" but the tricks which had always worked before, didn't work this time; they didn't unseat this rider. The cowboys who had assembled for a laugh got the surprise of their lives. They had witnessed a preliminary but finished exhibition by one of the greatest riders of all time. To "Nigger John" it was just another ride because he was not a "show-off", and conceit had no place in him. But he had won new respect from his fellows and from that time forward he met stockmen and others in the Canadian South-West on common ground. In later years when bronc-riding became competitive, "Nigger John" was recognized as the best on the Canadian side. There are old timers who state that "Nigger John" was never thrown by a bucking horse. In handling a rope or a gun, he was equally proficient. He took the conceit out of a lot of big steers of the four-year-old kind who thought they were too powerful to be man-handled; it must have been quite a shock to the pride of those steers to find themselves stretched on the ground, roped and helpless, all in less than 60 seconds after John Ware put the spurs to his horse and twirled his old lariat.

In the early years when "Nigger John" was with the "Bar

U", he usually carried his six-shooter. He was never guilty of using it foolishly but it could be handy in the encouragement of justice or in stopping an infuriated steer or convincing a horse thief that "Nigger John" meant business. When meat stocks were low and John wanted a prairie chicken, he elected to do his hunting with a revolver, which wasn't taking quite the same mean advantage of the wild bird as he would do if using a shot-gun.

It seemed that "Nigger John" could do nearly everything but swim. He said the "coal-dust" in his skin made him sink. But because horses can swim and he was nearly always astride a horse when fording a stream, he didn't worry. On one occasion, however, he found himself in mid-stream on one of those rare specimens of horseflesh that can't swim. It was the quick action of another cowboy with a lariat that saved John Ware's life that time. He was roped and safely hauled out while his horse was carried down stream to a watery grave.

"Nigger John" was on the "Bar U" Ranch when George Lane came. After a few years he went with the Quorn Ranch between Sheep Creek and Highwood River and ranged over the area later to be famous as the Turner Valley Oil Field. The Quorn Ranch had good stock, high class stock. The English influence was strong and Thoroughbred stallions were imported from the Old Country, also Hunter type mares and Aberdeen Angus cattle. "Nigger John" had no Oxford accent but he did become a great favourite at the Quorn and was given a good deal of responsibility. He was consulted about ranch policy, schooled the Quorn saddle horses and chased coyotes with the Quorn hounds. When English aristocracy visited the ranch, John Ware was in his element. He discovered that Dukes and Earls made first class companions.

But good men and ambitious grow restless and "Nigger John" itched to have a place of his own. The ranch he secured about 1888 or '89 was not far from the Quorn on the north fork of Sheep Creek adjacent to the ranch of John Quirk, another well known pioneer. Gradually his herd increased in size. He had good cattle but a hideous brand, "9999". It took quite a lot of cow-hide to provide a background for such a brand. Why he chose it isn't clear but some folk tell that he was 9 years old when the slaves gained their freedom and that he considered 9 to be his lucky number.

For some reason, John Ware didn't get along too well with the Indians and occasional stray bullets floated around his headquarters on Sheep Creek. But "Nigger John" was not afraid of the Red Men even though they were numerous and he was the only one of his kind in Alberta. Nobody ever had occasion to think that he was "yellow". "Nigger John's" pet dog disappeared one day when he was ranching on Sheep Creek. The Indians nearby were preparing for a feast and "Nigger John" had a premonition that his little dog was a candidate for the stew-pot. He bared his glossy white teeth and his curly hair stood more erect than usual; there was a wild negro up there in the hills. He made sure all the chambers in his revolver were filled and went out to reconnoitre. Sure enough, he found his dog at the Indian encampment. After an affectionate reunion between dog and man the darky had some useful advice for the Indian chief. If any Indian tried a trick like that on pet dogs again, he might find a lariat around his neck and a big brand with four nines in it being slapped on his left flank. As far as is known, "Nigger John's" dog was not molested again. I somehow think that John Ware regarded his lariat as being just as useful as his gun when it came to offensive or defensive warfare on the frontier.

This reminds one of an incident which occured when John Ware and one of his fellow ranchers were driving some "four-nine" cattle to a new pasture. A ruffian accosted them and claimed the good horse John was riding. John Ware wasn't easily fooled and he "called the stranger's bluff". He said, "If you can separate this hoss from me yo can have im but don't forget, yo're startin' this show". The stranger evidently decided not to press his claim and John Ware began to uncoil his lariat, muttering all the while, to his friend, "Wat yo say; think we should hang this hoss thief now or wait till next time we meet him". There was no next time because the stranger left the Canadian range.

Actually however, John Ware was a kindly and sympathetic person and until he was confronted with injustice he was the perfect gentleman. He loved dogs and he was gentle with horses unless occasion demanded otherwise. His chief aversion was snakes. He came in for a lot of teasing and took it in good part until a snake or something resembling a snake was used to torment him; then it was different; all of a sudden it was as though a match had been set to 200 pounds of super-explosive. The snake trick wasn't employed very often but the story is told about John Ware quite casually branding in a corral full of bulls when a tiny garter-snake slithering along the ground did what a herd of range bulls couldn't do, make big John hurdle the corral fence and take to the open range.

There weren't many girls of "Nigger John's" kind to choose from in that part of Canada but he made the acquaintance of a coloured girl from the East, who was visiting in Calgary. She liked the big, good-natured, black rancher. He drove into Calgary with a spanking pair of bronchos more often while she was there and went in for supplies once a week instead of once in three months which had been his rule. He took her riding in his democrat and once there was a near disaster. A thunder and lightning storm came up. A flash struck and killed both horses instantly while "Nigger John" and his future bride were left sitting unharmed in the democrat. He took the harness off the dead horses, threw it in the democrat and proceeded to pull the vehicle and the dark lady back over the muddy roads to town. The dead horses were left on the trail and traffic went around the carcasses until a permanent curve in the road came into existence.

When he recounted that experience and told of the number of bullets which had missed him and bad horses which didn't kill him, he was sure he had lived a charmed life. Surely the "four nine" brand had some of the same qualities as a four-leaf clover.

"Nigger John" sold his place on Sheep Creek and took prairie land on the Red Deer River, near Duchess. There he continued to run cattle, ride bad horses, and extend a helping hand to hungry and tired travellers who came his way. Allen Robinson told of stopping at John's one night in the spring of 1904. He was moving 100 brood mares for Gordon, Ironside and Fares. John's house was close to the river and in the morning they found the river had risen and the house was surrounded by water. They got a team and loaded John's wife and the pickaninnies on to a wagon and moved to higher ground. An hour later, the water was trickling through the windows and John said it was the first time he owned a house with running water in it. Next time Robinson called, the old 250 pound negro, was back at his old tricks, breaking a tough horse. John's wife was enjoying it. She laughed as the horse bucked, and called out, "You're doin' fine John. Yous an old nigga but you can shu show the young uns how to stay upstairs on a hoss".

Then in 1905, the sad news was circulated that his horse had stumbled in a badger hole and that "Nigger John's" neck had been broken in the fall. Farmers and ranchers over a large part of the agricultural West mourned the loss of a true friend. He was black outside but one of the whitest of pioneers within. Ask any old timer in Southern Alberta about "Nigger John" Ware.

Okanagan Ellis

When travelling to Winnipeg by plane in June 1943 I made the acquaintance of an old gentleman (G. C. Smith) 96 years of age. He was completing the journey from Vancouver to Winnipeg in less than eight hours. As we were gliding through the night admiring the magnificent illumination of that mighty Manitoba city, my new friend said, "That's a lot different from the Fort Garry I saw when I came here in 1872". On that first trip he was well over a month travelling from Toronto to Fort Garry by the old Dawson Route and he made part of it on foot, part by water and part in a Red River Cart. Today he came from the Pacific Ocean to the same destination in eight hours.

I find it a fascinating contrast but actually there are lots of striking parallels in this new land. At the moment I am thinking about Thomas Ellis and the strange and exciting changes which he saw and directed in his Okanagan Valley. I'm thinking of how he led the way in the change from wilderness to farming and ranching, and then to fruit.

But to start from the beginning; this Thomas Ellis was born in Dublin; no better place for an Irishman to be born. And to be sure, his was no ordinary family. The name of Ellis went with big enterprise and there was a family of 17 children. Thomas was the eldest boy. Things were a bit crowded, especially at meal time, and Thomas at the age of 19 decided to get out and make more room for the wee ones, "distant relations" as it were. Fascinating tales were being circulated about the west coast of Canada. They seemed to spell opportunity for those who would go out and fight for it. Tom Ellis and his pal, Andy McFarland were ready for a bit of adventure and secured passage on an old time sailing vessel. Ellis had to borrow money from his father. It was all paid back however, every cent of it. Thomas Ellis was like that. He expected to pay his debts and he expected others to do the same.

The ocean journey took not weeks but months. They

passed around the Horn and then north on the blue waters of the Pacific, to Vancouver Island. That was 1864, three years before Confederation, eight years before my old friend of the plane trip walked into Fort Garry, 21 years before the Canadian Pacific Railroad was completed. The coastal regions were occupied mainly by Indians and traders and a few gold miners. The country was still under the spell of that mad gold rush to the Upper Fraser in 1858 and the still madder rush to the Cariboo in '62. After a couple of years at the coast, Ellis and McFarland went up the Fraser and over the mountains to pitch camp in the Okanagan Valley. The valley was practically unknown except to Indians and a few miners who went in when a gold strike was made at Rock Creek a few years before (1861). The two young Irishmen began trading. Trade was profitable but not what one could call easy because there were no roads and any trade goods brought in or furs sent out, had to be transported over the Hope Mountains, usually by pack-horse. In any case, trading tea and flour for furs couldn't hold Ellis. He had some of the vision of a Hebrew prophet. He saw wealth in that soil and envisioned fat cattle coming off that grass. Of course there would be difficulties, lots of them. How would foundation stock be secured? And when cattle were established, who would buy them and how would one get the critters out? But when a man as stubborn as Ellis gets a notion, something must happen.

About the only cattle that had grazed right there in the Okanagan Valley, were a few milk cows turned out by the Okanagan Mission. They represented a back-wash from trade with the mines. Nevertheless, they seemed to thrive. Ellis was convinced so he and his partner managed to finance 20 head which they drove in over a rocky trail from Oregon in that first year. As time went on they secured a few more cattle from Americans going through to the Cariboo Gold Fields. The cattle multiplied rapidly, in fact more quickly than the market for them. Then to complicate matters, McFarland found it necessary to retire and return to Ireland. A short time later, Ellis went back to Ireland but for a different reason. He went to marry the sweetheart of his school-days and bring her to his Canadian ranch,—out where neighbourhood quarrels were unknown because the nearest white neighbour was 30 miles away. It was a drastic change for the Irish Colleen but she made it with grace and turned her hand at once to the great task of home-building.

Anyway, the Ellis herd was expanding rapidly and now grazing from a point north of the present Penticton, clear to the International boundary. Nobody was buying cattle and cattlemen were discouraged. But Ellis "dipped into the future" and he wasn't worried about markets. He did what I would expect a man like Ellis to do; bought more cattle. J. C. Haynes, later known widely as Judge Haynes, was building up a herd in the Valley. The two herds were expanding simultaneously but ultimately, Ellis bought the land of the Haynes Estate, 20,756 acres in all. How many of the Ellis and Haynes cattle were driven over the Hope Trail to the Fraser River in the pre-rail years, I don't know, but there were many. And when the cattle reached the river, they were placed on flat boats and taken to New Westminster or Victoria. The river boat, *William Irving* was the most famous in the stern-wheel fleet of that period and it carried a lot of cattle. Then came the railroad and it changed many things. The road-builders needed beef and cattle wearing the Ellis brand were sent east as well as west.

Man of many parts, this Ellis, and cattle represented but one of his triumphs. Every time I sink my teeth into a McIntosh Red apple from British Columbia, I think of him. It was exactly ten years after he arrived on Canadian soil that he planted the first apple trees in all the Valley. That was at the south end of the Lake, close to the present Penticton. Funny thing to do as nobody had thought seriously about growing fruit, and I can imagine that neighbours were ready to brand it a "crazy venture". But Ellis' dreams came true; his trees bore fruit. His was the first orchard in that Okanagan Valley which became world famous for its fruit. When the railroad was built, Ellis had apples as well as beef to sell.

The railroad changed many things but not the individualist Ellis. He was never very kindly disposed to the rails. He got along fine before they came and besides, didn't he come to this inter-mountain region to be away from trains and the like? Ah yes, Thomas Ellis did his own thinking and had a clearly thought out reason for everything, even if he didn't disclose it. He was of the strong, silent breed. He lived close to the Indians for many years and no doubt they made an impression upon him. On one occasion he did not see a white person for three months. He was friendly, yes, and had a good sense of humour but he never chose to use more words than necessary. Why should one, unless he has to round out a 15-minute radio talk? There was one topic, however, upon which he was more voluble, that was "votes for women". And he was opposed. "Sure the country will go to the dogs when women get the franchise." But I fancy that when seven daughters grew into womanhood, many of dad's views were changed.

Perhaps it was on account of being alone so much that he developed the habit of talking to himself. I would be willing to bet, however, that even when talking to himself, he used none but carefully chosen words and just enough to meet the need. It is said that he once travelled across the Atlantic without speaking to his cabin-mate, because, as he said, they had no common interests.

If anybody needed help, however, the quiet pioneer would be first to bring it; but it didn't pay to try to take advantage of him. Some visitors once pitched their tents on his land without getting his permission. It was the wrong thing to do and they experienced a sudden jolt one night when the master, single handed, raided and upset their camp. Later they presented letters of introduction to him and while they were still wondering who the night raider was, he invited them to enjoy the hospitality of the Ellis home for a week. Then they made a search for the ruffian but didn't find him.

Thomas Ellis was a hard worker. He kept long hours and his work was well organized. And was he methodical? When he was in England on one occasion, he wrote to order his steam boat *The Penticton* which plied between his town and the Okanagan Mission (Kelowna), to meet him at Vernon at a stated hour on a certain day. Captain T. D. Short of the Ellis boat was loath to make the trip. The boss might operate around the ranch according to his timetable, but he couldn't make that long journey from England on schedule.

But Cap. Short obeyed the order. He said afterwards, "I didn't expect to see Mr. Ellis, but came the appointed hour and blowed if he didn't step off the stage coach and the whole bloomin' family with him, right on time".

He had other qualities of the pioneer upon which I like to reflect. Until the last ten years of his life he was rarely ill, never in a hospital bed and never in a dentist's chair. If he did have pains and aches, I fancy that nobody but himself ever knew. When he was obliged to grapple with a human ailment, he insisted upon using his favourite remedies for sick horses. Sweet spirits of nitre gave good results in the horse barn and when he was a bit "off colour" he would sneak a little dose of it for himself.

One might suppose that so stern a man would have little patience with animals. Not so. His horses enjoyed the most thoughtful care. And long after he was unable to walk without a cane, he continued to ride his horse. Sometimes the Ellis home took on the appearance of a zoo because family pets were numerous. Orphan lambs and calves were standard equipment. And at one time or another there were coyotes, weasels, deer, a monkey, a parrot and a bald-headed eagle, to say nothing of dogs of all kinds.

Despite a crowded and busy life, Thomas Ellis had time for politics which he took very seriously and he read good books, mostly classical. He always had time to help folk in trouble, and he had time for church. His religion was of a practical type, yet a vital thing in his life. He built a small church in Penticton, known later as the Ellis Memorial Chapel, and ministers of all denominations were invited to preach in it. Even to the end of his life, he rarely failed to be in his pew for the regular service. He came on time, never earlier than necessary, and rarely late. One might expect that the bell which sounded the call to worship would cease to peal when the clergyman took his place in the pulpit. Not in this case. It stopped when Thomas Ellis arrived.

Here then we leave the record of one of the great Sodbusters of British Columbia. He "started from scratch" and saw his pioneer efforts develop into big industry. He died in 1918 at the age of 74. The Okanagan Valley in its lovely spring-time dress of apple blossoms is a most fitting memorial to Thomas Ellis.

A Barr Colonist Sodbuster

Forty odd years ago, on an April morning, Saskatoon blossomed into a tent city; the English had arrived. Business went into high gear because these Barr Colonists, train loads of them, were going to buy oxen and horses and wagons and stock up with provisions and push on over North-Westerly trails to a site selected for them on the fourth meridian. Every corner of England was represented and, I'm sure, every profession. There were as many points of view as one would have encountered in Hyde Park on Sunday afternoon. Some of the colonists had farm experience; the majority did not. Anyway they were making history.

But this is a story about one of them, a London cockney (born Oct., 1865) who admitted that he didn't know which of the implements of the farm was a binder and which a seed drill; and he wasn't very sure whether potatoes grew on trees or in bushel baskets. But when my friend Charlie Thomas set his hand to the plough, there was no turning back and he remained to become famous for his farming achievements.

To transplant one's self and family from the heart of Old London to the newness of the unbroken Canadian prairie was not a small matter. Charlie had been bred and reared right there in the Empire's Capital, and when the glowing story of Rev. I. M. Barr's plan for an English colony in Canada reached him, he was employed in an engineer's shop. He was 37 years of age. He had a wife and two children. He had completed his engineering apprenticeship and progress was of necessity slowing down; he was ready for a change. He had never as much as considered farming but Barr's scheme appealed strongly to his imagination. Barr had visions of getting a couple of hundred settlers; instead of that he got a couple of thousand. The response was a bit overwhelming. Anyway, on March 31, (1903), the Thomas family left Liverpool on the S.S. *Lake Manitoba* one of the boats chartered to carry Barr's party. The Thomases had severed all the ties with their old associations. Charlie had £80 in his pocket and some tough battles ahead.

After 11 days at sea and four or five on the train, the Colonists arrived at Saskatoon. The winter's snow had just disappeared. The roads and trails were impassible on account of mud but that didn't matter much because it would take days to assemble equipment and prepare for the long trail-journey to the "promised land". Charlie Thomas bought a team of horses and a covered wagon. Prices were high, too high, and Charlie thought that the infant metropolis should have been called "Soak-it-to-em" instead of Saskatoon. But, sure, the colonists had to have horses; they preferred to buy horses with the harness already on them because that would eliminate the perplexing mysteries of harnessing. At the end of the first day on the trail, when it became necessary to unharness the weary animals, some of the colonists were observed to be chalk-marking the horses. Why? To indicate where "the bloomin' 'arness" should go in the morning.

The trails were poorly marked and weeks of hardship lay ahead. They slept under canvas and if they couldn't sleep for the cold, they just shivered under canvas. They cooked and ate their meals in the open; they were lucky and shot a wild duck; they got stuck in the mud, lots of times, and had to unload the wagon to get out. It rained and then it snowed. There was hardship, sure there was, but they didn't discuss it much; they talked about the home they were going to build. If they longed for old Blighty, they did it silently. They saw discouraged settlers turning back every day, but the Thomases were not turning back. Then on May 20th, nearly a month after leaving Saskatoon, C. E. Thomas and family pitched camp on the quarter section that was to be their homestead.

A house enjoyed a homestead priority, so the newcomers built a log house and roofed it with what Thomas called "prairie shingles". It was one of those houses with a sod roof "where it rained inside the house for two days after it stopped raining outside". It was a modest home and plastered with clay, but they looked upon it with satisfaction and not a little pride and they had a gay house-warming when it was completed. Then Charlie Thomas dug a well and set up a flag-pole in the best British style. That was "round one".

So much, so good, but Thomas needed more equipment and he wanted some live stock. When a settler with some farm experience was going back to Battleford, "C.E." went along and simply duplicated all the purchases which the neighbour made. The neighbour bought an axe and so did Thomas; the neighbour bought beans and so did Thomas. But Thomas did more than that; at Bresaylor, he bought a cow in milk, a sow and 17 laying hens. He took possession on the return journey and for the balance of the way he peddled milk and eggs and collected a few cents that way. But the matter of extracting milk from the cow was a real chore and the cow as well as the Englishman must have suffered in those first attempts. Then to complicate the problem of milk removal, Thomas found that when he milked out in the open, the wind blew the streams of milk completely out of control and when he milked in the lea of a bluff, all the mosquitoes in the North West seemed to congregate for a feast of red blood.

The new animals were delivered safely and then a shelter had to be constructed for them. So a stable to accommodate two horses, one cow, a pig and the hens was built by driving two rows of fence pickets in the ground to form the inner and outer walls and packing the intervening space with hay. A roof was made by means of poles and hay and finally 25 cents worth of cheese cloth was tacked along the front to afford light and ventilation. The total cash cost of the stable was 25 cents, but it should be noted in passing that the Ayrshire cow Polly of Hillview who was champion butterfat producer in the prairie provinces about 1914, made her record in that lowly cow stable.

In spite of caution, the Thomas resources in cash were soon exhausted and there was poverty to fight as well as prairie fires and the trickery of an untried country. Said Charlie, "There's no police station here, no workhouse and no pawnshop so it's just up to ourselves". And looking back on it he said, "It wasn't all beer and skittles by any means".

Well, he broke a little land with his two faithful horses and the first summer passed all too quickly. The winter set in with fair fury but the settlers had plenty of wood. They had flour and they hoped to shoot sufficient game to keep themselves in meat. Most of them had guns; Thomas had a gun and was a good shot, but tragedy threatened when a complicated piece of gear, the ejector lever on his gun became broken.

What was to be done? There were no repairs in the country and the gun was an essential if the family was going to eat adequately. It was then that resourcefulness was put to the test. Thomas made a new piece, fashioned it out of a rail-road spike and did it without a forge and without a vice. I saw the job he did and still marvel at the quality of the workmanship. To heat the rail-road spike in the absence of a forge he dug a trench for the fire and used some hard knots of wood for fuel; and then to get a good draught on the fire, he jacked a wagon wheel clear of the ground, tied some sacks to the rim, and had the children turn the wheel, fan fashion.

The first winter was nearly always the worst one in the life of a settler; and the first winter produced lots of trials there in that district about the town called Lloydminster in honour of Rev. Exton Lloyd. Bishop Lloyd as he was known later, assumed leadership and gave great service in the community. Anyway, the winter was severe and feed supplies for the animals were scarcely adequate. Thomas had bad luck with his stock and no one can tell of it better than himself: the cow went dry, the horses died; a big wind blew the chickens away; and with a twinkle in his eye, the pioneer added, "so we butchered the pig to save its life".

The homesteader might get by without milk and eggs but he had to have power. Since the horses couldn't take it, Thomas decided to get oxen and he struck off 45 miles over the snow on foot, to buy them. Three weeks later he was back with a team of big Shorthorn-bred bullocks, one red and one roan. With the arrival of spring, the big oxen dragged the breaking plough through a small plot of ground that supported nothing but grass and buffalo for thousands of years. He had no disc or harrow with which to cultivate the newly broken ground so he used an implement of his own designing. It was just a large cluster of willow brush which the oxen dragged over the land until the surface was pulverized. He called it "flogging" and I fancy that the name as well as the implement was his own invention. And then while other settlers were planting their little fields to wheat or flax, Thomas planted onions, the idea being that there might be a good local demand. And local demand there was because Thomas collected 360 good Canadian dollars for his onions that fall. He was the "Onion

BARR COLONISTS

King of the North West". He was the Victor in "round two", in the competition 'twixt man and new country.

There was a steam threshing outfit down at Battleford, and because Charlie Thomas was one of the few in all the North West who knew something about steam, he was persuaded to go and run the engine. It was an autumn of characteristic western loveliness and Charlie Thomas learned western threshing methods. He returned to the homestead on the last day of October and found his fellow colonists busy with preparations for winter. They had bad news. It had been planned that provisions for the colonists would be floated down from Edmonton on the Saskatchewan River to Fort Pitt, but the scow met with a mishap and was wrecked 140 miles up stream. If the settlers wanted the water-soaked provisions, they must now drive west and freight them back. On the very day that Thomas returned from threshing, the call went out for volunteers to freight the supplies to the settlement. Thomas offered to go. He set out with ox team and wagon. For 21 consecutive nights he slept beneath the vehicle and then boasted that he knew the size and shape of every bolt and nut on the under side of a wagon.

Going up for the supplies he was travelling light and took a

SASKATOON, 1903

straight course but on the return he followed a devious route in order to have the best trail. One night when he was bedding down under the wagon, an Indian with two hounds came along and asked if he could share the blankets for the night. Sure he could, and before "rolling in" for the night, they partook a snack from the "grub box" in which Thomas carried all his food supplies. In the morning, when Charlie awoke, the Indian and hounds were gone, and so was the grub box. He was five days from home and now totally without food except for some of the bags of flour which had been rescued from the River. He discovered that by stirring this flour into slough water which he strained through a handkerchief, he could make a sticky and not very appetizing pancake which would at least keep him alive for a few days. And the only reward left by the Indian was a crop of crawling wee things that seemed delighted to make their home in his undershirt. While the oxen plodded on, Thomas scratched.

He bought more horses and oxen; in 1905 he had 4 horses and three oxen and he adopted the fashionable half mile furrows. Seven years went by and he had 100 acres of wheat land. But wheat had a limited appeal; it got caught by frost; it fell a victim to hail; it felt the sting of drought; it was a risky business. Thomas was for mixed farming. Dairy cattle looked good to him. His decision was Ayrshires, the hardy cattle from South Western Scotland, and he built up one of the best herds of that breed in the west. The Thomas Ayrshires won prizes at the fairs and they made worthy production records. C. E. Thomas was out in front in dairying and he became president of the Saskatchewan Dairy Association. He was one of the pioneers in cow testing. They called him "Babcock Charlie". Officials in the Department of Agriculture said, "We need that man for promotional work". He went with the Federal Department as a Dairy Recorder and Instructor in 1914 and two years later transferred to the Provincial Department to do similar work. He remained in the Provincial service until superannuated in 1931.

And all the while, he was taking pictures, making a photographic record of his farming achievements. Strange mortal indeed, who would bring a camera to the western frontier in 1903; cameras were about as common as Grand pianos in the homestead country. But photography had been a hobby with Thomas and his camera came with him. When he journeyed to England to attend the World's Dairy Congress in 1928, he took his album of pioneer pictures. When the London agent of the C.P.R. saw the collection which virtually told the story of the settler, he wanted to borrow it. "But," said Thomas, "that is only a private collection and I developed the pictures in my dug-out." Didn't matter where the pictures were made, the C.P.R. wanted them and Thomas loaned the album. Copies were made for the railway company's use and when the album was returned, Thomas was presented with a complete new set for himself. The pictures were used in connection with colonization.

Among the pioneer's treasures was a framed sketch showing himself leaning over a billiard table, making an expert shot. And over the signatures of a score of his admirers who gave it to him, was the title "Charlie Thomas, always a Straight Shooter". He had a justifiable pride in that gift picture.

The First Homesteader

When John Sanderson put down a precious ten-dollar bill and filed on a Manitoba homestead in 1872, it probably did not occur to him that he was making history. But he was. He was the first of a great army of land-seekers from remote corners of the world, to make formal entry for homestead land. Oh yes, there were settlers ahead of him; squatters they were and many of them remained to claim the land around which they had ploughed furrows. But Sanderson arrived there at Fort Garry in the year in which the Dominion Land Act was passed, providing for homesteads in the North-West, and he was first in line.

"Jock" Sanderson was a Scot, o' course he was, and he was born at Prestonpans in East Lothian (on Sept. 27, 1841). He was living testimony to the fact that "browes" and butter-milk were nutritionally superior to "browes" and whiskey. His schooling was brief. It had consisted of a little reading and a little writing but if credit had been allowed for class-room punishment, he should have qualified for a B.A. degree. In those days boys were expected to learn a trade instead of remaining long at school and so Jock Sanderson took to blacksmithing. The profession of "smithy" enjoyed a high rank in the life of the community and it called for stout men. But "Jock" Sanderson was silently nursing a determination to go to Canada and in 1867 he sailed from Glasgow on the good ship *St. George.* He sailed steerage, of course, and after three weeks he landed at Quebec and set out for Ontario.

A few years at Fergus in Ontario and away he went again, this time following the scent of homesteads in the new west. It wasn't a simple matter, journeying from East to West in those early days. From Collingwood in Ontario he went to Duluth by Lake Boat, then to Moorhead in Minnesota by train, to Frog Point by wagon and the final lap of the journey to Fort Garry was by river boat.

He arrived at Fort Garry on the 1st day of July, 1872, the day on which the Dominion of Canada was celebrating its fifth birthday. If Sanderson did much celebrating on that occasion, it didn't take him long to recover because the very next day he presented himself at the Dominion Land Office and filed on a homestead he had never seen. It was the brand of faith that should remove mountains. The Portage la Prairie land had been recommended strongly to him and that was where he was going to locate.

And now Jock Sanderson had a homestead. His next problem was to find it. The township survey had been adopted the year before and survey work was progressing favourably. But it was one thing to find Sanderson's farm on the map and quite another to find it in that limitless expanse of unoccupied land stretching westward from Red River to the Rocky Mountains.

When he arrived at Fort Garry he had $30.00. After he filed on the homestead, he had $20.00 left—not enough to buy the things he needed. But Sanderson had a sincere and honest face and on his third day in Fort Garry, he bought a team of oxen and a cart on credit in spite of the fact that he was a total stranger. Fancy that! The oxen were not well broken; they were like a lot of others sold at Winnipeg at that time, just partly educated to harness. Now a broken ox could be ornery enough but a pair of green oxen could break a man's heart and make him wish he had never left home. But Sanderson was young and game and struck off over a twisty trail, which later sported the proud name of Portage Avenue. Between Sanderson and the two green bullocks, a lot of new twists and bends were added to that famous trail that first day out. He knew he was going westward in the general direction of Portage la Prairie and he hoped to find the north east quarter of section 35, township 12 range 7, where he was going to pitch a permanent camp.

It took three days to make the 75 mile journey and to his surprise, he found the quarter section, five miles north of Portage la Prairie, without much trouble. As a matter of fact he expected to get lost at least a few times before he became located. Becoming lost on the prairies was quite a common complaint.

I don't know if it was Sanderson or one of his neighbours about whom this tale is told. The story as I got it, is that this particular settler was encountered on the prairie driving a team of oxen and wagon, with a hay mower in gear and cutting behind the wagon. "What's the idea," he was asked and the answer was this, "I'm a long way from home and when darkness overtakes me tonight, I'll at least have a swath of hay to keep me from getting lost." The pioneers *had* to be original.

As a matter of fact there weren't many neighbours and not many lamps burning in the kitchen windows to guide the wayfarer. There were Kenneth McBain and Hugh Grant, neither of them very close; and William Trimble who arrived that same spring, having made the long journey from Missouri by covered wagon. And let us not forget Neighbour John McLean, the first white settler in all the district. It was McLean whose letters in the Toronto Globe first attracted Sanderson to Manitoba. McLean was really quite a character—it was he who overthrew a government, if you could call it that. It was described as a Republican Monarchy, Portage la Prairie was the capital and the renegade Thomas Spence was the self appointed President. I fancy that not many people know that at one time Portage la Prairie was the seat of government of a Republican Monarchy. A government must have revenue so a customs tariff was adopted. Imagine that! But even though whiskey for the President was reported to be the chief cost in government administration, they experienced a most modern and familiar difficulty in balancing the budget. When things went too far for John McLean and a shoemaker called MacPherson, two Highland Scotchmen, went into action and the Republican Monarchy was knocked out. But that's another story; the point is that these same fighting settlers made good neighbours and Sanderson exchanged work with them, built a church with them and formed the first Caledonia Society west of Red River.

The first year on the homestead was always crowded with jobs waiting for attention. There were buildings to erect, land to break, fences to build and so on. John Sanderson built a house, a log house. Breaking some crop land was the next job and the big oxen dragged the breaking plough back and forth until a good-sized field was black. Then in October (1872), Portage la Prairie held its first fair, under the auspices of the Marquette Agricultural Society. John Sanderson had nothing to exhibit but in the next year, his first crop year, Sanderson was exhibiting Golden Drop wheat, garden produce and home-made equipment at the second Portage la Prairie fair. Golden Drop wheat, which is virtually unknown today, was popular at that time. Sanderson's first crop yielded 20 bushels per acre of hard wheat. That helped a lot because it meant something to sell, even if prices were poor, and homesteader Sanderson was able to depart somewhat from his potato and bannock diet when he came to his second winter.

That first crop was harvested with the old reaper and the sheaves were tied by hand. Threshing too was done the hard way, some of it was threshed by flail and the balance was done with a small threshing mill driven by ox-power. The best market for wheat was in Fort Garry and some settlers who had surplus for sale, simply placed it on a scow on the Assiniboine and floated it to market. The alternative was to haul the wheat to Fort Garry and peddle it or trade it to anyone who would take it. The Hudson's Bay Co. there took a lot of wheat but in most cases no money changed hands; it was a case of barter and every settler needed supplies.

Manitoba, by the way, was experiencing a plague of grasshoppers when John Sanderson came. It was the plague which created hardship and nigh starvation in 1868 and '69. His first crop in '73 escaped fairly well but the next was a victim. The insects descended in clouds; the sky was black and very little crop survived. To get seed for the third year, Sanderson went out and picked by hand, heads which the grasshoppers missed. It was a slow method of gathering seed but it was easier and cheaper than driving an ox-team to Minnesota for a fresh supply.

And a further reference to the homesteader's diet,— Sanderson sampled all the known varieties of pemmican, that meat and berry concoction of Indian invention. True enough, it stood between many a frontiersman and starvation. Sanderson's land was right on the path of the Indians who passed from the Assiniboine River to Lake Manitoba; his land was part of the "Prairie Portage" and Indians of various tribes and dispositions visited him. Some were pleasant; some were doubtful; some were coyotes in wolf's clothing. But they usually had pemmican and it was the medium with which they made payment to Sanderson for anything he gave to them.

Then came the notable year of 1876, notable for several reasons. It was the year of the Custer Massacre in Montana and when Sitting Bull and his mad warriors crossed into Canada, it gave John Sanderson and his neighbours something to think about when, if ever, they had insomnia. It was an experimental year in ranching in the Chinook Belt in Western Canada. It was the year in which Honourable David Laird was appointed first Lieutenant Governor of the Territories. To John Sanderson, I suppose the most important event of the year was not the Custer Massacre but rather his marriage to Sarah Green, daughter of one of his neighbours over on Portage Creek. But to the student of agricultural matters, the event of that year was the movement of a little cargo of wheat loaded on a flatboat on Red River and sent to Eastern Canada. It was the first western wheat to be shipped East,—1876, less than 80 years ago. The purchasers were "Higgins & Young, Importers of Boots & Shoes, Crockery & Glassware", and they had been commissioned to buy 5000 bushels of western wheat for the Toronto firm of Steel Brothers. The price was 85 cents a bushel but the West didn't have 5000 bushels of wheat to sell and the buyers had to be satisfied with 857 bushels. Imagine that, less than 80 years ago!

John Sanderson saw it all. He sold wheat when Billy Smith who had a steam grist mill in Portage la Prairie was the only one who would buy it. He sold wheat to T. B. Miller of Portage who sent it to Winnipeg by flat-bottom boat that year of 1876. He was an advocate of mixed farming when the only certain market for a dressed pig was in Winnipeg and it took six days to make the round trip with the ox team. And he was still there at Portage when a production of more than 500 million bushels of wheat was Canada's record, most of it grown in the West, to be sure.

And after all the years on Manitoba land, all the varieties of hardship, John Sanderson still contended that young people should stay on the farms. Said the lovable old pioneer with the grand championship crop of white whiskers,

"there is hard work there, but there is reward. There

> is satisfaction in a well ordered farm with clean fields and good beasts."

And in his 89th year when they asked him if he would care to do it again, what did he say? Sure he would do it again. "I would like nothing better," he said. That was John Sanderson, the homesteader who came to Portage la Prairie seven years before the West had a railroad and was there until his death in 1930.

I am proud of the picture I have of the log house with the venerable pioneer standing beside it. The house lies "four-square", every log carefully hewn and dovetailed. It symbolizes the modesty and thoroughness of John Sanderson. It symbolizes pioneer stability. I imagine I see a lamp in that window on a dark and blustery night. It's an invitation to the traveller no matter what his colour or his social rating may be. It is an invitation to share the warmth of a pioneer shelter and share the blankets and bannock and bacon and the contents of the porridge pot nearly big enough to scald a pig in.

JOHN SANDERSON—*Homesteader Number One*

Norman Lee

Chilcotin Pioneer

In between the mountain ranges of British Columbia there is a vast, rugged and beautiful "cattle kingdom", called Chilcotin. Only a few people know it well—many Canadians are quite unaware of its wonders and beauty. From the time of the gold rush to Barkerville about 1860, there were cattle along the Cariboo Trail but in that less accessible hinterland of mountains and hills and valleys, west of the Upper Fraser, in that territory called Chilcotin—there was no activity until the '80's.

To-day some of Canada's mightiest cattle ranches are there in the Chilcotin. When the Gang Ranch, for example, outfits 20 or 25 riders to do the June round-up, the task ahead is a big one. They can expect to find cattle with the Gang brand, seven or eight thousand of them, anywhere in the 2400 square miles of rugged country over which they range. Quite a good sized back pasture, I would say. And when steers from the Chilcotin ranges are ready for market, they don't enjoy the luxury of lower berths in stock cars spotted close to the home corrals. They must be driven over long and dangerous trails; they will cross the Fraser by bridge or ferry and probably go on freight cars at Williams Lake. The trail journey may be one of fifty miles and take four or five days, or it may be two hundred and fifty miles and occupy three or four weeks.

That is Chilcotin and the Englishman Norman Lee was one of the trail-blazers. He came as a mere youth in '82. From England he took passage to New York, crossed the continent to California and then turned northward to Vancouver. He got work with the C.P.R. a while before the last spike was driven at Craigellachie. He acted as chaperon to a train load of Chinese labourers, punched cattle in Nicola Valley and then hired with the Hudson's Bay Company at Kamloops. The idea of ranching appealed to him and he recognized profit in trade with the Indians; so, he and his friend Hugh Bayliff decided to push into virgin territory, far beyond the horizon.

It had the ear-marks of a fool-hardy venture, but Lee was long on courage.

In that spring of 1887, they loaded their pack horses and started up the Cariboo Trail, that left-over from a deflated gold rush. It was the twisty trail leading northward through Ashcroft and Clinton. It was a trail which led some to fortune and a lot to failure. After a while the two adventurers left the Cariboo Trail, went west, swam their horses across the hard-bucking Fraser River at Chimney Creek and continued westward toward the coastal range for days. They halted about the present site of Redstone and set up to trade in furs and run cattle. Trading furs and raising cattle was their idea of mixed farming. Except for a trading post started by Tom Hance, theirs was the first in all the Interior west of 150 Mile House. Chilcotin Indians would come 200 and 300 miles with furs and the trading business was good. Although cattle were hard to get the partners got a few together and called themselves ranchers.

Lee's partner got married and in '94, Lee moved to conduct business for himself at Hanceville not far away. His cattle went with him; the grass was good; the range was unlimited and the herd grew. When Lee needed supplies, he hauled them in behind a four-horse team by way of Gang Ranch from Ashcroft. When he had steers to sell, he drove them out over the same trail.

In those days anyone living in that country experienced strange adventures and some narrow escapes. Lee had plenty of both. He knew what it was to be lost in the wilds. He knew how it felt to play hide and seek with a hungry bear in the Chilcotin woods, and he knew how it felt to have a freight wagon slipping away from under him and rolling over a mountain side. (To me, there's an idea for a first class nightmare). Napoleon once asked a soldier what he did in a certain campaign and proudly the soldier replied that he survived. Lee did well to survive.

But for sheer daring and bravery, the great cattle drive of '98 was the crowning adventure. It was the year notable for the Klondyke Gold Rush. People of all races, all ages and all morals, descended upon wild and wonderful Dawson City. The majority went by Skagway on the coast and over the difficult mountain route. In any case, food prices at Dawson soared to unheard of heights. Gold was more abundant than beef. Potatoes were 75 cents each; eggs were twelve dollars a dozen with no guarantee that the purchaser would find a fresh one. And beef was a dollar a pound.

That market for beef was a challenge to cattlemen like Pat Burns and the Tuxfords of Moose Jaw, and Norman Lee. But how could it be delivered? It was out of the question to freight anything so perishable as fresh beef over the mountains from Skagway. The alternative was to drive the herd from the coast to some point on the Yukon River; or, attempt what was still more hazardous, driving cattle overland from Central British Columbia to some far northern point from which cattle or beef could be rafted to Dawson City. Lee decided to attempt the drive northward. He would at least know why it couldn't be done. The great drive of '98 began from Lee's Chilcotin range on May 17th. He had 200 cattle, 30 pack and saddle horses, five cowboys, a horse wangler and the inevitable cook. For the journey ahead the policy was to split the big herd into smaller bands of about 40 head, with a rider in charge of each. The cattle drove better that way, particularly in the bush country. Each morning they would start the cattle before sun-up. The wrangler with the spare saddle horses would go ahead and halt when he found a good feeding ground for the noon stop. Then the pack-train and cook would go ahead and locate a site for the night camp. At first they averaged ten or twelve miles a day but when in rougher country, speed was lower.

There were two or three other cattlemen attempting to make similar drives and Lee mentions them in his diary which it was my pleasure to study. He says, "Of the cattle that started from Chilcotin, Jim Cornell was about a week ahead of us with seventy-five head, Jerry Gravelle about three days with one hundred and we heard that Johnny Harris with his two hundred was trying hard to catch us up."

Well, every day presented new problems. One day it would be fallen timber on the trail; another day it would be rain and sometimes it was the prevalence of poison weeds. Lee reminds us through his diary that night-herding "in the pouring rain is the reverse of pleasant". I would think so. They came to the Mud River and planned to swim the cattle across. But an Indian argued about the dangers and persuaded them to hire his ferry. Then Lee made the discovery that the artful Indian had actually built a dam on the stream to force travellers to use his ferry. He made the discovery in time and simply drove his cattle down stream and crossed quite easily below the dam. But they did lose some cattle from poisonous plants. Lee was advised to bleed the poisoned cattle "by chopping off pieces of their tails and feeding them bacon grease". Incidentally the advice was not taken seriously.

They halted to rest the cattle at Hazelton, far north on the Skeena. Lee's blueprint called for three days at Hazelton but there was neither a ceiling, a ration nor a permit attached to the purchase of Hudson's Bay rum and some of the cowboys weren't ready for the trail for another three days.

Farther north there were new trials. Feed shortage in some sections made travel slow. Worst of all, the horses were playing out. According to Mr. E. D. Sheringham who accompanied Lee on that journey, the horses became victims of mud fever and some lost their hooves. In order to spare them, any supplies not considered essential were discarded, but the horses continued to get weaker and most of them died. Still those stout-hearted cattlemen were not licked. They drove forward, on foot and arrived at Telegraph Creek on September 2nd. There was Jim Cornell who had started earlier, operating a butcher shop and selling his beef. He had decided not to go farther. But Lee's plan was to drive on to Teslin Lake, there to slaughter and raft the beef across the lake and down the rivers to Dawson City. And sure enough, the cattle arrived at Teslin Lake on October 3rd, about four and a half months after leaving the home range.

The rest of the story adds up to tragedy. One called McIntosh went ahead to build two rafts, each 40 feet long and 16 feet wide. The slaughtering began and on October 17, the two rafts loaded with beef carcasses were eased by a fair wind out on to the lake. They had two days good sailing but on the third day, disaster. Up came a gale and before it subsided, both scows were wrecked on the rocky shore. It was 60 miles back to Teslin and the meat was practically valueless. They did try to salvage a little but it was not worth while and none ever reached Dawson City. Harris with his beef was ahead of Lee a few days and escaped the storm, but his cargo was "frozen in" about 200 miles above Dawson and it too was a complete loss. Jerry Gravelle's beef suffered the same fate.

The agricultural frontier has produced many stirring tales but none more stirring than that of Lee's cattle drive of some 1200 miles. He arrived back in Vancouver sometime in January, ready to begin again. And he did begin again. You can't keep a good man down. He got support from some Vancouver wholesalers and back he went to his beloved Chilcotin, to trade, and raise cattle. His herd grew to nearly 1000 head. In 1902 he went home to England and married. In 1913 he sold his ranch and the 700 or 800 cattle on it and went to live in Victoria. In 1915, he "joined up" but he was too old to go overseas.

One of his misfortunes was that the Real Estate streptococcus got into his system and the result was not good. He thought that others were honest like himself, and some were not. In 1919 the ranch came back on his hands. But it wasn't the ranch he left. The fences were wrecked. The trading business was down and there wasn't even a milk cow on the property. Norman Lee was back on the ranch to "do it all again". But it wasn't so easy this third time and cattle prices were dropping.

He went about his work as usual. He made plans. He worked hard. He arose early each morning. Most pioneers were early risers. Nobody should waste time sleeping after the sun is up. When a guest arrived from England, expecting a luxurious rest, she got the call to arise at 6:00 a.m., just like others who lived about Norman Lee.

Norman Lee who died in the spring of 1939 was one of the Inter-Mountain characters as well as a great pioneer. I heard one man say that "Chilcotin lost a lot of its colour when Norman went". A fascinating personality, a fine sense of humour. I can picture him with a little lad, a nephew I think, who was holidaying at Hanceville one summer. The little man didn't get all the mud off his face after being in for a swim. Norman Lee suggested a wash. The lad argued as all lads will that he had washed. "Then", asked Norman Lee, "what makes that lemonade so muddy?"

His was not a story of great fortune. With some of the Sodbusters, everything to which they turned their hands succeeded. Not with Lee; his reverses must have been nearly as numerous as his successes. Yet he progressively broke new trails and made them better for those who followed. He had boundless courage and he could "take it on the chin".

I believe that anyone who could direct that herd of wild cattle over those hundreds of miles of still wilder country, losing everything, without going insane, had super-human qualities. And after that notable drive with all its losses and hardship, he recorded quite refreshingly that he arrived back at Vancouver with "a roll of blankets, a dog and a dollar". What he didn't record was that he traded his coat for a passage back to civilization for his faithful dog which made all of that terrifying trip with him. Yes, Norman Lee could "take it on the chin". Either Lee caught the "Spirit of the Chilcotin" or he created it. Really though, it would seem that the unbeatable spirit of Norman Lee became the "Spirit of the Chilcotin."

And here is a tribute to his notable cattle drive, penned by Leo Bates.

"Bogs to the right of them, woods to the left of them,
Mountains in front of them, hoofed the two hundred.
Stormed at with many a curse, while trails grew worse and worse,
Tongue lashed in prose and verse, limped the two hundred.
Far off their white bones fade, and the brave charge they made,
All Hanceville wondered.
Honour that gorgeous spree
Honour brave Norman Lee,
Spavined two hundred."

Another Unknown

It would be quite wrong to give the impression that only men of distinction deserved a place among the Sodbusters. Actually, the Sodbuster heroes were common men, for the most part quiet men. They were good at minding their own business. They constituted the backbone of a young nation; but they are too soon forgotten. For that reason it seems expedient to draw out an average or sample specimen from time to time, and thus do honour to that host of pioneers whose names as individuals will never appear on the pages of history. That's why I choose, "Another Unknown".

The editor of "Who's Who" never heard of this one. Here was a Sodbuster who never won a sweepstake for wheat. He never won a championship for bulls and he never won an election. He won a homestead and a lifetime sentence tending his soil and fighting weeds and growing food to nourish human bodies. About the only picture of him to survive is a tintype made at the local fair at least half a century ago. But he is typical of an army of brave men who congregated with him on the frontier in the '80's. And I choose him because, as it happens, I know his story particularly well.

He was eighteen years of age when he arrived in Manitoba (in 1889). He had no money but he had the confidence of youth. He would stop at Brandon and work long enough to let him complete his journey to the ranch country. The pot of gold at the end of his rainbow was one thousand dollars he was told he could earn herding cattle or sheep for three years. He took a job on a farm at Chater. He had testimonials from Ontario, good ones which said "this young man is not afraid of work", and he was hired at $20.00 a month. That was considered big pay and there were no Income Tax deductions. But half of the monthly pay went back east to help the folk there and what remained was his reward for 30 days of hard labour at fifteen hours a day. His boss at Chater was a bachelor and as a cook he was no better than the worst of them. He could make tea and an indigestible some-

The Big Outfit at Brandon, 1899, "Another Unknown" the Owner, fourth from the left.

thing that might have been a cross between a bannock and a bismark. The meat wasn't of the Grade A kind. It was salt pork and the longer it reposed in the barrel, the saltier it became. In maggot season our young Sodbuster concluded it better to close his eyes and produce a temporary dim-out until the meat was eaten. The hens it seems, found that same meat barrel situated in the shed, to be a fine place to roost. That was all right except that last thing at night somebody had to turn the hens, heads to the centre.

Next year he heard about a job selling trees and shrubs for Cavers Brothers of Galt, Ontario, on a 20% commission. It appealed to his Scotch nature and he bought a horse and cart and started. But selling trees to homesteaders who didn't mean to remain long in the country was like selling woollen underwear at Palm Beach. The real tragedy came when he was obliged to drive through a flooded creek. The harness broke and the turbulent water soaked his order books and floated some of them out of the cart and away in the direction of Hudson's Bay. It looked like the time to quit the nursery business and he went back to a North Brandon farm at $20.00 per month.

The trouble was, it would take a long time to save the cost of a farm that way. But he got the farm, first a quarter section and then another. One of those quarters was all raw land when he got it in the spring but with two walking ploughs and a lot of energy, the 160 acres were all broken that summer and backset that fall. Those walking ploughs cut a furrow of only 12 inches, but a Scottish neighbour who was ready to share his experience, remarked hopefully, "The more seams, the more lice". If it were so that the more seams one had in his clothing, the more parasites could be accommodated, then it might follow that the more furrows there were in the field, the more wheat should result, or something like that.

Financing was always a problem in those years. Cash was a commodity homesteaders talked about but never saw in abundance. The plough-share became dull and it would cost two dollars to get it sharpened. The settler had a load of hay which he could spare so he took it to town, hoping to sell it for six dollars and thus pay for the sharpening and also pay for a pair of beef-skin mocassins which he needed. But it was an unlucky day. The cast iron share fell from the load of hay and broke. There was only one thing to do, have the share welded at additional cost of a dollar and some lost time which would mean a livery bill and a hotel bill. Then it rained and the hay got wet so Alex Trotter bought the wet load for five dollars. He went home with a sharp plough-share but with an over-all debt of $1.75 and no beef-skin mocassins.

After a couple of years on the new farm and the sale of some frozen wheat, this specimen pioneer paid a visit to his home back east. Proud he was of achievements on the homestead. Pals of his youth glanced in admiration of the boy who had won the first round in the struggle with pioneer Western hardships. Sure he had some of the bulldog breed in him, the kind of bulldog which wouldn't stop for 50 miles of unbroken snow. When he was returning to Manitoba in that spring (of 1894) his train became snowbound in a March blizzard. For two nights and two days it was completely stuck at Belmont, about 50 miles south east of Brandon. The railway company was furnishing the passengers with two meals a day but the travellers were becoming tired of each other's company. When the homesteader from Brandon could stand the inactivity no longer, he consumed his noon meal, checked his grip and struck off through the storm, on foot. Leather boots without rubbers didn't make the walking over the unbroken trail any better. At first he walked on the railroad grade and then the country roads, and both were bad. He walked to Wawanesa the first night and after a brief rest, he was on the road again and was in Brandon at 12 o'clock noon. He completed a 50-mile walk through a March storm in exactly 24 hours. And he didn't ask the railway company for a refund on his ticket either.

Farming was proving profitable if one could just get the crops harvested before the frost, since the soil held the accumulated fertility of a thousand years. Our Sodbuster made some money and then came the machine age and he put all his savings into a threshing outfit of the newest and biggest design. Manufacturers were competing to see who could build the mightiest steam engine and the biggest separator. The newest gadgets on threshing machines that year were self-feeders and wind stackers. His outfit consisted of a Minneapolis engine and a separator with a 40 inch cylinder. It was the first west of Portage la Prairie having both self-feeder and blower. Homesteaders came for miles to see the monster in action, to see a separator building its own stack and eating up sheaves which didn't have to be forced into its throat. The only trouble was that the new feeder didn't work and had to be discarded. So instead of having four men pitching sheaves into the automatic feeder, they had to be satisfied with eight men at the feeder end, four pitching from the loads to the tables, two cutting bands and two forcing sheaves into the cylinder. When noon time came and the threshing crew descended upon the farmer's kitchen, 23 ravenous men sat down to test the food resources and the patience of the good wife. But when things were going well, that big outfit threshed a lot of wheat. It threshed 1000 bushels in three hours one time, to say nothing of the bushels which went into the straw pile. That record stood a while and when the big outfit had to move from one farm to the next, it broke another record, a record for slow motion. And it usually broke a few bridges, because bridge builders hadn't reckoned with any such mechanical monstrosity. Indeed the same outfit went through the 18th Street bridge at Brandon on one occasion and after that if the river was to be crossed, the outfit was placed on a flat car at Chater and sent across on the rails.

Strangely enough the big outfit didn't ruin the old timer and it didn't drive him crazy. Some who bought threshers weren't so lucky. Anyway by 1908, he had a nice bank-roll and because it was fashionable to retire when one could, he sold his farm, held a sale at which T. C. Norris was the auctioneer, and went to live in the city. There were business opportunities and there was every inducement to speculate in city property. It would be easy to make money that way. But was it? There is just one thing wrong with real estate booms, they don't wear well. When this one backfired, the retired farmer was holding too much property. He felt a new yearning for the land. He became homesick for the farm. He would go back to the land, for there he would find new confidence. He would start again, and he did. But by this time the frontier had receded 400 miles to the North West and there in what was called Northern Saskatchewan he began from scratch to do it all again. His lawyer said, "What! you going to township 44? Should be the best place in the world to grow icicles; but what else can you grow?"

Well, the retired Sodbuster was on his way back to the land. He had no cash but he managed to make up a car load of so-called "settlers effects", two old "fox-meat" horses, a Jersey which had been the family cow in the city, a box of hens, a lot of furniture, a lawn mower, and the elder son as a stow-away. Yes, they called it "settlers effects". The freight train stopped at Dauphin for a few hours and the settler seized the opportunity to replenish his supply of bread and cheese. But when he was absent, the car was supposed to be unattended, the train conductor entered the box car, removed two of the best hens from the box and left with his prize in a bran sack, while the stow-away son watched it all from his hiding place behind a crate of furniture and had the good sense not to make a protest which would have cost the family a train fare.

The new farm up there in township 44 had no cultivation, no fence, no house, no well, and no lawn on which to use the mower. What the new farmstead had was good soil, a lot of trees and an opportunity for heavy work. The furniture was piled around a small clearing in a cosy bluff of poplars and within that enclosure, the newcomers set up two beds and called it home. Nobody could say the roof leaked because there was no roof. However, it wasn't a bad place to live, just as long as the weather was fine.

And so, for a second time the pioneer was developing a farm. He bought another horse, Old Bill, noted for great age and chronic indigestion. He dug a well. In fact he dug six wells and each time alkali water that would make a dose of Epsom salts taste like orangeade, bubbled in; and he built a stable and tied the Jersey cow inside. His first crop was fair, the second was frosted; the third was rusted; the fourth was hailed 100 per cent. But he stuck and saw the frost hazard diminish and the rust demon licked. Soon he went in for cattle. He bought three pure bred Aberdeen Angus cows and built a herd. Later he took some of his cattle to England and saw them sold at Smithfield. He exhibited at the local fair; was made a director and then president.

The Provincial Live Stock Board recognized the contribution he made in breeding good cattle and presented him with a scroll and said, "Long Live the Pioneer". And he did live long because he belonged to a hardy breed. He was in a hospital bed just once, when he had his arm broken in a tussle with a bull. But when he had to be there for a few days, he told the doctor to make the best use of time and give him an overhauling. So they set his arm, did a minor operation and pulled all his teeth. He was the pioneer; rugged individualist; the kind that blazed trail. And after he had more than fifty years of service to Canadian agriculture behind him, he retired for the second time. He sold his machinery and equipment but not his horses. They were not for sale. His order was that they would never leave the farm on which they had served. And they didn't. They were superannuated right there on their home farm. But in retirement, the pioneer continued to get up at 4:30 in the morning and disturb the peace of the community. He had done it all his life and no one could stop him.

I said I wasn't going to identify this Sodbuster. I've almost changed my mind. I'll tell this much about him. He gave me my first spanking.

My Friend Ole

The tiny island of Iceland has had an influence out of all proportion to its size; and that's the way it was with my friend Olaf Olafson. He wasn't very big; that's so, but he was mighty in spirit and his originality and progressive ideals made him one of the best known members of the fraternity of pioneer ranchers.

But Olaf Olafson was not always a rancher; indeed his experience was as varied and colourful as the material in Joseph's coat. Olaf was born in Iceland. He was the oldest of a family of five left fatherless when he was eight. It was at that tender age that he left home to make his way in the world. Live stock had an instinctive attraction for this Nordic lad and his first job was herding sheep. Herding sheep in Iceland had one thing in common with herding on the Canadian range; it was a lonesome life. To stay with it long, a man would go crazy or he would become a philosopher. One thing sure, he could learn to do his own thinking and certainly Olafson learned that lesson well.

At the age of fourteen he quit the sheep. He took to sea. At first he was a cook on a fishing smack that sailed the Icelandic waters. A few years elapsed; young Olafson became a seasoned seaman. But he wasn't satisfied and at twenty he came to Canada. He arrived at Brandon in 1887 but nobody wanted to hire a sailor. The "prairie navy" which made a little history on the Assiniboine and Saskatchewan Rivers, was in decline. Farm work was the only employment available and the immigrant lad hired with Robert Hall of Griswold at five dollars a month. The work was very new. He was required, among other things, to milk cows. "Imagine a sailor milking cows". True, he had milked sheep in his native Iceland but milking cows was different. The "stripping" method which involved only two fingers on each hand was the only one he knew; when it produced friction, it called for lubrication and the resourceful Olafson found a means of supplying that. But when it was discovered that the milk delivered at the house was discoloured and tainted with what seemed to be tobacco juice, Mrs. Hall protested; and the embarrassed Ole was obliged to change his methods.

The spring of 1892 found Olafson in the boom town of Moose Jaw and it was there that he began railroading. Nothing was more foreign to him than bragging but, with a glint in his eye he did boast of being the first Icelandic train conductor in all the world. Quite right; it is a big world, but I'm sure his claim is correct because there were no railroads in Iceland.

When the railroad bridge at Saskatoon was shifted by ice in the spring of '98, Olaf Olafson was the conductor of the work train sent to make repairs. About the same time, the Saskatoon ferry was carried from its moorings and lost. The only remaining communication between Saskatoon and Nutana was the railroad bridge which was under repair, but the C.P.R. officials offered assistance and train conductor Olafson ruled the traffic for a matter of two weeks. He sent a train across the river southward daily at 9:00 a.m. and one back at 4:00 p.m. It was good fun, this thing of being local controller of transport, and it was long before the sport of appointing controllers struck Ottawa.

Indeed his reputation as a railroader went far and it was known that here was a man who could meet any situation. He was serving as brakeman on one occasion when told by the conductor to remove twelve hobos riding on the front end. That was a big order and it was plain that the conductor didn't want the job. Olafson didn't see why he should get into trouble if the conductor wouldn't support him. So instead of attempting to force the issue with the men, he said to them, "boys, this is a hell of a place to ride; why don't you go back and sit in the coach". They did go back to the passenger coach and then the conductor had the unpleasant job of dealing with them. Olafson was like that; but if it was really his fight, he would never back up.

This Olafson was a lover of horses. He was not long in Moose Jaw before he owned a good mount. He was a member of the first Moose Jaw Turf Club and was one of the 40 members who each bought an acre of land, about the present location of the Moose Jaw Exhibition Grounds, for a turf park. His chief recreation on idle days was to ride westward from the town, out into the hills and look down upon Lake Johnston. There was a lure about it; there was more,—there was a challenge. "Why become tied down to a damn railroad when there's so much grass calling for cattle and horses?" The idea was gradually getting a strangle-hold on him.

In the meantime, Olafson induced certain members of his family to come to Canada. His mother and sister were at Brandon and were easily persuaded to proceed farther west and settle on land where the grass was free and good. That was '97. Early the next year, Olafson founded his ranch herd with 25 Shorthorn cows which he bought from Mr. Hawkes of Balgonie. The little herd was trailed west to Olafson's adopted cow-country, and a Shorthorn bull was bought from Fred Speers. Before the next breeding season the bull was lost in a fire but Ole said the loss was more apparent than real because he got a better bull, a Hereford, and if you ask me, he continued to get even better bulls as long as he was in the business. That's why he had good cattle.

Grass was plentiful and the herd grew. In 1903, Olafson quit the "road" completely for his beloved grass country. His friends said, "Ole, you'll get lost in those hills". I can hear his disdainful reply,

> "How can I get lost? I've got Lake Johnston on the south of me, Lake Chaplin on the west, the C.P.R. on the north and Wood Mountain trail on the east; I can't get lost."

Like other cattlemen, he lost heavily during the memorable winter of 1906-7 when some of the big outfits like the "Turkey Track" counted their losses in the thousands of head. To add to the grief of that season nearly 100 head of Olafson's cattle went out on the lake and went through the ice. He said it should have ruined him, "but it didn't", and very shortly some 700 head of cattle and horses were again on the books.

It was then that settlers were flocking to the West in large numbers. Free land was a powerful lure; and that some of it was unsuited to farming didn't seem to matter, much. The grass country was threatened and so was the security of the ranchers. It called for action, united action on the part of the cattlemen.

It was then that the Saskatchewan Stock Growers' Association was conceived and Olaf Olafson was its father. He wrote to Ottawa for a list of those holding grazing leases in the province and he was advised that such a list would cost five dollars. It was Olafson's money that went to pay for that list, but he circularized all whose names were on it and a meeting held in Moose Jaw in 1913 marked the birth of the organization. Next year Mr. Olafson was elected president and no government or administrative body having a difference with the stockmen could rest during his term of office. When one government official told him he was making himself "very obnoxious", my friend replied with a chuckle, "thank you, thank you, that's the encouragement I need".

The Province was totally without a public stock yards when the Saskatchewan Stock Growers' Association was formed. Olafson was one who thought such an institution should be provided. They got the Southern Saskatchewan Co-Operative Stock Yards when an Act of the Legislature was passed on February 15, 1919. Olafson said it took a lot of talking, but most of the agricultural folk knew how well Ole could do that. In debate he was composed and refreshingly sarcastic. Sometimes he used words he had difficulty getting his tongue around but at least he always had them in the right places.

When I think of the Moose Jaw Feeder Show, I think of Olafson. He was very proud of it. He was part of it from the beginning in 1923 and saw it become one of the biggest of its kind in the world, a great live stock classic bringing the breeders and feeders of cattle and sheep together annually. And incidentally there were few better cattle coming to that show year after year than those "white faces" wearing Olafson's own brand the "N7F".

He wanted co-operative marketing. He advocated grading of all live stock. He fought for more attention to preservation of the grass country. And let there be no doubt about his determination; only those who opposed him on the floor of a convention or elsewhere knew the power in his punches and the stubborn spirit behind them.

I love that fighting story about Olafson the railroader which appeared in the Moose Jaw Times Herald one day back in 1895. It was about the desperadoes who attempted to hold up a train between Moose Jaw and Swift Current. Here it is in part.

> "Little Ole Olafson, of Conductor Burton's crew, tackled the gang on the blind end of baggage van, just as the robbers were in the act of pulling the cord to stop the train and perchance, rob and kill the passengers. Ole warned them to desist; they showed a fight. He pluckily faced them with a pistol in one hand and determination in his eye. His valiant front cowed the gang and they turned tail, sprang into space, and have not been heard of since."

That's the paper account dated May 17, 1895.

His was a full life and a fair share of reverses were written into his log. As he looked back upon nearly 60 years in Western Canada he said, "I guess they can't hit me with anything I haven't been hit with before, unless they try sympathy". But there were triumphs and satisfactions. It was with pride that the lad who was left fatherless at the age of eight was able in after-years to support his father's family and bring the mother to Canada where she enjoyed more than 20 years of well earned comfort. It was a matter of satisfaction to him to see his own family growing up as good Canadians. I remember the twinkle in his eye when telling about one of his boys, said; "he doesn't drink; he doesn't

"MY FRIEND OLE", (right)

with

MR. EDWARD EVANS

smoke; he doesn't talk much; but then he's got a good mother".

Olaf Olafson was the stockman selected to receive the Saskatchewan Live Stock Board's annual honour on one occasion. They talked about his fearlessness, his vision and his great sense of humour. It was all true. And a lot could have been said about his quiet generosity. I conclude with a story from Olafson's railroading experiences, told by the late Dr. Rutherford. I think the little Icelander was in Brandon or Moose Jaw. Anyway he had charge of a train. Owing to negligence on the part of a member of his crew, there was an accident and a car was smashed. Conductor Olafson was called to account for the accident and while he refused to disclose the details of the accident, he insisted that he was responsible. Olafson's superior said, "Now I'm convinced that your trainman was to blame but if you refuse to inform us of the facts and insist on taking the responsibility, you'll have to be fired". Ole said, "I know that; you can fire me". And they did fire him. Afterwards somebody said to him, "Ole, why did you do that when you weren't to blame?" The big little man replied, "If you want to know, I'll tell you; I've just got my mother to support and the other fellow has a big family". That's just one more reason why I'm proud I knew that noble little sodbuster.

Pioneer at the Prairie Gateway

The story about Archibald Wright and Mary Ramsay who became Mrs. Wright, should be something of a double feature. Separately and together their lives were linked with an astonishing number of Winnipeg and district milestones. They saw the old Indian trail that followed the Red River become Main Street and they saw the trail that flanked the Assiniboine, become the bustling and modern Portage Avenue.

Mary Ramsay saw Red River quite a bit ahead of the man who became her husband. Her parents came to Fort Garry from Scotland, came by way of Hudson's Bay in 1848. They were three months on the way and three weeks in the ice-flows. Next year Mary was born within the walls of old Fort Garry (Aug. 27, 1849). And she died ninety years later (March 1939) at approximately the place where she was born; but in the meantime, her birthplace had grown from a frontier outpost to a proud metropolis of nearly a quarter million population.

But don't be misled; Mary Ramsay did not live in town or city for long. When she was seven years old, her father secured a grant of land on the Assiniboine, from the Hudson's Bay Company. It extended from where Riverbend School now stands, to Notre Dame Avenue, and there the Ramsays broke sod the hard way and made a home.

Young ladies liked to travel in those days, as in these, and in 1868 Miss Mary made a trip to Fort Carlton on the North Saskatchewan River. Horse and cart constituted the means of travel; 'twas a most modern and acceptable method and futhermore a horse is always good company. She left Fort Garry on September 2nd and arrived at Fort Carlton on October 2nd. From the time she left the Red River Settlement she saw no cultivation whatever, not a furrow in all that distance. But on the return trip in the following spring she saw some ploughed land near Portage la Prairie, probably the work of Kenneth MacKenzie.

It was while Mary Ramsay was visiting at Fort Carlton

that a man came into her life. He was Archibald Wright, a young harness-maker who had seen a lot of the world. He was a Scot who went to Ontario and then to the United States where he made war harness for the Southern Armies during the Civil War. After that he drove a mule team from the Mississippi River to California and tried mining. From there he went north with a horse between his knees and landed in the Cariboo in British Columbia. He next went to Fort Edmonton, stopped to make hay for the Hudson's Bay Company, and, still travelling on the weather-deck of a horse, he drifted to Fort Carlton where "bang", "boy meets girl".

Archie Wright and Mary Ramsay liked each other from the start, and, if Mary was going to return to Fort Garry, that would be Archie's destination too. He traded horses, got a fresh little bay mare, blind in one eye, and rode on to Fort Garry. That little mare, by the way, lived to be 27 years old and as recently as 1927, some of her offspring could be identified around Winnipeg. Mary made a fast trip home too and later in the year (1869) they were married. But the honeymoon was most rudely interrupted. In the third week of married life, the bridegroom was taken prisoner by Louis Riel who was leading the Red River uprising. Prison diet was pemmican and tea. It was perfectly clear that a jail was no place for a man with a brand new wife so when Col. Wolseley and his troops arrived on August 23 (1870) and the insurgent leader had disappeared, Archie Wright left the jail. The young couple started life again and moved to the corner of Portage and Main where the James Richardson office now stands. There Wright opened a harness shop and over the shop the Wrights made their home. Hon. John Norquay and others who were good judges of home cooked meals, were frequent visitors.

During the next few years, the Wrights were to witness one notable historic event after another. There was the tri-weekly stage service between Winnipeg and Abercrombie in Minnesota which began in 1871. And there was the arrival of the steamboat *Selkirk* the next year. Yes, Mrs. Wright and Maggie Murphy were sitting on the walls of Fort Garry, braiding each other's hair late one afternoon when they were startled by a strange whistle. It sounded "like somebody blowing in a bottle". In a few minutes the steamboat rounded the bend. And then such excitment! All the able-bodied folk rushed to the river to welcome Jim Hill's riverboat. It was an event of great moment. It marked a new era in transportation. It practically ended those Red River Caravans in which fifty or one hundred Red River carts would travel together, carrying freight north and south.

All the while there was a growing demand for harness for horses and oxen bought by landseekers and "Harness-maker Wright" was busy. Work came so fast that customers had to wait their turns. An Ontario man drove in from Minnesota and tied his team at the corner of Portage and Main and hung the harness and collars on the wagon while the horses rested for the last lap of the journey. But one of the local cows which enjoyed the privilege of grazing on Main Street came along and ate the straw out of the dilapidated horse collars. Now a de-strawed horse collar in 1875 could be as big a barrier to progress as a blow-out tire in 1948 and when the restless landseeker learned that he must wait several days for repairs, there was threat of a new Red River Insurrection. But the repair job was done well, you can bet and the same settler returned years later and wanted collars that would wear "like those which Wright rebuilt for him".

Winnipeg was incorporated as a city in 1873 and Wright was an alderman on the first council. The first mayor, by the way, was Frank Cornish. As mayor he was also police magistrate and they tell that on one occasion he formally laid a charge against himself for disorderly conduct on the previous night. He pleaded guilty to the charge and then fined himself $5.00. That was the brand of legal integrity which obtained in early Winnipeg. There is no record of how His Worship was celebrating on that night of misbehaviour but it was just about then that the last of the Annual Dog Meat Feasts was held by the Indians at Fort Garry. It was attended by 200 Indians and everybody knows you can't have a banquet without inviting the mayor.

Still there was no railroad to connect the Gateway City with the outside, but on an October day 1877, the Steamer *Selkirk* arrived from St. Paul with a welcome cargo. The riverboat was towing a barge and on it was Manitoba's first locomotive, the Countess of Dufferin which stands today in a place of honour in front of the C.P.R. depot in Winnipeg. With the caboose and flat cars which came too, Winnipeg could now boast a train, but still no railroad on which to operate it. A holiday was declared and everybody was merry because at least it gave promise of things to come.

The rails from the East did reach Winnipeg in '79 and the western brand of optimism appeared. Nothing could stop progress now. Wright couldn't make harness fast enough for the incoming settlers. Winnipeg boomed. The boom reached a peak in 1881 and '82 when real estate was sold privately or by auction, just like home-cooking at a church bazaar. But unlike the sales of home-cooking, a bar-room was a popular setting for the auction. Jim Coolican the Real Estate King was supposed to take his baths in champagne.

Admittedly, it was fashionable to tell tall stories about progress. Wright had a neighbour who adopted bucksawing firewood for his livelihood. Advancement was slow in that profession but the newcomer caught the Spirit of Winnipeg and wrote home to tell the folk in Ontario that already he was going about Winnipeg with a fine "horse and cutter". What he didn't explain was that the horse was a saw-horse and the cutter was a sharp buck-saw.

It was during that unparalleled boom in 1881 that Archibald and Mary Wright moved to their farm on the south side of the Assiniboine River. It was right against the present City Park, about four miles west of the old fort. It was a 2300 acre farm with seven-eighths of a mile river frontage; a big farm at any time. Part of that property ultimately became the present Tuxedo Park (sold to Tuxedo Park Co. in 1906 at $150 per acre) and in 1905, Wright sold 117 acres to the Provincial Government for the first Manitoba Agricultural College (now Osborne Barracks).

Anyway it was to Wright's farm on the river that were brought the first Holstein cattle to come to Western Canada. They were only two in number, a bull called Lord Selkirk and a heifer, Agnes Jane, but they were pedigreed and they cost Wright $600 in the United States in that year of 1881. No monkeys in a circus cage ever created more interest than those two bovines when Wright exhibited them at an early show at

St. Boniface. Indeed their coming to Manitoba was almost as significant in the life of western agriculture as the delivery of that first locomotive, Countess of Dufferin. They were the forerunners of a breed which was to occupy first position in the great dairying industry in this land. Mr. Wright continued to breed and boost Holsteins until his dispersion sale in 1905 and at times he had 100 or 150 black and white cattle on his farm. It was Winnipeg's first big dairy farm with 30 or 35 cows being milked regularly.

The same year that Wright imported the pure bred Holsteins, he brought 80 head of other cattle from Minnesota. About 20 were oxen, because he was determined to bring his new farm under cultivation quickly. He bought a 24 inch breaking plough, biggest thing of its kind seen in the West. With this mechanical leviathan he was going to try ploughing scrub and smaller trees right under without the usual axe-work. Sure it would take a lot of power; he hitched twelve big bullocks to that plough, six pairs strung out tandem. They were hitched with yokes and a big chain down the middle to the plough. The oxen weren't really driven at all because there were no reins; but while one man handled the plough, another attempted to guide the oxen with the aid of a long whip and some assorted language. That outfit was able to plough through almost any root and upset some big stumps.

Archibald Wright was also the first to grow sweet clover in the West and he had other "firsts" in his farming record. He was interested in sweet clover because he was interested in tanning and read that the seed from a plant called sweet clover, contained tannic acid which is useful in that process. He sent away for seed in 1882 and the crop grew well, but nobody guessed about the great place of importance it was going to fill as a feed crop and as a soil building crop in western agriculture.

It seemed that this man Wright was always trying to grow new things. He was conducting a private experimental farm several years before the Dominion Experimental Farms were set up. He tried various varieties of cereal grains, and garden stuff. He hand picked some of the grain seed and exhibited it at Winnipeg shows in the '80's. He gave sugar cane a trial, and water melons; he even tried peanuts. I'm not sure about cocoanuts. And with fruit he had the same insatiable curiosity.

Along came an agent for fruit trees and shrubs. Wright had a bit of the horse-trader in him and said, "Here's a proposition. I've got the best site in this country for an orchard. You supply the trees and we'll divide the profit from the fruit we grow". That was 1881. The deal was on. The trees were set out but somehow they didn't care for this strange climate, and there was no profit to divide. The tree fruits were a failure, but somebody had to experiment and make the mistakes or we wouldn't be far along today in the search for hardy fruits.

Strictly speaking the fruit project wasn't a complete failure because some bush fruits did well and the rhubarb did fine, and they managed to produce an apple, yes one apple. But that solitary apple came to an untimely end. Wright had an old horse which had been raised in Ontario and when the animal recognized the apple, he dashed to the tree and devoured the fruit which evidently brought colthood memories.

Archibald Wright the sodbuster and experimenter died in March 1912. The man who gave his personal note to ensure building Winnipeg's first public school and the man who fought for a Hudson's Bay Route, was a booster to the end. Proud he was of the mighty city whose foundations he helped to lay and just as proud of his associations with Manitoba agriculture upon which he left a vivid imprint.

ARCHIBALD WRIGHT

Pioneer at the Prairie Gateway

Clement Cornwall

Ashcroft Pioneer

This Clement F. Cornwall was one of the first farmers in the Interior of British Columbia. He was a Sodbuster, indeed he was, but an unusual one. He was one of those Englishmen who would not allow the hardships and heavy toil of the frontier to interfere with his recreation. I would bet that no job about the farm could prevent Cornwall from having his 4 o'clock tea. Yes, this strange combination of farmer, sportsman, and politician who went to the new and wild country about the present town of Ashcroft, managed to take a good bit of old England with him.

There he was, cultivating land, irrigating and building roads ten years before there was any homesteading on the prairies and twenty years before the C.P.R. was built. But that didn't prevent Cornwall from playing cricket and racing horses; and strangest of all, imagine this pioneer "riding to hounds" in between the ranges of the Rockies, years before British Columbia became a province; red coats, imported dogs and everything needed to make the lives of the Ashcroft coyotes as short as possible.

Clement Cornwall sailed from Southampton on April 17, 1862. He was 26 years of age (Born, June 18, 1836) and he was bound for the west coast of Canada, via Panama. His companions on the boat included everything from criminals to clergymen. He arrived at Victoria on June 2nd (1862). He was disappointed; Victoria was dull. But he wasn't staying long; he was going to follow the crowd; he was going up the Fraser to hunt gold.

He bought two horses and crossed to New Westminster. It was a town with 100 houses. There he loaded up with provisions and took the Lillooet Trail. His decisions were more important than he realized. He was plotting the course for an important agricultural enterprise, and didn't know it.

There were lots of gold-seekers on the trail, but still it was primitive. One never knew what he might see when he went around a bend in the trail. It could be a pack of Indians or it might be a grizzly bear. The last thing Cornwall expected to see was a pair of camels, but sure enough, he met them laden with packs. Yes, camels were taken to the inter-mountain country for packing to the mines; but they weren't successful. Cornwall was surprised but his horses were more than surprised; they were frantic and tried to run away.

He swam his team across the swollen Thompson River and on June 30th he passed a grassy plain which was well watered by creeks. What's this? He almost forgot about the gold. He pushed on up the trail but he couldn't forget that grassy land and next day he rode back to take another look. It looked even better this time and he decided to pre-empt 320 acres and abandon the quest for gold. He marked the land and away he went to Lytton to enter his claim. The site which he and his brother chose for their farm was five miles south-west of the present town of Ashcroft. They called it Ashcroft Ranch after their old home in Gloucester-shire, England.

Instead of mining for gold, Clement Cornwall was now going to farm. Plans had to be revised. He had a lot to learn and there was nobody ahead of him to help, so Cornwall would learn the hard way. But this Cornwall was a student. He studied the situation. Said he, "It looks like good country for cattle but it's dry and we had better consider irrigation for cultivated crops". Fancy that. He dug a garden plot, and before he was there many weeks, he and his brother and his helpers were diverting water from nearby streams to irrigate it.

Now, he needed power and breeding stock. He bought a cow and calf but they were wild and wouldn't stay home. They wanted to go back to Oregon and Cornwall had no fences to hold them. He started for Kamloops one day to buy a team of oxen, but before going far he met a man driving a team of horses, "a black and a yellow roan". The owner was leaving the country and since Cornwall wasn't particular about colour combinations, he bought the team and the traveller went on toward New Westminster afoot.

As the weeks went by, Cornwall became convinced that he was right. He bought another 1800 acres of land and (on December 5/62) he bought 20 cows and 20 steers and heifers for spring delivery from a Mr. Stroud of Oregon. The price was to be double the cost of the cattle in Oregon, but not in excess of $60.00 for the cows and $20.00 for the two-year-olds.

Traffic to the mines was increasing and Cornwall and his brother found themselves living on a primitive but important thoroughfare. And the road was getting better. The Cariboo Wagon Road was one of the most famous pioneer road-building undertakings in history and Walter Moberly and Edgar Dewdney were largely responsible for the great effort which was to link Yale and Barkerville. In his diary for November 1, 1862, Clement Cornwall records that "six large pack trains passed during the day". And as winter approached, many of the packers' horses and mules were left with the settlers to be wintered.

Somehow, the pioneer's first winter in the country was always tough; at least they always said so. Cornwall's experience was no exception. The house was none too well finished and when he awakened many mornings, the blankets were white with frost. Cornwall rode over the countryside a good deal that winter, hunting for horses and hunting deer. When he returned on many occasions, his mustache and beard were so frozen together that he couldn't open his mouth. Being denied the right of "free speech" is about the worst thing that can happen to any Englishman.

This strange bachelor homesteader actually hired squaws to come and do his washing, $2.00 worth in one day. Two dollars would have bought all the clothes some of the homesteaders had. On Christmas day, the Cornwall brothers prepared a stylish meal for themselves and "dressed for dinner" according to the best English custom. New Year's day called for more festivities and they treated themselves to a "sliding party" on the lake. They had no skates so they just slid.

With the spring (1863) there was increased activity on the Cariboo Road. Cornwall recognized an opportunity and broke into the business of operating a Road House to serve the gold seekers. On that long trail which terminated at Barkerville, road houses were a necessity. They accounted for an exciting chapter in the history of the frontier and if they could talk they would tell strange tales, some of robbery and some of murder. Men might make a fortune playing poker at one road house and lose it at the next. Great place to study human nature; Cornwall saw miners with $20,000 worth of claims, coming out utterly broke, and he saw English gentry sharing beds with the dregs of humanity.

Cornwall now had plenty of power, about a dozen horses, 4 oxen and a mule. He hitched them in every conceivable combination. He planted barley and wheat and timothy and clover. He released the irrigation water and the crops did well. Then in that autumn of 1863, he planted winter wheat and irrigated it. He was constantly trying new crops and plants. It seemed that every person returning from Victoria had to bring seeds for Cornwall. "What in creation is he doing with all those seeds?", they asked. The answer was simple. He was testing them in this untried soil. He got alfalfa seed; called it "stuff that costs 40 cents a pound in Victoria", and it took hold. It was probably the first alfalfa seeded between the province of Ontario and the Pacific coast. In April, 1867, he went to Victoria and returned with apple trees, and then he got raspberries and strawberries and melons and made them grow in the new country.

There were reverses too. The cows calved too soon and losses were heavy. Dry summers withered the grass and feed was sometimes inadequate. Beside that there were grasshoppers. Grasshoppers took crops and pastures in parts of of the British Columbia Interior in 1943, and '44 and more recent years but that was not the first time because the pests descended in swarms that summer of 1864 and devastated some of the crops. It was a period of trial and error but the errors pointed the way to better methods.

Cornwall got sheep and then pigs. He erected a sawmill and set up a grist mill. In three and one half months after the middle of September, 1866, some 35 tons of wheat were gristed. Early in 1867, according to Cornwall's records, "a man came who is going up to Soda Creek to run the new grist mill there". I mention it now because that mill, north of Williams Lake, still stands. The water is running around its turbines and the mill is rusting in idleness, but it's a great monument to pioneer workmanship.

All the flour from those early mills was needed to supply travellers on the Cariboo Road and bran and potatoes were fed to Cornwall's pigs to make "Bacon for Barkerville". He surely had the first threshing machine in that same area. Not a very big one, true, but it was a threshing machine and settlers came such distances to see it that they had to rest their horses a couple of days before returning. It was a six-horse power machine and horse driven. Yes sir, with favourable conditions it might thresh 300 bushels in one day. And Cornwall's wheat that fall (of 1867) went 43½ bushels per acre.

New Westminster held the first agricultural Fair in all the west of Canada in the fall of 1867 and Cornwall was an exhibitor. He actually had the nerve to send samples of wheat and Indian corn from his homestead away up there in the wilds, but he won first prize with each. That was all the encouragement needed. Next year he secured a reaper. Wonderful invention too, and when Cornwall harvested that fall, he had one man operating with a cradle, one with the reaper and 13 Indians binding by hand.

One day in October, 1867, Cornwall wrote this in his diary, "Saw a coyote. I should like immensely to have a few hounds to rattle the beggars about a bit." Cornwall had a faculty for getting what he wanted and before many months, he was placing an order for hounds in England and requesting the Hudson's Bay Company to bring them out. Four were shipped around the Horn and three arrived safely (on Sept. 3/68) at a cost of £65. As the hunters "halloa" sounded through the valleys for the first time, the Indians must have wondered what tribe of savages had descended upon them. For 20 years, Cornwall rode that countryside with his beloved dogs. The fame of the pack reached England and several times, hounds were sent out by the Duke of Beaufort. A local Indian was elevated to the position of Master of Hounds. He was known as Cornwall Harry and folk said he spoke with a distinct Oxford accent until he died.

Yes, Cornwall's hounds furnished lots of thrills and a few spills. On one occassion after a long run through woods

Cornwall discovered that he and his pack were following the scent of an Indian rather than a coyote. We can suppose the Indian wasn't entirely in love with the situation either. Another time, a distinguished visitor in Cornwall's hunting party had the embarrassing experience of falling off his horse and rolling down a hill right into the midst of the hounds who were in the act of finishing off Mr. Coyote. The honourable member of the legislature came to a stop amid more sharp teeth and bad tempers than he had ever met in politics.

Cornwall became a good stockman. Seven years after he settled at Ashcroft, he had 400 cattle. And he got them the honest way. Too many cattlemen of that period were looking for stray calves to brand. But not Cornwall. When he did make a mistake, he recorded it in his diary (May 1, 1873) "I fear I have branded a calf belonging to someone else". He branded himself an honest man. And he could hold his own in a horse deal. Governor Musgrave came up for some shooting (Oct. 1869) and before he left, Cornwall sold the Queen's representative a bay mare for $120.00. The mare cost Cornwall $40.00; 300% isn't considered a bad profit.

Sooner or later, the best men are overtaken by matrimony and on June 8, 1871, Clement Cornwall was married. Then, for some time, according to his diary, he was occupied with papering the sitting room, framing pictures, hanging curtains and cultivating posies. What a revolution in the life of an outdoor man!

And who else in all the settled areas of the West would have sponsored an annual horse race in 1869. He called it the Derby and the first running of the classic was there at his own Ashcroft on October 13, 1869. The Derby was well organized with starter, judge, clerk and stewards. White people and red flocked to Ashcroft and it was won by a bay stallion called Gladiator. Other events that day were Colonial Stakes, Governor's Purse and Hurdle Race, and Cornwall's horse Blue Jack won the Hurdles.

Clement Cornwall was closely in touch with political progress in his adopted province. Quite early the Governor named him magistrate. When he accepted that post, along came his official supplies, a few legal forms and a lot of handcuffs and leg-irons. Later, he was Stipendiary Magistrate and County

Court Judge (1889-1907). Under date of April 7, 1868, he mentions receiving the mail and then he writes in his diary "The Capital is moved to Victoria so goodbye to unlucky New Westminster lot owners". It was about the same time that a great meeting was held in Victoria requesting British Columbia's admission to the newly created Dominion of Canada and asking as a condition of entry that a wagon road linking Lake Superior and the head of navigation on the lower Fraser, be built. A railroad was too much to ask.

From 1864 to 1871, Cornwall was a member of the Legislative Council and when British Columbia entered Confederation in that latter year, he was appointed to the Canadian Senate. There he remained until 1881 when the pioneer who broke trail away up-country and planted the first seeds of agriculture in that part, was named Lieutenant Governor of his province. It was a fitting honour. And when his term of office expired (in 1887) what did he do? He returned to his beloved Ashcroft Ranch where he made his home for another 20 years. When he died in 1910 he was buried on a slope overlooking the scenes of his earliest farming efforts, right there on the Cornwall Ranch.

Man of principle, was Clement Cornwall. If he worked on Sunday in those early years, it was because he had become confused in the days of the week. That happened now and again when settlers were isolated on the frontier. And he believed in fair play. That was why his political life brought him such great respect.

"Twelve Foot" Davis

Somebody is sure to ask why "Twelve Foot" Davis is included among the agricultural pioneers. Well, one might as well make it clear on the outset that Davis was not a farmer in the strict sense but at least he was a pioneer in an area which becomes increasingly important in agriculture. And certainly the story is one which should be written into the agricultural records of this land. Besides, I like the story.

Some folk have visualized this well known character of the early Peace River district as a giant. He wasn't twelve feet tall. He wasn't a giant except in a point of generosity and friendliness. Actually, "Twelve Foot" Davis was a small man. How did he get his title? Like this; he belonged to Boston and in 1849 he followed the Gold Rush to California. He was one of the famous "forty niners" who crossed the continent by "prairie schooner", sporting the motto "California or Bust". A few years later Davis was attracted by the reports of gold in the Cariboo area of British Columbia. Yes, he was one of the thousands who went in over the Cariboo Trail in the early sixties.

And he was using his head all the time. After looking things over, he got a "hunch" that two of the best claims were bigger in surface area than they were supposed to be. So under cover of darkness one night, Davis made some measurements of "Discovery Claim" and "Number one From Discovery". Sure enough; his guess was a good one. Those who had these claims had staked 12 feet more surface area than that to which they were entitled. He lost no time in registering his claim to those 12 extra feet and managed to take $20,000 worth of gold from that little plot. Hence the name, "Twelve Foot" Davis.

From mining in the Cariboo, Davis turned to trading in furs. At first he was with the trader P. Dunlevy who had a post on the upper reaches of the Fraser and who made his first excursion into Peace River in 1873. But almost immediately Davis took up trade in the Peace River on his own account. His supplies and trade goods, he took in from Soda Creek there on the Fraser River and worked upstream to a point well north. Then they had the Giscome Portage to contend with and all supplies had to be carried over the height of land to a stream flowing toward the Arctic rather than the Pacific. From the Parsnip River, the Davis flat-boats passed into the Peace River, the mighty stream whose name is a memorial to early efforts to keep peace between the Cree and Beaver Indians. Still Davis' troubles were not over because there was a 14-mile portage around a dangerous canyon, just above Hudson Hope.

When going up stream, the power required to move a boat, loaded or otherwise, was generated by bread and fish and beans fed to a crew of nine husky men. There were eight oarsmen and one steersman and they were usually Indians who were hired for the purpose. And when they came to a fourteen-mile portage, the freight had to carried on the backs of the same sturdy helpers. Davis was a powerful fellow and always carried a bigger load than his men were expected to carry. Two hundred pounds was the customary load for Davis when they were on portage.

Finally the year's supplies would be delivered at Dunvegan or Peace River or some other point in that north country. And in due course a load of furs would go back to Soda Creek by the same route and then on to the Pacific coast. And let nobody suppose it was an easy trip whichever way the Davis crew was travelling. There were usually two boats making a journey together and each would be loaded with six or eight tons. Two months or more was the customary time to move a cargo of furs from Dunvegan to Soda Creek and it took just as long to move a load of trade goods back to Dunvegan. Sometimes an early winter would see his boats "frozen in" on the Peace or Fraser. Finally, "Twelve Foot" Davis used Edmonton as his base and made at least one trip per year from his Fort Vermilion post to Edmonton.

The Indians grew to trust Davis; indeed they loved him and brought their best furs to him. Thus his competitors found it difficult to trade near him. An Indian would give Davis a bale of beaver skins or mink or fox and agree to take settlement when the freight came in, six or eight months later.

And six or eight months later, there would be a perfect understanding between trader and Indian. There were no written records, no receipts and no statements; but the Davis memory never failed. An old Indian with whom Davis did business died; 10 years or more later the son came to trade. Said Davis to the young Cree, "Your father gave me three beaver skins and died before I settled for them; I'll pay you now". It was an example of Davis' honesty as well as Davis' memory.

Wherever Davis was living or camping, there were food and shelter for the traveller, no matter what the colour of his hide. And there was a light in the window at night so that it would be easier for the traveller. He probably didn't have blinds and curtains but I'm sure he would never subscribe to the modern idea of pulling the blinds in the evening. And the fame of his food went far. Hadn't he been an apprentice to a cook in old Boston and he liked to display his kitchen skill. As a maker of "Johnny Cake" nobody in all the north would challenge the supremacy of "Twelve Foot" Davis.

Anyone in trouble in that country came to Davis. If he couldn't help, he would at least try and he became recognized as medical and dental advisor as well as guide and friend. The story is told of an Indian woman who came to his cabin, groaning and pointing to one particular molar in her lower jaw. Obviously she wanted help for a bad tooth. Davis had a pair of forceps which could be used to pull any tooth but the squaw who was making lots of signs but no understandable talk, refused to co-operate as one suffering from toothache might be expected to do. Davis and his helper, Tom Barrow I believe, held a conference and concluded that the tooth must come out. So, while Barrow held the squaw, Davis extracted the tooth. Madam Squaw became really hostile and left in a rage. Soon however, she returned, this time with another squaw. The explanation was now clear. A tooth had been removed from the wrong squaw. The first squaw had no tooth trouble but was simply making a futile attempt to enlist help for her friend who really had a severe tooth-ache. So the traders made another extraction. But Davis was never able to make amends with the first victim, whose demonstrations had been so sadly misinterpreted.

Yes, that was the only brand of dentistry practiced on

some parts of the frontier. It was about that time that Rev. John McDougall, the well known missionary who was at Fort Edmonton, had a troublesome tooth. He poulticed the tooth and even tried treating it with a hot iron; but finally he made an overland trip to the nearest dentist, at Fort Garry, about 1000 miles away.

In his later years, "Twelve Foot" Davis was blind. But he didn't stop trading. So much of understanding existed between Davis and the Indians and so completely did he enjoy their confidence that he didn't need his eyes in order to trade fairly. For several years the totally blind trader made his annual trip from Fort Vermilion to Edmonton to sell his furs and buy his supplies.

Davis had his own ideas about things. Of course a man has a right to his own views and when Osborne Scott was making a journey up the Peace River with the blind frontiersman in 1896, much of the conversation had to do with the shape of the world. Davis believed the world to be flat. He was sure of it. "If it was round, how could anyone stick on except at the top." No youngster was going to talk him into believing that he lived on the dangerous slopes of a round world.

Yes, Davis was an uneducated man, couldn't read and couldn't write but he had something that can be better than a cloak of education; he had a great and kindly heart; he had a love for his fellows and an urge to be fair. Somebody asked him the secret of his numerous friendships in the north, among red men and white, and Davis replied; "I dunno; maybe its because them fellers all need smiles and they need grub and I keeps a big stock of both. And so I just smiles at 'em and feeds 'em." Mighty practical psychology; more effective perhaps than all the wisdom packed in a four dollar book on making friends. It might have a lot to offer us in our national and international planning because Canada as a nation has great resources in both food and good will. And the world needs both.

"Twelve Foot" Davis died in 1900 at Grouard in the Peace River District which he loved so dearly. (The date of death as shown on the tomestone is believed an error and should read 1900 instead of 1893.) His last testimony has been quoted many times. It will bear repeating. He was asked by a lady from the Anglican Mission if he was afraid to die, and he replied, "No ma'm, I'm not afraid. I never killed nobody, never stole from nobody, never hurt nobody intentional, and I always kept open house for men who were tired or hungry. No ma'm, I ain't afraid to die". In his lifetime he made lots of money but somehow he couldn't hold on to it when there were needy people about, and he died penniless.

They buried Davis there at Slave Lake but in accordance with his last wish, his friend Jim Cornwall saw to it that his bones were removed to a spot on a high hill overlooking Peace River Landing. It is a picturesque setting looking down upon three rivers, a setting Davis loved. The stone they placed upon his grave carries an epitaph which tells the whole story. In a few words it tells why "Twelve Foot" Davis is remembered as a great pioneer. Here it is:

"H. F. Davis
born
In Vermont
1820
Died at Slave Lake
1893
Pathfinder, Pioneer,
Miner and Trader
He was every man's friend
And never locked his cabin door."

No, he wasn't a farmer in the ordinary sense. And you can brand this sketch as a cross between a sermon and a bed-time story if you wish; but just the same, this Davis was the pathfinder in what is today a great agricultural community. True, he was blind in his latter years, but by his own testimony he could see a lot. He could see his old home in Boston; he could still see, with his mind's eye, the grandeur of the Peace River. And he could see more than that; he could see new homes and roads and schools and churches there in his north-country; he could see fields of ripening grain and pastures stocked with cattle and sheep. He prophesied that Peace River would one day feed multitudes.

Funny little man, of course he was. He would look a bit

of a curiosity at a four o'clock tea but out in the open he was smarter than most people. He could whinny like a mustang and howl like a coyote; and he could build a fire and cook a bannock while most folk would be hunting for the cook book. Whether he should be classified as an agriculturist or not doesn't seem to matter so much; what's most important is that somebody branded him the "first dairyman in all the Peace River"; he peddled "the milk of human kindness". Yes,

> "He was every man's friend
> And never locked his cabin door."

THE "TWELVE FOOT"
DAVIS STONE

Motherwell

Statesman in Overalls

When he prodded two sulking oxen into Assiniboia, a little in advance of the rails, he was just Bill Motherwell. It wasn't long until he was winning new titles and he had a lot of them. By the beginning of the century they called him "the fighting farmer from Sintaluta". Then he was Honourable W. R. Motherwell and Dr. Motherwell. Best of all, in later years, he was hailed "the Grand Old Man of Canadian Agriculture". There can be only one at a time with that most endearing of honorary degrees. But looking back over it all now, I would suggest still another title. I would name him "Statesman in Overalls". Somehow he could bring more dignity to a pair of overalls and a five-tined fork than anybody I have known. Ashamed of those symbols of honest toil? Not Motherwell! He was proud of them.

His coming to the prairies and all the hardships that went with the frontier, wasn't a matter of necessity. He graduated from the Ontario Agricultural College in 1881 and might have accepted professional work amid the comfort of old Ontario or gone back to the security offered by the home farm there in Lanark County (where he was born in 1860). But college degree or no college degree, he was going to start from scratch and make his own way out west.

Fresh from College, he went to Winnipeg and got a job building the C.P.R. Next spring (1882) he bought a pair of oxen and a wagon and struck west into the North West Territories. He swung north, crossed the beautiful Qu'Appelle Valley, chose a piece of land that had what he wanted and built a sod house. He hid his college diploma and began the struggle with tough sod and a tricky climate. The survey wasn't completed but Motherwell couldn't wait. He marked his farm boundaries where he thought they should be and began to plough. When the survey was completed, it was clear that Motherwell had ploughed the road allowance and part of an adjoining homestead. But that didn't matter much because he went ahead and cropped the land anyway for a couple of years.

The first crops were frosted and Motherwell concluded that live stock were needed. Back to Ontario he went in '84 and he returned with some grade Shorthorn cows and a pure bred bull. He was always a staunch supporter of fairs and exhibitions and the newly purchased Shorthorn bull was exhibited at the fair at Indian Head that fall and won 1st prize of $10.00. Somebody asked him what he did with the prize money and he answered "bought a wedding ring and quit batching".

During the Riel Rebellion Motherwell did freighting for the troops. All the while he was developing his farm and extending cultivation. Wheat was losing some of the risk attached to its culture; but the problems of marketing diminished only a little. Farmers were not always permitted to load grain over the loading platforms and when they went to the elevators, they were often cheated. There was injustice and farmers were hostile but they had no leader. And then they discovered one, Motherwell would lead the fight. And was he a fighter? His father once whipped him for fighting at school. But later when the father learned that the boy had just cause for his actions, dad apologized and said, "Son, don't be afraid to fight if you know you are right". No one could ever say he was afraid to fight for his principles, whether it was a matter of farmers' rights, temperance or church union. And when he was stirred by injustice, I tell you he could teach a Bengal tiger some tricks.

Here is the story of the famous struggle which gave rise to the Grain Growers organization. The Manitoba Grain Act provided that farmers would be permitted to load their grain directly from a platform into freight cars and thus "short circuit" the elevators. In 1901 there was a shortage of freight cars and to make matters worse, the distribution clause in the Act seemed to be ignored by the railroads. If farmers couldn't get cars, they were at the mercy of the elevator companies and some of them were undoubtedly guilty of excessive dockage, short weights and unfair grading and prices.

Some of Motherwell's letters to the press came to the attention of Wm. Whyte (later Sir William) vice-president of the C.P.R. Said Whyte to Thomas Acheson, "who is this rebellious homesteader? Better go up there and see what you can do to pacify him. Tell him, if he has a complaint to come to Winnipeg and see me." My friend Thomas Acheson went up, a bit uncertain how he would approach this so-called rebel. He drove out to the farm by livery. Motherwell was driving a team in the field. The C.P.R. man thought better than to bother him in the field so tied the livery horses and waited until the farmer's team was brought to the stable and unharnessed and fed for the night. Mr. Acheson made his first advance but he got a cold reception. He mentioned weather. He talked crops but Motherwell was foxy. Then the visitor got a view of the new church and manse just across the way and said, "you can be proud of your new church". Then he added, "My father was a minister and I was raised in a manse". That broke the ice. The Presbyterian Motherwell was won over at once and was ready to talk. That was the first meeting between Motherwell and Acheson who were later very good friends.

But Motherwell lost none of his determination to see this marketing difficulty through. Says he to his friend and neighbour, Peter Dayman, "there's only one solution to this wheat blockade and that is farmer organization". Peter Dayman nodded a bristly chin, but how is organization to be achieved in this new land of scattered settlers and no practical means of communication. Motherwell and Dayman burned a lot of

MR. MOTHERWELL

Courtesy of Mrs. Miriam Green Ellis

midnight kerosene and blackened a lot of lamp chimneys before they concluded that farmers were really mad enough for action.

It happened that Premier Roblin of Manitoba and Premier Haultain of the North West Territories were to be at Indian Head on Dec. 18, (1901) for a public debate on the matter of Assiniboia becoming part of Manitoba. It seemed a good time to get a group of farmers together and find out if they would support organization. Motherwell and Dayman wrote letters to every one they knew and a big crowd came to town. Sure enough, the farmers were mad. Some said it was too late for organization and that bullets were needed. But anyway, they organized, called themselves the Territorial Grain Growers' Association, and Motherwell was provisional president. Then when the first regular meeting was held at Indian Head a few weeks later, (Feb. 1, 1902), Motherwell was elected president, with nothing provisional about it.

In a short time, as we trace his career, we find him accepting J. W. Scallion's invitation to address meetings in Manitoba and the result was the Manitoba Grain Growers' Association. The fight against "Elevator Monopoly" continued and reached a climax in the fall of 1902. The new west had a big crop and the freight car famine was serious. Agents were not keeping "order books" as required by the Manitoba Grain Act and farmers often "missed their turns" for cars. Elevators were getting cars which should have been allotted to farmers who wanted to do their own loading. Motherwell demanded a show-down. He went to Winnipeg with protests and returned weighted down with assurances of better treatment. But better distribution of cars failed to materialize. The railroad agent at Sintaluta was one who failed to furnish cars in accord with the Act and the farmers swore out affidavits. The fat was in the fire. The farmers were going to court. They decended upon Sintaluta from miles and miles around. Some slept in the livery barn and some bedded down in their wagon boxes. At least they were going to be there for the showdown, and see what a young farmers' organization could do against a mighty railroad company. It looked like David against Goliath. But those who came to Sintaluta that day were not disappointed because the farmers won their case and the railroad agent was fined $50.00. It was a great moral victory and the Grain Growers' Movement swept over the prairies and so did the name of Motherwell.

In politics, Motherwell had something in common with Abraham Lincoln. Both started with defeats. The Canadian statesman contested the North Qu'Appelle seat for the Legislature of the North West Territories in 1894 and lost the election. That wasn't all. He lost his deposit too. He lost about everything but his fighting determination. Two years later he ran again, and again was defeated. But Motherwell was never a quitter. Many years later (Jan. 1940) when finally retiring from politics, he said, "When a man drops out at the age of 80, people can't say he's a quitter". Those first two attempts at politics were before the birth of the Grain Growers' movement. By 1905, it all looked different. The farmers in North Qu'Appelle wanted Motherwell and when the province of Saskatchewan was created, he was elected to the first Legislature. He became the first Minister of Agriculture in the newly formed province and continued at that important post until 1918. His resignation then was in protest against certain provincial policies. One year later he resigned from the Legislature to be a candidate in the Federal Election. But he lost the election and again had the experience of losing his deposit. Abraham Lincoln had three political defeats and Motherwell beat him by one. He had four. But by 1921, Motherwell's defeats were over. In that year he was elected to the House of Commons and became Canada's Minister of Agriculture in Prime Minister Mackenzie King's first cabinet. From 1921 until his retirement in 1940 he won five Federal elections, (1921, 25, 26, 30 and 35,) and for nearly 10 years he was Minister of Agriculture.

At Ottawa he was known as a reformer and his policies left a permanent imprint upon the character of Canadian agriculture. Restricted areas for the control of tuberculosis in Canada, were the first to be started in the British Empire. Pig grading was started during his period of office and so was the grading of many agricultural products, beef, butter, eggs and so on. He gave leadership to the organized fight to defeat stem rust of wheat. He supported the Hudson Bay Railway. And so it goes. Nor did it follow that he always voted with his own political party. Many will recall, for example, how he supported the Marketing Act in 1934, although other members of his party were opposed. One of his last political fights in the House cost him his best cane. The walking stick, it seems, came to its end when it crashed down on somebody's desk, just to add a bit of punch to his argument. I've sometimes wondered if the cane was really aimed at the desk.

Soil was sacred to him. He was part of every movement that had soil conservation as its purpose. He was president of the International Dry Farming Congress in 1913 and president of the International Irrigation Congress in 1916. He wanted to see more grassland and the concluding sentence in a letter I was happy to receive a short time before his death was this, "We must grow more grass if we wish to continue growing grain or anything else on our wind-swept open prairies".

Innumerable were the honours which came to him. He might have been Saskatchewan's Lieutenant Governor but he said he wanted no "three-cornered hats and feathers". He never wanted to be considered old. In 1928 the University of Saskatchewan, the prairie University he did so much to encourage, bestowed the honorary degree LL.D. upon him. It was for eminent services to Canadian agriculture. And then thoughts went back to the formative years of the University when Motherwell was Saskatchewan's Minister of Agriculture and the relationship between the College of Agriculture and the Provincial University was being debated. Mr. Motherwell at first favoured the Ontario plan where the Agricultural College was separate from the University, but when the evidence was placed before him, he gave his approval and support to President Murray's unorthodox plan to place the Agricultural College at the very heart of the University.

Of course there was another side to Motherwell, the more private side if you like. He was the kindly and sympathetic soul. He had been a good ball player. He was always a good farmer. When neighbours admit that, it must be true. The massive stone house standing on the Abernethy section farm was a symbol of Motherwell stability and it testified that the Motherwells came to stay.

When he was retiring from public life in his 80th year, friends presented him with a large portrait of himself (by

Ernest Fosbery) and a fine banquet was arranged for the presentation. Then there was the matter of where the portrait should hang. Some suggested the Legislative Building at Regina, but Motherwell had something to say: "No", said he, "If I have my way, the picture will hang at the University right by that of my old friend and neighbour, Angus MacKay". And that's where it hangs. It was Angus MacKay who nominated Motherwell for the Presidency on that stormy day when the Territorial Grain Growers' Association was born at Indian Head.

He died on May 24, 1943. Hundreds gathered at the little local church to pay tribute to a beloved pioneer. It wasn't given to many to reap such breadth of experience as was his, to come into the country by ox-cart and remain to become one of the nation's law-makers. That was W. R. Motherwell, an outstanding farmer, an able statesman, and a great Canadian.

Sheridan Lawrence

Emperor of the Peace

I somehow picture one with the fascinating name of "Sheridan Lawrence" as the hero of a three-act play, perhaps a dashing lover, but more likely a "two gun" sheriff, or a general home from the wars. Well, Sheridan Lawrence was the hero, right enough, but not in the theatre. His stage was the north country, those far reaches of Alberta which were new sixty years ago and are still pretty new to most people.

He was the frontiersman extra-ordinary. They dubbed him "Emperor of the Peace". The northern territory which felt his influence was bigger far than the empires ruled by many proud monarchs in history. But let's get back to 1886, the year following the completion of the C.P.R. The Lawrences from Waterloo, Quebec, step from the train at Calgary. The boy Sheridan is sixteen years old but big and powerful for his years. He is already broad shouldered and square jawed. And dad Lawrence who had fought with the Northern Army in the Civil War, is taking his family into the distant north where he had the year before accepted an assignment to teach at the mission at Fort Vermilion, wherever Fort Vermilion might be. The Lawrences know a bit about Fort Vermilion. They know it's about half way between Calgary and the Arctic Circle and they know they must spend weeks on the "poop-deck" of an ox-wagon before they reach the place. Dad Lawrence had a brother "E.J." teaching farming at the mission at Fort Vermilion at that time. Strange that anybody would consider farming so far from civilization!

Of course there was no railroad north of Calgary. And not even a decent trail north of Edmonton. But the Lawrences loaded up and headed north. One yoke of oxen hauled a brand new Watrous steam engine, another team hauled the family wagon and the third team a load of mixed equipment. What lay before them was a 900-mile journey and it represented weeks and weeks of driving by day and sleeping close to mother earth at night. They forded the Red Deer

River and got along fine, except that the oxen drawing the Watrous engine got stuck. From Edmonton North, there were more difficulties however, until at Peace River Crossing they made a big raft and moved on with all their worldly belongings for the last 300 miles. Young Sheridan was taking cattle north for his uncle, two pure bred Shorthorn bulls and two pure bred cows.

Somewhere along the trail, the Lawrences met up with the Scott family bound for the same destination. Rev. Malcolm Scott who later became Archdeacon Scott was going as a missionary and his family was with him. He too had live-stock for the north and his two children, Osborne and Julia had two wee pigs which were being bottle fed with the utmost punctuality. Important pigs, indeed, because they were going to establish their species in a territory where no pigs had been before. Trouble was, these little pigs brought from Red River wouldn't stay little and Osborne and Julia had to make the crates bigger every few days.

Sheridan Lawrence pretended to be interested in those pigs but actually it was the blue-eyed little girl who was feeding them that he glanced at so shyly. And each time he peeked at her, she seemed to be peeking at him. Old Dan Cupid had something up his sleeve, sure as fate. It was romance on the trail and fourteen years later, Sheridan Lawrence and Julia Scott were married (Westbourne, Manitoba) and they re-dedicated themselves to their adopted north country.

The same Mrs. Lawrence is to be remembered as one of the notable pioneer women of the North West. She was re-sourceful. She was a woman with culture, and was religious.

When the upper millstone became loose, it was she who adjusted it to make certain it was level with the nether or lower stone. How did she do it? She flooded the nether stone with water and froze it. Then she set the upper stone in its bracket with melted lead from a tea caddy. In 1900 she had an organ brought in on sleighs and later a piano was delivered the same way. If twenty people dropped in at the hour of prayer, you could depend upon it, there would be a Bible for each one. That was partly accounted for, of course, by the fact that there were many children in the Lawrence family, fifteen altogether, eight daughters and seven sons who all lived to be proud of their north country. (The youngest born 1922). To Sheridan Lawrence, it was the ideal size for a family. He "wouldn't take a million dollars for any one of those children and he wouldn't give two cents for another". When most of the babies were born, the doctor was about four hundred miles away. Yes, and the doctor was still that far away when the family experienced an epidemic of small pox, and sixteen members were sick at one time with only Mrs. Lawrence to look after them.

From the very beginning, Sheridan Lawrence saw the north country as a land of opportunity, a land which must one day be developed for farming and other enterprises. And didn't he take the lead! He could have been considered a one-man Chamber of Commerce. In his little Empire there in the north he was not only farmer and rancher; he was trader; freighter; butcher; miller, and lumberman. He alone had the answers to all the questions about Northern Alberta. Whether they concerned farming; furs; fishing or something else. Then the pioneer was named a magistrate, and a benevolent magistrate he was.

In the famous year of '98 he was going to the Klondike to mine for gold but plans fell through. So instead, he walked to Edmonton and used his savings to buy a turbine engine; a threshing machine; a flour mill and a saw-mill. It took months and a lot of scheming to freight those new and heavy machines to their destination by way of Athabaska. It was one thing to buy such ultra-modern machinery and get it home; it was quite another to put those strangely new fangled machines together for the first time. Assembly was by trial and error at first, and pieces of saw-mill were sometimes fitted on to the steam engine, and parts of the threshing machine were bolted to the flour mill. Finally however, the machines were in working order and they marked a new era in serving the needs of the north.

Lawrence opened a store at Fort Vermilion and one at Hay Lakes, 120 miles distant. He and his family long maintained a regular freight service between those two points. Supplies from the Lawrence farm; flour; cured meats and so on, were sold to trappers and Indians and others through the stores and Hudson's Bay Company. Such supplies replaced those which the Hudson's Bay Company formerly brought in from the outside. In one winter, the Lawrences slaughtered 160 pigs and 80 cattle. All the meat was for use at home or by others in those far latitudes. That winter they cured some 3,000 pounds of bacon and a ton or so of hams. In some years, 100 tons or more of flour made from wheat grown on Lawrence's own farm, would be sold to traders and trappers and others in that part. There was no other market for a long time and most trade was on the basis of barter, except when Indians got treaty money.

Furs constituted an important factor in trade and Lawrence handled tons of the best furs to come to Edmonton for many years. For example, the modest Lawrence arrived quietly in Edmonton in the spring of 1924 with bales of fur from the winter catch; 3,000 muskrats; 1,000 beavers; 365 mink; 122 lynx; 96 cross-fox; 24 silver fox; 128 skunk; 476 ermine; 121 red fox; 20 wolf; 17 marten and a few otter and wolverine. Quite an assortment I would say. That particular delivery brought $22,000. Lawrence knew every trapper and settler between Peace River and the North Pole, and they knew him. Many of them ate flour and meat grown on his farm and many of them slept under his roof one time or another because Sheridan Lawrence kept open house on the banks of the Peace. He once remarked that there would be no fur traders in Heaven, but those who knew Sheridan Lawrence were pretty sure there'd be at least one exception.

He operated about a thousand acres of land but no-one could accuse him of being a wheat farmer. He did cultivate a few hundred acres of grain annually but sometimes he had 150 horses and as many as 300 cattle. When he had more cattle than were needed in the north trade, he sent them to Edmonton, which was no very small undertaking. I think of him starting out (in 1924 for example) with 65 head of cattle. They had to be loaded on a scow and towed upstream by the once noted steamer *D. A. Thomas*, floated to Peace River where they would be transferred to freight cars and hauled to Edmonton. In 1926, Sheridan Lawrence was in Edmonton with 41 pigs, the first ever shipped from Fort Vermilion. They came the same way, river boat to Peace River and freight car to Edmonton.

Lawrence often travelled on the steamboat *D. A. Thomas*. It seems that he sometimes took that boat in a journey upstream and returned on a craft of his own making. One traveller returning south from Fort Vermilion told of the boat getting a signal to stop and a big man coming aboard. In one hand, this big fellow, identified as Sheridan Lawrence, carried a leather grip, and in the other, a heavy parcel well wrapped. He was going to Peace River to do some business which he said would take him 10 minutes after he was there. The business at Peace River was completed and with no loss of time he was observed to return to the river with an armful of supplies, a can of gasoline and that same heavy parcel. But there would be no boat scheduled to return for several days. Lawrence knew that. He had considered everything and wasn't waiting for a boat. He commandeered some lumber and in a few minutes he fashioned a craft that looked like a cross between a scow and a rowboat. He climbed on with his supplies and as he floated away from the shore he was seen to unwrap the mysterious parcel. It contained a small outboard motor or "kicker". This was clamped to the back of the craft and Sheridan Lawrence waved "good-bye". Those who knew him said, "He'll do it in 30 hours and except to boil some tea, he won't stop till he gets home".

Oh yes, there was lots of work on and around the Lawrence premises and Lawrence said it was nice not to be handicapped by darkness in the summer when they were busy. I have a mental picture of Mr. and Mrs. Lawrence in those early years, sitting down for their first relaxation of the day after the children were all in bed. There were the potatoes to peel for the next day and one would peel while the other would read aloud. That was their relaxation. It took a lot of potatoes to feed 17 Lawrences and so mother and dad were able to get in a fair amount of reading.

They tell of Lawrence hiring a man for his farm when in Edmonton one summer. The man wanted to know something about the number of hours he would have to work each day. Lawrence chuckled to himself and said, "Oh, from daylight to dark will be all we'll expect of you". That seemed fair enough but when the new hand went north with his boss, he got quite a shock. The sun sneaked over the eastern horizon at 3 A.M.

and didn't "knock off" until 9 P.M. And all through those nights in June and July there was practically no darkness. The joke was on the new-comer, but he had a sense of humor and said he would remain with Lawrence for the winter when he could draw his pay for working two or three hours before dinner and two or three after.

Quite a few Canadians have heard about the school Sheridan Lawrence built on the north bank of the Peace. The Government didn't build schools for people who went so ridiculously far from everything. But Lawrence had a habit of doing things for himself. He built miles of graded roads and highways on and away from his farm because they wouldn't be there if he didn't make them. But this outpost of learning became famous as Lawrence Point School, where grades one to nine were taught. Any man with fifteen children and ideals like those held by Lawrence, needed a school, and a few boys and girls with other names attended. Lawrence Point School was a sturdy log structure and it was equipped as a modern school should be. It had good desks, a library, maps, text books, gramophone, and a flag pole. And there was an able teacher who lived with the Lawrences. The first teacher by the way was a very talented lady, Miss Waghorn of the family which gave its name to Waghorn's Guide. Everybody at that school studied music and most of the pupils learned to play the piano. Imagine Lawrence Point School, far off on the banks of the Peace River, achieving fame for discipline and efficiency; the bell rang at 9 A.M., not a minute before or a minute after but at 9 A.M. Children congregated; they came from barns, garden or fields and fell in line to march in an orderly way in to the school. Then there were morning hymn and Bible reading and studies for the day. That was the way Sheridan Lawrence did things on his frontier. Among the honours which came to the mud-chinked Lawrence Point School, was Miss Margaret Lawrence's distinction of winning the Governor General's gold medal for grade eight standing, in all the Peace River Inspectorate.

After Lawrence built the school, he proposed building a church. The church service was often held in the Lawrence home when a minister came that way, but now Lawrence would build a real church. He did, and then somebody asked if he was going to hire the minister too. He said, "No, but I'll supply a congregation". And when all the Lawrences went to Church, a congregation was assured all right.

The Peace was Sheridan Lawrence's country. He was farming there successfully long before those in the outside world even considered the Peace River for settlement. He heard it argued that farming so far north could never be successful, and he laughed. To him it was like standing beside the Alaska Highway and arguing that it couldn't be done. Any country that would permit the Lawrences to live so fully and independently must be good country. "Enough variety in climate that nobody can get tired of it," said Lawrence, "and everything grows." He said it was a lot of bunk when some writer was romancing about the killing frosts and wild Indians and ferocious wolves of that land. Lawrence never saw wild and dangerous Indians and there were no wild animals which he considered more dangerous than his own herd bull. To prove that he meant it all, his years of retirement were spent right there in the north, his north, the development of which he had watched for over half a century. There were hardships, yes, but hardship never blocked the progress of resourceful pioneers. He slept many nights in the open. He once walked the 800 miles from Fort Simpson to Fort Vermilion in a month and a day. He scorned luxuries like tents and pillows when he was on the trail. A lot of the Sodbusters were like that.

Anyway, he proved to the world that you can grow nearly anything on that northern soil. One of his hopes which was not fulfilled was a railroad to Fort Vermilion. He argued for a rail link with Edmonton or the Pacific coast but it didn't come and on that point, the elder Lawrence was neither happy nor pleasant. He did see a telegraph line completed in 1931. That helped a lot, but still such a vast and productive country as Lawrence's North deserved a railroad. At least the six-foot, 280-pound Emperor of the Peace said so and who in all the north would argue with so determined, so courageous and so kindly a pioneer.

Seager Wheeler

Searcher for Seeds

Fate plays strange tricks on people and nations. If Seager Wheeler had been one inch taller, he probably would never have seen the prairies and the little Western town of Rosthern would have missed a lot of good advertising. Somebody else would have won the International wheat championships and progress in Western Canada would have been slowed up at least a little. If Seager Wheeler had been one inch taller, he would have gone to sea with the British Navy as he wanted to do. When a man can set out to be a sailor and end up a dry-land plant breeder, it's safer not to make too many guesses about anybody's future.

He grew up amid the fisher folk (born Jan., 1868). He liked flowers and "growing things" but actually he knew a lot more about boats and fish-nets and sea-boots and things than he did about farming. His home was a lowly fisherman's cottage on the rock-bound coast of the Isle of Wight. From the high cliffs at Chale Bay, Blackgang, the boy Seager watched the boats which plied the "Seven Seas". He saw ships in distress. He saw drowning people snatched from wet graves by his brave kinfolk. He gathered treasure washed ashore from sunken vessels. He heard strange tales about the Blackgang pirates who operated from caves near home. He was filled with the romance of the sea. He would join the "bloomin' nivey" and enrich the family traditions.

But the best laid plans sometimes go wrong and Sig Wheeler wasn't big enough to be accepted for the navy. In spite of all the stretching and expanding he could do, he was an inch short. It was a bitter disappointment to a boy whose heart was set on it.

While he was still smarting from disappointment, there came a letter from an uncle who was so bold as to settle on land in the North West Territories of Canada. The letter had a lot to say about homesteads and opportunities. Sig Wheeler had never thought seriously about farming anywhere, least of all in far-off Canada, but now the idea fired his imagination and before the family realized what was happening, the young blood was on his way to join the Uncle at Clark's Crossing wherever that might be. It was the spring of '85 and before the 17-year-old immigrant lad reached his destination, the lid of bloody rebellion was blown off on the South Saskatchewan. Clark's Crossing which was north of the village of Saskatoon sprang into prominence. The Crossing was on the route taken by General Middleton and his troops on their advance from Qu'Appelle to the scene of the rebellion.

Well, young Seager found his Uncle's homestead. It was like all the rest of the homesteads. It had a log hut and there was no luxury. It was 180 miles by bad road from a railway. To get minor supplies, somebody had to cross the river. That was simple enough when Clark's ferry was operating or when the river was frozen over, but it afforded problems in spring and fall. Several times Seager Wheeler was obliged to cross on foot when the ice was breaking up in the spring. No boy raised as he was beside the sea could be afraid of the water but the big chunks of ice which pitched and jammed could crush a man quickly. Twice Wheeler narrowly escaped death when he was tossed into the icy water while making a crossing. On one of those crossings he had groceries for the homestead, mainly a dollar's worth of sugar. Sugar wasn't rationed in those days but dollars were; at least they were awfully scarce and in order to protect the precious package, Wheeler held it above his head and dodged the cakes of ice while the uncle helped to get him to shore.

That first winter was very severe but it passed and with the seed time came new hope. The uncle had 25 or 30 acres broken ready for seeding. Cropping methods were primitive. The seed was planted broadcast and covered by dragging willow brush over the field. Hay for the horses was cut with a scythe and raked by hand and Seager Wheeler helped to cut the first crop with a cradle and tie it by hand. He was there 18 months and then went to Moose Jaw for the express purpose of making some money so that he might return to Clark's Crossing and take a homestead for himself. He got construction work with the C.P.R. and saved his money.

The '80's on the whole were pretty dry and Moose Jaw

settlers had no crop in several years. Seager Wheeler was impressed, however, with the speed at which the settlers could recover from their reverses. He said that serious drought conditions prevailed in 1884, also in '85 and '86 but in '88 Moose Jaw had a bumper crop and "most of the settlers retired and moved into Regina to live". Dry years did not change Seager Wheeler's determination to take a homestead. In 1890 he bought a pair of oxen and a wagon load of supplies and along with his mother, set out for a homestead on the Saskatchewan River, 18 miles North-East of Saskatoon. Their first home consisted of poles placed upright around a dug-out in the river bank. It wasn't artistic and it wasn't stylish, but it was their own, and its protection was a welcome relief after the outdoor camps along the trail from Moose Jaw. But Seager Wheeler would provide something better and the very next summer he built a tidy house with logs he hauled from across the river.

Seager Wheeler had arrived at Clark's Crossing practically penniless and if ready cash was the determining factor, he was still penniless a year later. To make a few dollars he undertook to repair a broken telegraph line between Saskatoon and Humboldt. Although he had never been in a saddle, he undertook to ride a horse over the 75 miles between Saskatoon and Humboldt in one day. He thought he would never recover. For a week he wasn't comfortable standing and it was torture to sit down.

The homesteaders would do a lot for a dollar. But after the first year, Seager Wheeler had something with which to trade. He hauled his first load of wheat to Saskatoon when the thermometer registered 35 below, and sold it for 25 cents a bushel. Actually, the sale of buffalo bones represented a more profitable and certainly less risky business than wheat and much of his first income was secured by gathering and selling bones. The rails reached Saskatoon in 1890. Immediately there was an important trade in buffalo bones which were scattered over the face of the prairies. They sold at $8.00 a ton and represented more net profit in terms of beans and bacon and overalls, than wheat.

He got his title to the homestead, but he wasn't entirely satisfied with the location. So in '98 he bought the Rosthern farm on which he won fame, from the C.P.R. at $3.00 per acre. It was 5 miles from Rosthern. To it he drove his little herd of 25 head of cattle; he planted trees; he struggled with Red Fife wheat but it usually froze before it was cut. But in spite of the low price of grains, he kept on sorting and hand-picking the seed. Yes, he would work outside all day and pick wheat by lamp-light for much of the night. Notwithstanding long hours of devoted toil, he almost lost his farm to the Mortgage Company. Frozen wheat at 23 cents a bushel didn't improve his financial position much, but a friend in Rosthern came to his rescue and quite unknowingly did western agriculture a great service by keeping Seager Wheeler on his land.

Then things took a turn for the better. He got married (1908) and got regular meals. He got some Preston wheat from Dr. William Saunders. This new variety could beat Red Fife to maturity, and once he got 60 bushels per acre from it. Still he hand picked the seed until his eyes were sore. Neighbours laughed; but then, they'll still do that.

About this time, the Secretary of the Canadian Seed Growers' Association, L. H. Newman went out of his way to pay "that young Englishman at Rosthern" a visit. Wheeler and Newman took quite a fancy to each other. It was harvest time and they went out into the fields and studied the crops and experimental plots. Newman took time to demonstrate better experimental technique and Wheeler was a most receptive student. From that time forward his methods were the next thing to professional. They bore fruit and the Canadian Seed Growers' won a devoted supporter.

In his field explorations of 1910, he found something unusual in his Bobs wheat, a head that was strangely superior, probably a natural cross. Anyway it got good care and from that head came Wheeler's Red Bobs, a variety which survived well in Western Canada. It ripened early, was a high yielder, and the master said it was the wheat he had been hunting for. Next year (1911), his eagle eye fell upon another unusual head of wheat in his field of Marquis. It must have been a mutation. It bred true and that was the beginning of Kitchener wheat which won the Sweepstakes at the International Exposition at El Paso, Texas, in 1916.

There were lots of medals in the Wheeler family but they

were mostly for life saving off the rocky shores of Wight. In 1910, Seager Wheeler started collecting trophies of another kind. Indeed everybody must have been tired the day they cleaned silverware at Wheelers in later years. Wheeler had to be coaxed to start showing seeds and the first exhibits went to Regina in 1911. From then on he didn't need any urging. Later that year he scored the first International win, when his sample of Marquis wheat was champion at the New York Land Show. Not only did the wheat win a championship, but it won the thousand dollars in gold offered by the C.P.R. And that story is worth telling.

James J. Hill of the Great Northern Railway offered a gold cup valued at $1000.00 for the best wheat grown in the United States. No sir, Hill would not allow Canadian growers in that competition. But Sir Thomas Shaughnessy of the C.P.R. said, "All right, if you won't, my railway will give $1000.00 in gold for the best hard spring wheat, grown on the continent". Wheeler was the victor and people in distant parts of Canada and United States took out their maps to see just where Rosthern was located anyway. The presentation of $1000.00 in gold coins was made at an elegant banquet in Calgary and then Seager Whealer was able to pay for the C.P.R. land he bought a few years before, with C.P.R. money.

Winning International Sweepstakes for wheat became somewhat of a habit with Wheeler and he did it no less than five times. He did it with Marquis in 1914 and again in 1915. In 1916 he was hailed out but he won the International Sweepstakes just the same with a sample of his Kitchener carried over from the previous year. Then for the fifth time he won the supreme honour in 1918 with Red Bobs. It was in that latter year that Queen's University conferred upon the little farmer from Rosthern, the honorary degree of Doctor of Laws. No more popular degree had been conferred by any University.

Actually Wheeler never restricted his activities to wheat. He won with oats, and barley and forage crops and even potatoes. And in later years he turned his thoughts to fruits. What he did to improve cereal grains for the mid-western provinces, he duplicated in his determination to find suitable fruits. The Dominion Government recognized the value of his work with fruits and granted an exceedingly well merited subsidy.

Then one day in 1935, Seager Wheeler said to his wife, "Lillian, it's 50 years since I came to Canada and I haven't seen my native soil in that time, wish we could take a trip home". Well, somebody dropped the hint to Sir Edward Beatty and it wasn't any time until the Wheelers learned that they were to have a trip to England with the compliments of the C.P.R. It was a great journey and the little Doctor told me that the prettiest sight he saw on all the trip was the appearance of his own Isle of Wight as he recognized it through the mist over the sea and the mist in his own eyes. The next best sight to greet the Wheelers was the home farm at Rosthern which seemed to welcome them on their return.

They said Seager Wheeler never grew old. He was too busy to grow old. When approaching his 70th year, he was as proud of his baseball team, the Rosthern Wheat Kings, three times winners of the Provincial Championship, as he was of his wheat trophies. In fact he was honorary president of the Rosthern Hockey Team as well as the baseball team for as many years as I can remember. When I met the pioneer on the street in Saskatoon, I said, "What brings you here today?" And the answer was "Baseball; those kids wouldn't come without me".

And didn't he have the broad view of agricultural betterment? His own words make that clear. Here they are:

> "It is not sufficient to plan how many bushels of grain can be taken off in a single season with no forethought of the future. The soil is ours to make or mar and we should aim to leave it, when the time comes for us to pass it on to a future generation, practically in as good or better condition than when it first came under our hand."

I salute that staunch little sodbuster who remained at Rosthern until his 80th year and then went to enjoy his ease at the Pacific Coast.

Sinton of Regina

On May 17, 1944, I attended a birthday party in the City of Regina. It was a happy affair, birthday cake and all the trimmings; it was Robert Sinton's 90th birthday and it marked his 66 years in these Western provinces.

Yes, it was in 1878 that he said "good-bye" to his Beauharnois County home, in old Quebec. He was going west, to break new trail out where the buffalo and the Indians had never heard the whistle of a railway locomotive. Young Sinton travelled by rail to Sarnia, boat to Duluth, then rail again to Fisher's Landing on the Red River in Minnesota, and finally stern-wheel river-boat to Winnipeg. At Winnipeg he stopped long enough to buy a pair of oxen and some outfit as was the custom among the landseekers. Guessing where the C.P.R. would be built was a popular pastime in those days. Everybody wanted to get land which would be close to the rails, when they came. Sinton staked his bet on the area now marked Rapid City and drove on westward to locate a homestead.

That first summer on the frontier was filled with toil, but otherwise was rather uneventful. The first winter, however, was different. It was savage and there was a blizzard which was not to be forgotten. Robert Sinton was almost caught in that storm. One of his neighbours, Johnny Dunbar, was half a mile from his buildings and was frozen to death while trying to find his way home. Homesteaders turned out to search. And when they found the body they made a rough coffin and buried the victim beneath the floor of his cabin, the only place they could dig, with the inadequate tools available.

The Canadian Pacific rails were being extended westward but those who envisioned Rapid City as a mighty metropolis were due for disappointment because Brandon was on the route and Rapid City was not. So, when Sinton and some of his neighbours, (including the Grassicks) got title to their homesteads in '82, they "pulled up stakes" and moved farther west. Robert Sinton had graduated from the ox-team class to horses and on this westward journey he was driving a pair of buckskin ponies; tough ones they were, tough like all buckskins are suppose to be. The Grassicks pitched camp at Fort Qu'Appelle for a few days. Sinton climbed the Pilot Butte hill and got a view and an inspiration. Rumour had it that Fort Qu'Appelle might be fixed as the capital of the North West Territories but their decision nevertheless was to drive on to Pile of Bones Creek.

A month after my old friend arrived at his new destination, the first railway train steamed in and then the place was renamed. The little town shook off its undignified name of "Pile of Bones" and became Regina. There was no Land Office and since possession was considered nine-tenths of the law, "squatting" was the rule. Sinton went about three miles south and got good land. But it was dry. It was so hard to get water for the house that he would sometimes drag a sheet in the dewy grass until it was wet and then wring the water from it into a bucket. But from the beginning, he was more interested in mixed farming than in wheat alone. He got an idea from the Mounted Police and went into dairying and poultry and sold his butter and eggs to the force.

Early in the following year, Regina was declared the capital of the North West Territories, instead of Battleford. Lieutenant-Governor Dewdney arrived to take up residence in August (1883). There was rejoicing around Regina but elsewhere the choice of the new site met with a rather mixed response. There was one prize editorial from a Winnipeg paper which Mr. Sinton carried and read on selected occasions in later years. Those selected occasions were mainly when he visited Saskatoon because he found the editorial was more popular in Saskatoon than in Regina. Anyway, here it is as I got it from him:

> "One thing is certain, Regina will never amount to anything more than a country village or town for the simple reason that in neither its position nor its surroundings is there anything to give it the slightest commercial importance. Situated in the midst of a vast plain of inferior soil with hardly a tree to be seen as far as the eye can range and with about enough water in the miserable little creek known as Pile of Bones, to

> wash a sheep, it would scarcely make a respectable farm, to say nothing of being fixed upon as a site for the capital of a great province. The place has not a single natural advantage to recommend it".

That's the editorial. I'm glad I can say "I didn't write it," but Mr. Sinton often pointed with pride to the fact that the same Regina, his Regina, was host city to the World's Grain Show exactly fifty years after that caustic editorial was written.

In 1885 the thing that settlers feared more than prairie fire, happened. It was rebellion with Indian sympathy on the opposing side. Homesteader Sinton offered his services and he and his team were put to work at once, hauling ammunition to the scene of the shooting. He was at Fort Carlton when they decided to abandon that post following the skirmish at Duck Lake (March 27, '85). When the rebellion was over, Mr. Sinton kept on freighting for the Police. Freighting over those long and lonely trails in winter wasn't what you'd term fun and there was no feather bed to look forward to at the end of the day. When the thermometer said "40 below" in January, 1886, Sinton was seen leaving Regina for Prince Albert, just as in fair weather. He would make the round trip in twenty-eight days. And here is his own description of the luxury affored by a night-camp on the trail:

> "(We would) try to reach a bluff every night. To shelter our horses we removed the snow with shovels down to the grass in the shelter of a bluff, banked up the snow for further shelter, blanketed the horses with two covers each, one under and one over the harness . . . . For our own shelter, we followed the same plan of digging down to the grass, completing the structure by throwing a heavy canvas over our snow bedroom. What with hay and robes, in addition to a log fire at our feet, we spent the night in such degree of comfort as one may imagine."

In '86 Robert Sinton began dealing in horses. The settlers needed more power and Sinton would buy range horses in Montana and drive them overland to Regina. One of his early purchases consisted of 150 head which he swam across the Missouri River where the city of Great Falls now stands.

On one occasion, it was raining at nightfall, so he decided to seek shelter at a cabin occupied by a character known as Dutch Henry. Sinton knocked at the door; knocked again; knocked a third time. Then it opened just a little and out came the barrel of a gun. He explained what he wanted. A gruff voice told him he could sleep in the stable. He did but it was raining about as heavily inside as it was outside. He thought that his skin would turn the rain better than it would stop bullets and concluded that a nice soft bed of wet hay wasn't a bad place to sleep.

He had another narrow escape on one of those Montana trips. When he bought horses he would pay cash for them but sometimes he neglected to get a proper receipt. As he was preparing dinner on the side of the trail one day, some armed men rode up and asked to see the "bill of sale" covering the horses. The visitors were none other than Montana Vigilantes, settlers who took the law in their own hands, determined to stamp out rustling and other forms of crime. But that didn't make them any more attractive to Sinton, when he didn't have a "bill of sale". They meant business. With no particular ceremony, these strangers escorted him down to the river and showed him two birch trees; said they "hung couple of hoss-thieves there a while ago", and the rope was ready for another "necktie party" if Sinton couldn't produce evidence of having paid for the horses. But luck was with him; John Henderson, the very man from whom he bought the horses, happened along and explained that this Canadian's horses were acquired honestly. It really spared Mr. Sinton a bit of unpleasantness, and probably a very serious dislocation in the region of the neck. Then the leader of the group had the nerve to suggest that if Sinton was paying real money for horses, he had some for sale.

Robert Sinton told me of another strange experience when buying horses in that summer of '86. He called at a Montana village named Choto on Sun River and made contact with an intelligent half-breed who seemed to know the district and the ranchers very well. When this chap learned that Sinton was from Canada, he said he too was from there, "from Batoche on the Saskatchewan River", to be exact, and his name was Gabriel Dumont. Sure enough he was Louis Riel's right hand man, Adjutant General or something in the North West Rebellion. Sinton remembered that there was a reward for the capture of Gabriel Dumont, but he decided to stay in the horse business and leave the capture of fugitives to the police.

As time went on our pioneer expanded his farming operations. He survived the dry '80's and then the economic hardships of the not-so dry '90's. "Ninety-one" furnished a bumper crop and put good folding money in settlers' pockets. Sinton finished threshing that crop on New Year's Day. But it gave them all new ideas and Sinton made up his mind to get some pure bred stock. I fancy he was about the first to bring pure bred Hereford cattle to his part. The Hereford was hardy and Sinton concluded that it would be appropriate for the prairies. He secured foundation stock from John Sharman of Souris and built his herd of pedigreed cattle up to 200 head. And of course he had commercial cattle. For a time after '93, Balderson and Sinton were supplying beef for the North West Mounted Police. The firm of Gordon and Ironside was beginning to build a big export trade in cattle about that time and between 1893 and 1902, Robert Sinton was buying agent, working the area between Regina and Medicine Hat.

There have been few men who have influenced agricultural organization as much as Robert Sinton. The Saskatchewan Live Stock Breeders' Association was formed through his efforts in 1905 and he was the first president, serving until 1909. In that latter year, the association was superseded by four provincial associations, Cattle Breeders, Horse Breeders, Sheep Breeders and Swine Breeders; but in the new set-up, there was to be a unifying body known as the Live Stock Board and Robert Sinton became the first president. He tried politics (in 1906); he was on the Regina City Council for nine or ten years after 1900; and he was president of Regina's first Winter Fair organization. At least that's a partial record of his achievements in leadership. In proposing the principle of Community Pastures at a National Live Stock Convention in Ottawa in 1908, he showed something of how far ahead of his time he was in his thinking. The Community Pastures became a reality, but not until many years later.

In the course of time he was acquiring more and more land around Regina. Land which is now part of the site of the

Provincial Parliament Buildings was bought by him at an average price of about $9.00 per acre. But he didn't sell it at nine, not by any means. I don't know all the details but as I heard him tell the story, his price on 500 acres was $150.00 per acre. Those proposing to buy the land with a view to reselling to the government for a building site, said the price was too high. They wouldn't pay it. But they said to Mr. Sinton, "When you change your mind on that price, we may buy". They came back and said, "You asked us the exorbitant price of $150.00; now have you changed your mind?" Sinton replied, "Yes, I've changed my mind; I want $250.00 an acre now". That was a jolt but they really wanted the land and they found that here was a man they couldn't bluff; so they said, "How long is that price good for?", and Sinton's answer was "60 seconds". They must have worked fast because they bought the 500 acres.

The first time I saw Mr. Sinton, many years ago, he was discussing the superiority of Clydesdale horses. The last time I saw him he was talking Clydesdales and if I meet him in Heaven, I'm sure conversation will turn to this breed of horses which he loved. In 1908 he went to Scotland to buy Clydesdales and before the first Great War, he made nine more trips. If you had asked him about it, I fancy he would have pronounced Gartley Bonus, a champion at the Scottish Highland, as the best of those he imported.

It was in 1920 that Dean Rutherford, William Gibson and Robert Sinton were backed with $25,000.00 of Provincial money and sent to Scotland to purchase the best stallion or stallions available, for Saskatchewan. Two young horses were secured and then the devoted Sinton announced that he was not much interested in the luxury of a first class passage back to Canada; he was going to travel "with the horses". He did that and saw his beloved charges safely delivered.

Yes, he was a distinguished pioneer and at the age of ninety-four he was still out in front, still attending agricultural meetings, still walking four to six miles a day. Somebody at the party on his 90th birthday, sizing it all up well, said, "If it would make for better farms or Church welfare, you could be sure of Robert Sinton's support". I shall think of him always as a great Canadian.

"Dreadnought Joe" Wylie

The Maple Creek country in South-Western Saskatchewan has a personality all its own. Perhaps it is the rich history of the old cow town, or its proximity to the lovely Cypress Hills. But I doubt if that is the explanation. More probably it is the imprint of those solid pioneers like William Abbott and Lou Fauquier, and Bill Pollock; yes and the Cheesemans and Gordon Quick and Joe Wylie. Hardy and determined men they were. They were young men when they came; young like the country, and they remained to see a mighty transformation.

As for this Wylie, his correct name was David James, but somehow people wouldn't accept the family choice of names and he was best known as "Joe"; sometimes it was "Dreadnought Joe". Anyway, Joe Wylie was an Englishman, born in the county of Shropshire (in 1859). With 21 birthdays behind him he left his native England to seek fortune on the frontier of British North America. He halted to get his wind at Winnipeg; but that place was too highly civilized and he went on to Rapid City and Oak Lake; and then farther westward, beyond the end of the steel, to Medicine Hat where the Indians had not given up all hope of annihilating the whites, and inviting the buffalo back. It was the 5th of November, 1882, when he arrived there at the "Hat". He crossed the river. There was no bridge but he crossed anyway. The lack of a bridge didn't stop "Dreadnought Joe". He used his Red River cart. He removed the wheels and strapped them on the under side of the cart to increase the buoyancy and then climbed in and paddled.

Joe Wylie located a piece of land near Medicine Hat but he didn't remain long on it; instead he travelled back for a formal introduction to the upstart village of Maple Creek. That was '83 and the rails of the C.P.R. had reached there that year. Freeze-up in the previous fall had halted railroad construction just a few miles east of the present town site and a few workers decided to make their winter camp at the present site of Maple Creek rather than return to Manitoba or Ontario.

The contracting firm of Langdon and Sheppard built a warehouse in which to store equipment and one, Sam Brady, speedily erected a log boarding house on what is now Pacific Avenue. The town had a population of 12 and about half of the number lived with Sam. Mid-way along in the winter, Sam Brady's ambition got the better of him and he decided to call the "joint" a hotel; the only difference however, was that his rates went up. But if a stranger came to Maple Creek, Sam Brady could always sell him a "room and bath", a room in the hotel and a bath in the creek. That was the Maple Creek which greeted Joe Wylie on his arrival.

Then like a chill from the north there swept over the prairies word about the North-West Rebellion. The Maple Creek settlers were in a bad spot because the local Indians so far outnumbered them that there wouldn't have been enough white scalps to make decent trimmings for the buckskin mocassins in Cypress Hills. Those Cypress Hills with their peculiar and varied plant and animal life were long a rendezvous for the red men. But the settlers organized and every able-bodied man stood ready. Wylie served with the Rocky Mountain Rangers. There was no doubt about his fighting qualities. He could fight either way,—with a gun or without it. They tell of the time he became involved in an argument about a horse race in Medicine Hat and had to "clean up" single handed six Frenchmen before his horse was officially declared the winner. He came from a fighting family. Was not Barbara Wylie who shook all England in the fight for woman suffrage a sister? She was one of Mrs. Pankhurst's window-smashing lieutentants and she believed in being thorough.

Joe Wylie took the position of foreman on the Sir John Lester Kaye farm and ranch at Kincorth, a few miles west of Maple Creek in 1888. But he was critical of the efforts to grow wheat. The "Wheat economy" had been officially unveiled there in Saskatchewan's Chinook belt in the year of Joe Wylie's arrival at Maple Creek, when Lou Fauquier and "Corky" Jones brought in a threshing machine. Wonderful contrivance it was, and driven with a "horse power". The very next year 650 bushels of wheat were shipped out to the Indian Farm at Fort Qu'Appelle. It was Wylie's contention, however, that while the prairie land west of Swift Current was admirably suited to grazing cattle, sheep and horses, the policy of destroying the sod and cultivating grain in many sections was a waste and an unpardonable sin. His connection with the English company was severed in 1891. He turned to hay contracts for the Mounted Police and then to work for Harry Fauquier who was running cattle and farming east of Maple Creek. While working with Fauquier, this future cattle baron acquired the first cattle of his own and he dreamed of the day when he would be completely occupied by his own ranching operations.

Joe Wylie went to England in 1896 and organized the Maple Creek Cattle Company. He returned to Canada and on behalf of the company, he took over the Oxarat Ranch south of Maple Creek. Lovely and interesting setting it was. It was the ranch established by that colourful Frenchman, Michael Oxarat, and it was the first ranch south of Cypress Hills. It was on that site that the I. G. Baker Co. made hay to fill Mounted Police hay contracts after Fort Walsh was established in 1875. It was close by that the so-called Cypress Hills Massacre was perpetrated in 1873, when a little group of traders from south of the line came looking for horses which were allegedly stolen by Cypress Hills Indians. Some 200 Indians encamped near Farewell's Trading Post on Battle Creek refused to give up the horses and the heavily armed visitors opened fire and ruthlessly cleaned out most of those in the camp. It was this act which culminated the plan to police the plains. Oxarat had come north with Montana horses in 1884 and spent a short time in jail, a reminder that customs duty was supposed to be paid on incoming horses. But Oxarat said there were worse places to spend a few quiet weeks than in a Canadian jail and when his holiday period had expired, he decided to remain in the country. He knew the kind of a ranch he wanted and gravitated to the Cypress Hills. He built a log cabin and then drove in 300 horses from Montana. But Oxarat didn't stay with broncho horses. It might have been better if he had. He got racing stock and Thoroughbreds. They were good ones but race horses are peculiar since they can be winning races and still losing money. That's what Oxarat's horses did and the losses were heavy. Well, Oxarat's health failed and he died when on the way back to France in 1897. It was then that Joe Wylie's company got the ranch and Manager Joe Wylie took over. The deeded property was still held by Mrs. Oxarat but Wylie's company secured an option to purchase and in 1899, the transaction was completed.

The ranch was quicky stocked with cattle. In 1899, Wylie made one of his occasional visits to Montana and returned in June with 234 horses. Receipts in his files show either that horse values were very low or Wylie was a clever buyer. Some of the horses cost as little as $5.00 each and the average price was about $13.00. Anyway that Montana foundation produced many useful horses which were sold in the farming districts where settlers needed power. The company's cattle numbered up to 2000 head. For many years Wylie exported large numbers of cattle to Britain; some of them wore his brand, the "double lazy H" brand (⌶) and some didn't.

Few men contributed more to the political life of the prairies in the formative years than Joe Wylie. Not that he was always successful in politics; he wasn't. He took his first fling at politics in 1902 when he was a candidate for the Legislative Assembly of the Territories, and he was defeated by Horace Greeley another old timer in the Fort Walsh and Maple Creek area. But when the election of 1905 approached, Wylie's hat was once again in the ring. This time he was elected and took his seat in the first Saskatchewan legislature. Everything around Maple Creek is dated from that election night in 1905 when the ranchers came to town to celebrate Joe Wylie's victory. Some of the old buildings haven't needed red paint since.

Wylie was returned to the legislature in 1908 and again in 1912. In 1917, he received a political defeat from A. J. Colquhoun and in 1921 he was an unsuccessful candidate in the Federal election. But whether in politics or not, D. J. Wylie was most active in seeking better legislation for ranchers and farmers. The western cattlemen have not forgotten that Joe Wylie, while president of the Saskatchewan Stock Growers' Association was the spear-head of many a campaign for greater security on the range. In 1921 when beef prices were at a low ebb and producers across the prairie provinces were facing extreme difficulties, Wylie was the one chosen to represent the Western Stock Growers' Association, the Interior Stock Growers' Association of British Columbia, and the Saskatchewan Stock Growers' Association, and to carry the cattleman's cause to Ottawa.

On September 12th, he presented his case for greater security, longer leases and lower lease rentals to Prime Minister Arthur Meighen. Wylie proposed a five-year cancellation clause instead of a three-year clause. He proposed a land rental of two cents per acre instead of four and remuneration for fences and other improvements where there would be a change of lease ownership. The Minister of the Interior had to be convinced. Somebody down there hinted that this western cattleman was seeking concessions because he had large personal ranching interests. To that, Mr. Wylie replied magnanimously,

> "In order to prove the fallacy of that and in order that the stock industry should not suffer, ... if the cancellation of my leases will induce the Minister to take a different view, I am prepared to cancel them."

Mr. Wylie died in September, 1932, at the age of 73 years. It was the passing of one who left a great and indelible impression upon western agriculture. Man of judgement and justice he was indeed. And when "Joe" Wylie said "play cricket", he simply expected the other fellow to play fair, just as he always did. Ask any old timer in the Chinook belt.

Old Doc Shadd

Dear old, black, Doc Shadd! No one who knew the Carrot River Valley in pioneer years could forget him. Quite obviously he wasn't typical of any particular class or group on the frontier. He was just Doc Shadd, but that doesn't lessen in any way the country's debt to him.

Strange combination; medical doctor; farmer; negro. Kinistino and Melfort were not the places you'd expect to find him. As for his qualifications for a place among the Sodbusters, there is no doubt in my mind. Whether he was doctor first and farmer second, or farmer first and doctor second, doesn't matter. What counts most, is that he was a progressive farmer and no pioneer ever served his fellows on the agricultural frontier with more Christian devotion. He was "God's right hand man" and it gives one a lot of satisfaction to tell about him.

Alfred Schmitz Shadd was born in Chatham, Ontario, (in 1870). The father had grown up in slavery in the deep south and there at Chatham, the Shadds were farmers and poor folk. When the lad was through public school, he was required to go to work. But he was determined to get more education. He had hoped to study Medicine, but that was a secret because people would only laugh at the negro boy's big ideas. By hard work he got his matriculation and then normal and some college classes. But the medical course cost a lot of money and young Shadd had to make his way. He would do anything to make a dollar and there were times when he would work all day and study all night. There were times too when the total food for a day consisted of three bananas; a banana and a drink of water for breakfast, a banana and a drink of water for lunch, the same for the evening meal and a drink of water before going to bed. No wonder he hated bananas in later years. But he had a double objective, a medical practice and a farm.

The time came when he had to interrupt his medical course in order to get more funds. There was a job open for anybody who would teach school near a place called Kinistino, five hundred miles beyond Winnipeg. Shadd said he'd go anywhere for real money. The settlers out there heard they were going to have a school teacher, but they didn't know he was black. Word about his colour did reach the Kinistino district ahead of the teacher and hands went up in horror. "Will we let our children go to a darky teacher?" and "who will board such a teacher?"

Well, when J. M. Campbell who drove the mail stage from Prince Albert, arrived at Kinistino one day in the spring of 1896, he unloaded the new teacher. The local women whispered rather more than usual and the children manouvered into position to peek at this novelty. One wee girl who was so bold as to get on his knee, moistened a finger in her mouth and then tried to rub some of the blackness from Shadd's face. The local people concluded they could put up with it for a summer but then they made some discoveries. This handsome young man was good natured; he had a laughing personality; he was altogether magnetic, and he won their confidence.

The problem of a boarding place was solved. Charlie Lowrie the post master said "sure" he'd take the dark lad and it marked the beginning of a long friendship.

School was held in the Agricultural Hall where they also held agricultural fairs and socials and political meetings. And on Sundays it was Presbyterian or Methodist or Anglican Church (Dr. Charles Endicott was a student minister at that time and had his Sunday).

But nobody took that "Medical student" stuff very seriously, until one day a man up at the Birch Hills had his head split open. "Can't possibly live" folk said, but the darky teacher asked to be excused from school for a day. He worked patiently and somehow closed the wound, and the patient lived. Who'd have believed it? From then on the school children had a holiday or two every week while the teacher was away trying to keep life in some sick homesteader.

Shadd's contract with the school expired and he returned to the East to the University of Toronto to complete his medicine. Again there was a struggle to break down race prejudice. In his first class, a group of students refused to sit in with a "nigger". But Shadd was allowed to speak. He told those fellow students that he was not a "nigger" or a member of a travelling minstrel show. He was "an Abysinnian" and proud of it. He told of his struggle to get an education and he concluded by reminding them that he would undertake to fight and lick anyone in the University who considered himself a better man. There were no takers. Instead, Shadd was accepted and his fellows grew to like him until it could be said that he was the most popular student in the graduating class.

He graduated with honours that spring of '98. And then what did he do? He was on his way back to Kinistino. As he travelled westward, a stranger who wanted to make conversation said, "Going West, eh! Going to open a barber shop, I suppose". Shadd turned his new valise over to expose the newly stamped name A. S. Shadd, M.D.; and then he said, "No, I'm going to teach school and doctor homesteaders and in my spare time I'll do some farming for myself". His return to Kinistino was a most welcome event because he was to be the first medical doctor in all the Carrot River Valley community.

And didn't the news spread fast; "Shadd is back and he's a full fledged doctor". He moved in with his friends the Lowries and in their farmyard he erected a two-roomed log structure. One room was his bedroom which he called the "chamber of silence" and the other was his surgery which he called "chamber of horrors". If there was to be an operation, Mrs. Lowrie, his landlady, might assist and perhaps administer the anaesthetic. Calls came from far and near and sometimes when he arrived at a destination, he would discover that the patient was a horse with colic or a cow with milk fever. He would have a case at Birch Hills and a rider would reach him about an accidental shooting at Fort a la Corne and then a tired and sweaty team might overtake him to bring word that a baby was expected down about Melfort.

There were endless tales about exposure and hardship, nights on the trail and sometimes no trail. Nobody could ever remember any complaining, no matter how long the trip or how low the temperature or how poor the prospect of payment. My friend Francis T. Graves who knew him intimately in those years, said Shadd was remarkable, "never dull, never tired, never sick". He accepted everything with grace, except his short curly hair.

He loved that northern district from the beginning and in 1902, he bought his first farm. It was on the Carrot River, just south of Kinistino. It had deep, black soil; should be good because it was the same colour as himself. There in the spring of 1903, he set out the first crab apple trees that anybody had the nerve to bring to that part. And they did well, surprised everybody. The farm became the doctor's home and headquarters. From there he drove a single seated democrat and a team of wild and fast ponies. He would drive himself and always sat square in the middle of the seat. Pretty soon he secured a second team and one team would be recovering from a long journey while the other was in harness.

When he was on the Kinistino farm, a young Mounted Police officer lived with him. There was the time when the "mounty" caught some young chaps shooting game birds, prairie chicken out of season. The officer seized the chickens for evidence and placed them in a bag and hung them in the doctor's cellar. Then he laid a charge against the boys. The doctor learned the story. He knew those boys, decent lads really and he didn't want to see them in serious trouble. He knew where the bag containing the evidence was hanging and something must have happened to it because when the bag was untied at the trial, three old barnyard hens rolled out on the table. The case was dismissed and those decent boys who were the doctor's friends were spared the embarrassment and shame of a conviction. I hope they said thanks to the Doc.

In 1904, Doc. Shadd moved to Melfort and very shortly he bought another farm 16 miles east of Melfort and north from Star City, called it Craigbog Farm. There he brought pure bred Shorthorns and good horses and some of the first sheep in the district. When he could get away with it, he would steal out to the farm and plant trees and work with the cattle. He hated to see so many native trees being cut down, and tended his fields the way a good doctor would care for a patient. He seeded tame grasses and followed a crop rotation. He had a lot to do with the formation of the Melfort Agricultural Society and was the first president. He started the

Farmer's Elevator Co. which built some of the earliest elevators in that part.

He got his start in pure bred Shorthorns from Tom Sanderson of Kinistino and then went east to the Canadian National Exhibition at Toronto in 1912 to buy the best bull available. His selection was Bandsman's Choice, a prize winner in the senior yearling class, and was he proud of the white bull for which he paid $1000. Progeny from that bull were sold all over Northern Saskatchewan and had a big influence upon the quality of the farm cattle.

In 1907 he went to the Old Country for post graduate studies at Edinburgh and London. But it was an expensive year because the big hearted doctor couldn't keep his money when he saw so much evidence of poverty, and he had to borrow money to bring himself back to Canada.

What a figure he was in the Kinistino and Melfort community! His energy was unlimited. As if his big medical practice was not enough he operated a drug store for a time and engaged in journalism (started the Melfort Journal). He served terms on the Melfort Town Council and School Board. He was in everything. He tried politics but it didn't go so well. In the provincial contest in 1905, he was a Provincial Rights or Haultain candidate and his proposals at that time show how forward in his thinking he was. Here's an extract dated November 28, 1905,

> "We should also undertake in our own behalf the building of a line of railway to Hudson Bay at once. By the word 'we', I mean the Western Provinces. I don't think the Ottawa government will be in any haste to do this work, and I don't think we can wait."

He argued for control of public lands and resources for the Province and about schools, he said,

> "In countries like this where men of every race and creed are coming to make homes, a system of national schools for all little children would be the best way of making good Canadian citizens of them."

And all the while, he was taking long rides and fast rides to relieve the sick. I have information about one of those fast rides behind a team of colts which had never had harness on before. I knew the man who drove that time and they didn't stop for ditches nor even for barbed wire fences, but they got there before it was too late. He drove through floods when everything floated out of the democrat except himself and he crawled across the Saskatchewan River on his belly to get to a sick-bed one time when the ice was too thin to hold a man on foot. Along about 1910 he bought a car, a little red Reo runabout, the first car in that part. He was proud of it and he drove it to the limit of its speed. The horses took fits when they saw it coming and there were lots of run-aways. But the Doc said the same little red car saved more people than it killed.

Folk wondered if he slept. He never gave up, at least not until he reached the end of his tether in 1915. Appendicitis caught up with him and they took him to Winnipeg. As he lay on his deathbed, he placed his fingers on his pulse and said, "that old pulse is going to quit on me, and my work is only half done".

And it did stop on March 9, 1915 and a shadow fell over all the homes in the Carrot River Valley. The frontier had lost a friend; a sympathetic doctor; a poor collector; and a progressive farmer. And the funeral which was held in the little town of Melfort was one never to be forgotten. The service was arranged for All Saints Anglican Church where the doctor had been a warden for years. But the church couldn't begin to accommodate those who wanted to pay a tribute. So they quickly arranged for an overflow service to be conducted simultaneously in the town hall. The church was full, the hall was full and hundreds of people of all races and creeds whose hearts the doctor had ruled, stood outside. The funeral procession of autos and buggies and wagons was a mile long.

An editorial in the Melfort Moon (March 17, 1915) summed it up pretty well,

> "No drive was too long; no night too dark; no trail too rough to deter the doctor when the call for assistance came . . . . Rich or poor, he made no distinction and nobly he performed his duty."

That was old Doc Shadd.

Cross of the "a7"

A lot of "book larnin" was considered quite a handicap to the man on the Western Frontier. The victim was usually difficult to acclimatize. He was the hot-house plant transferred to cold soil. He could spell words as long as Mississippi and call the English poets by their first names but he couldn't build a camp-fire and he couldn't throw a lariat to catch a gate-post. Too often he couldn't even crawl through a barbed wire fence without losing part of his pants.

There weren't many who suffered from over-much of the so-called "edecation", but Albert Ernest Cross was one who came with an academic "ball and chain" that should have dragged him down. He had grown up amid culture in old Montreal where his father was a distinguished judge in the Court of Queen's Bench in Quebec. From secondary school, young Cross went to Business College and went to one of the good colleges in England for three years (1875-78). Still he didn't have enough so he attended the Ontario Agricultural College (1879-81). But Ernest Cross worked for what he got. His course at the Agricultural College cost him exactly $25.00 in cash. He made up the balance required to finance his way to a degree by working on the college farm. Finally, he qualified for a V.S. degree from the Montreal Veterinary College ('84).

Obviously, his training was not for ranching. Nobody had reckoned with a strange decision on the part of the youngster to cut himself adrift from the comforts and social opportunities of a big city and accept the freedom and hardship offered by the frontier. But weighted down with diplomas and college degrees, he arrived in Calgary in 1884, and went right to work with the British American Horse Ranch, a subsidiary of the famous Cochrane Ranch. He was to be book-keeper and veterinarian. About the time he got the feel of things he was also assistant manager under W. D. Kerfoot. What he did with his spare time between 4 a.m. and 10 p. m. isn't recorded but he must have done some scheming because the very next year he started doing things for himself. The foothills got into his blood; some of us know how hopelessly incurable that can be. He took a homestead on Mosquito Creek, about five miles from the present site of Nanton, 55 miles from Calgary. He built a log house with the most modern type of mud roof. He called it home. It seemed that every traveller who ever sighted the smoke from that cabin about meal time or bed time, turned in.

Things were shaping up all right. He got a 50,000 acre grazing lease on the Little Bow and adopted the "a7" brand. Now, he had a ranch and a brand but no cattle and no money to buy the cattle. But he borrowed some money and bought 500 head for a foundation. He bought more; he must have bought at least 501 because he secured the grand champion Shorthorn cow at Guelph in 1886 and transplanted her to the foot hills where this aristocratic matron was forced to accept the indignity of a branding iron.

The winter of '86-'87 in all its fury settled down upon the range just as Cross was getting started. Like the other ranchers, he lost cattle, lots of them: 60% of his cattle perished but the grand champion cow from Guelph didn't. When a big storm was brewing and the herds were beginning to drift, Cross caught his champion and tied her to the corner of his log house. There she remained until the storm was over. Indeed many of the good Shorthorns for which the "a7" ranch was later famous descended from that old cow which was storm-anchored to the log house. And if the whole truth were known, the same cow which made loud protests when the branding iron touched her delicate hide, probably held her head pretty high in bovine social circles on account of that "a7" decoration she was wearing.

In the spring of '87 there weren't many cattle to round up. Most of them were dead. Beef carcasses lay everywhere and for a brief spell, there were no hungry Indians. But the cattlemen had to have a round-up just the same and Ernest Cross, George Lane, Dan Riley, and some others of ranching fame found themselves riding together. It was the beginning of life-long associations. Cross demonstrated the stuff he was made of one night during round-up when the saddle horses took fright and made a successful dash for freedom, from their rope corral. A horseless round-up gang is about as useful as a car with an empty gas tank. Without saddle horses, the cattle would quickly drift and the round-up effort would be undone. The camp was 100 miles from the home range in the foothills and Cross knew that the stampeding remuda or horse herd would go back there unless turned quickly. He was young and agile and he struck off at something between a walk and a trot. Ten miles from camp he got ahead of the band. One old mare was determined to lead the wild band back to "Bar U" and would not turn. But Cross could think fast and knew what to do. He had his "six-shooter". He just dropped the ornery old mare and left her for the coyotes. The band was then turned rather easily and he brought it back to camp. Cross became the cook's hero and qualified for the best favours. He ate off the cleanest plate and he got the freshest of the prairie chicken eggs after that.

For several years then, Cross was the boss of the Mosquito Creek Round-up wagon. That may not seem such an exalted office but it called for a leader who knew what to do. He had to know the hills and understand the ways of cattle and horses and men. His good horsemanship was recognized from the time he worked with the Cochranes. He could ride the bad ones and in later years he was an enthusiastic supporter of polo. He sold a lot of horses to the Mounted Police. He brought in a Cleveland Bay stallion and many of the colts from that horse had the type and size wanted for police patrol. There was just one difficulty, Cross' horses were often pretty wild and the police didn't want wild horses. Cross found however, if these wild horses were ridden hard from Nanton to Calgary, they lost much of their spirit, temporarily at least. Then the thing to do was show them to the police right away and sell them before they had time to recover from the long journey and become wild again.

But evidently those questionable horse deals didn't do his reputation with the Mounted Police any lasting injury because in 1899 he married Helen Macleod, eldest daughter of Col. James A. Macleod who was the second commissioner of the Police in Canada. It was Col. Macleod who travelled westward as second in command with the original force that established historic Fort Macleod beside the Old Man River.

At any rate, wild horses held no terror for Cross. If he

couldn't ride them, at least he knew the best way to fall off. On one occasion he broke the only lamp chimney in his homestead cabin and rode across to a neighbour to borrow one. On the way home his horse bucked and Cross went off. But lamp chimneys didn't grow on trees and with no thought of easing the fall for himself, he held the precious chimney aloft and saved it. After all, a broken bone will repair itself but not a broken lamp chimney.

The neighbour, by the way, to whom he went to borrow that chimney was Billy (W.E.) Cochrane, one of the frontier characters. It was this Billy Cochrane who encountered an Indian butchering one of his steers. He jumped from his horse and, "beat up" the Indian. Then he reported the slaughter of the steer to the Mounted Police. "Can you identify the Indian?" was the question the Police put to Billy and the answer was, "Certainly can; I marked him". Billy Cochrane had been accustomed to marking his calves by splitting the left ear and as the police were to discover, Billy had marked his Indian the same way. But then poor Billy was hailed before the magistrate, Col. Macleod, on a charge of mutilating one of Her Majesty's subjects.

The "a7" herds grew bigger and they grew better. Cross used none but the best sires. The majority of ranchers were using Herefords but he was mostly for Shorthorns and got the greatest degree of size in his cattle. He obtained a worth while advantage from cross-breeding at times. Galloway-Shorthorn crossbreds and Hereford-Shorthorn crosses were quick growers and vigorous cattle. Sure enough, they had that somethng called "hybrid vigour" and Cross sold his steers for the most money year after year.

No human hide was ever packed with more vibrating energy than that of Cross. He was never dormant. Even when he was sick, he was scheming. The pioneers didn't get sick often and didn't always admit it when they were sick but Cross had a nasty tussle with an outlaw appendix and it was when convalescing in a Montreal hospital in 1891 that he made important plans for future business. He became interested in industry and in the next year he organized the Calgary Brewing and Malting Company. Then he took a whirl at politics; that was in 1898 and he won the seat in the Legislature of the North-West Territories for east Calgary and sat with the Hon. Frederick Haultain.

Came 1912. A. E. Cross, George Lane, Pat Burns and Archie MacLean, Alberta's "Big Four" cattlemen were together in the Ranchman's Club in Calgary one day. They talked about the old cattle range which was passing. Too much good native grassland, yes too much, was coming under the plough in the mad rush to grow wheat. There and then, those mighty men in the Cattle Kingdom decided to perpetuate the skill and colour of the early West in a Rodeo at Calgary. They secured Longhorn steers from Texas. They brought in Indians and bad horses and the best cowboys in the country. They all backed it financially, and the show was a huge success. It was more than that. It was the beginning of the great annual ranchland classic for which Calgary is now famous throughout the world.

If I knew nothing about the history of Turner Valley on which the "a7" cattle sometimes roamed, and were asked to guess the men who did the spade-work in that famous oil field, I would say that A. E. Cross would be one of them; and I'd be right. He was one of the originators and backers of the Dingman Oil Well, original discovery well, and he was still a backer and supporter after others became timid and withdrew. That's about the way I would expect it to be. Cross was a sticker; that's the reason the bad winter in the '80's which took sixty per cent of his cattle, didn't stop him.

Yes Cross had his fingers in no end of activities in and around Calgary. He was one of the founders of the famous Ranchman's Club of which I spoke. He was a pioneer in the Western Stock Growers' Association and served both as secretary and president. He was one of the early directors of the Calgary Exhibition and was its president for a term. He was president of the Calgary Board of Trade in 1908, and so on. But when a stranger asked him his business, his answer was always the same, "a cowman".

Outwardly he was the shrewd business man whose calculations were "sure-fire" but to those who knew him, he was sympathetic and understanding. Anyone in need could count on reasonable help from Cross. To one man I heard about, he loaned one hundred dollars and the money never came back.

Somebody criticized his judgment in financing such a useless fellow. Cross replied that he hadn't expected to get repayment, but without the loan "that man's wife and three children might have been hungry".

Cross died in March 1932. He left Alberta a lot different than he found it, a lot better for the foundation which he laid in farming, ranching and industry. He was the Indians' friend; he was the Prince of Wales' friend; he was everybody's friend.

"So when a great man dies,
For years beyond our ken,
The light he leaves behind him lies
Upon the paths of men."

Longfellow might have been thinking about Sodbusters.

Walter Lynch of Westbourne

The new west had two notable experiences in 1870. One was rebellion and the other was the arrival of Sodbuster Walter Lynch. Lynch arrived at Fort Garry just after the Red River Uprising under Louis Riel had been smothered. The settlement at Fort Garry had a population of 300; there were two doctors, one policeman and no lawyers. The people were still exercised about the insurrection. Lynch was interested in homesteads and more interested in a farm than in local politics. He knew what he wanted in the way of land. He went on to Portage la Prairie, on foot of course, and then north to the shores of Lake Manitoba. There it was, just what he had hoped to find, good soil, and with it water and grass and hardwood. He would return to Ontario and prepare to move the very next spring.

The journey homeward was not uneventful. He was carrying some money and when he met up with a suspicious looking stranger who tried to be friendly, Walter Lynch was a bit worried. So just as a precautionary measure, Lynch pulled out his old pistol and staged a little demonstration of sharp shooting. The stranger seemed to lose interest and departed. A little farther along Lynch learned that the man who was his audience for the pistol shooting show was a desperado who was wanted by the police.

In due course Lynch was back in Old Ontario. His enthusiasm for the opportunities in Manitoba attracted a lot of folk in and around Lobo Township. Very next spring he was leading a party westward. It took weeks to complete the journey and they finally arrived at the infant Winnipeg by River boat. Walter Lynch was accompanied by his brother William. There were others in the party too, David Morrison and John MacKay and John Chantler and Roderick MacKenzie and bride, James Stewart, and David Stewart and others who were to become stalwart settlers in the new land. Lynch was Irish but most of those with him were Highland

Scotchmen. Oh, yes, there was Donald Stewart, too, who was very close to Walter Lynch through many years in Manitoba.

This Donald Stewart, by the way, brought a trotting mare with him from Ontario. The folk from Lobo Township liked a good driving horse. On the first day out of Winnipeg, the Lynch party halted to rest at the mission at St. Charles. The mare attracted the attention of a young priest there and Stewart was asked what he would take for her. Actually he hadn't considered selling her but he said he would take $200. Then he learned that Bishop Tachè was at the mission and wanted a horse. The Bishop was invited to come out and see the mare. He came and was told by the young priest that the price was $200. The Bishop was cautious. He replied in French, thinking that no one on the Stewart party would follow the conversation and said he liked the mare very much and would gladly pay the price named. But one of Stewart's friends (David Morrison) understood French and the conversation was relayed to Donald Stewart in Gaelic, with the hint that since the Bishop fancied the mare so much, the price might be stepped up to $250. But Donald Stewart had said $200 and that was final in spite of opportunities. The Bishop bought the mare and the money paid was sufficient to cover the transportation fares over Jim Hill's railroad as far as Fisher's Landing on the Red River, for all of Stewart's family.

Well, Lynch led his party westward and then North along Rat Creek. For himself he chose land right on the creek and built a log house about three miles from the Lake (Lake Manitoba). It was a picturesque setting and there the cattle and other live stock which Lynch brought from Ontario were turned out to graze. Kenneth MacKenzie had brought the first pure bred Shorthorn bull to Manitoba but Walter Lynch in that year of '71 brought the first pedigreed cows of the breed, and thus laid the foundation for the first herd of pure bred cattle of any breed west of Winnipeg.

For a time the Indians were a source of worry to Walter Lynch and his neighbours at Westbourne. When Lynch began to break some land for cropping and had made one round with the plough, an Indian decked in war paint came and sat on the furrow, with his gun resting over his arm. The nature of his protest was very clear. It looked like a grim contest between the newcomer and the native. Would the Indian move when the plough team approached, or would Walter Lynch go around that sulking heap of human dynamite? It was a tense moment but Lynch decided to "call the Indian's bluff" and almost drove over him before the red man seemed convinced that Irishman Lynch was going to overturn straight slices of prairie sod in spite of obstacles. That Indian departed and came no more.

But other Indians came. Yes, a short time later a band of angry natives arrived at the homesteads of David Morrison and Walter Lynch. The homesteaders held a two-man caucus and lost no time about it. It was clear that the Indians came to give the two settlers notice to quit or to forcibly oust them from a favourite camping ground and they were deadly serious. There was no time to waste as life and property were at stake. As usual, Lynch had a solution. Said he, "These red skins are fearless and they wouldn't hesitate to kill, but they're awfully susceptible to good food. Let's feed them". So out came the good food brought from Winnipeg and the good smoked hams brought all the way from Ontario. The hams were boiled quickly and tea and preserves and everything good were placed on the grass and the Indians feasted as they had never done before. Instead of being warlike, they became friendly; they forgot their complaints; they smoked their pipes and shook hands with their host and left in the best of spirits. They never returned except on one occasion when they wanted more food. There was proof that it would work with red men just as girls say it works with white men,—the way to the heart is through the oesophagus.

Walter Lynch and his fellow settlers brought some sheep to that district. Probably they were the first sheep west of Red River and when Indians saw those strange creatures for the first time, they staged a different kind of a show. They were filled with fear and one Indian was found hiding in the branches of a tree while the harmless "woolies" grazed peacefully below.

In his search for a farming site, Lynch had deliberately passed good wheat land on the open prairies to get the best location for mixed farming. And as a mixed farmer he was out in front for many years. A record of the prize winners at the very first Portage la Prairie fairs will confirm the progressive nature of the man. He was out with his Shorthorns, or Durhams as they were called in those days, when Portage held its first fair in 1872, and again in 1873.

In '74 the Lynch family decided to try a change. Walter Lynch sold his cattle and the family went to California, but a few years later (1883) they were back on the same Westbourne land and Walter Lynch was laying the foundation for another herd, this time a better one.

The first bull used in the new herd was called Cupid. He may not have resembled the Valentine designers' conception of Cupid, but still I would consider it quite an honour to the Roman God of Love to have a good Shorthorn bull named after him. That bull did have a royal pedigree. He had been bought from Richard Gibson of Delaware in Ontario, and he belonged to the noted Duchess family of English Shorthorns or Dual Purpose Shorthorns. But Lynch like many other breeders of that period was shortly to be converted to the Scottish or beef type Shorthorn which was the creation of that Scottish master Amos Cruickshank of Aberdeenshire. And so the next sire in the herd was a big roan called Silverskin which Lynch bought from the Watts of Salem. Then he secured a bull whose name is familiar to students of breed history, a red bull called Village Hero. This one proved to be a great breeder and a splendid show bull.

Lynch's new herd was much in the public eye. He sold young bulls over a big part of the West and his old friend Archie Stewart took the herd to the western fairs and exhibitions and won notable honours.

The homesteaders of that period knew their neighbours for miles and miles. Walter Lynch was said to know every settler for fifty miles around him. Among his special friends was a young Irishman who was homesteading over near Minnedosa. His name was Pat Burns and one of the first steers which Pat Burns bought in Manitoba was from Walter Lynch. No clinches were barred when those two Irishmen began to buy and sell cattle and they did it a number of times.

Once when Burns visited the Lynch farm, Walter had no cattle ready for market. But Burns pleaded to buy something; he simply must buy something; he had been driving all day and had bought nothing and it would be unlucky to let a day go past without making some kind of a deal. So rather than allow a fellow Irishman to lose his luck, Lynch sold him a clucking hen and a setting of eggs. But after the hen had made the long journey from Westbourne to Minnedosa, in a flour sack, she had pretty well forgotten about her avowed intention to be broody and she ended up by becoming Pat Burns' Sunday dinner.

Yes, here was a man who held the respect of all on the frontier. They came to him when they needed advice and they came when they were in trouble. Walter Lynch could "witch a well" and Walter Lynch could make a pretty good job of doctoring a sick cow. His counsel was good and his sense of humour helped. One Irish neighbour came when he was worried about his estate. The man had several farms and several sons and came asking Lynch to make out a will for him to sign. He wanted the boys to get the land, yes; but he wanted no "monkey business". He was afraid the boys might become over-anxious to get possession of that good soil and said, "Now, Mr. Lynch, can't you put something in that will, so that if I don't die, the boys won't get my land". Mr. Lynch assured him that if he could just manage to keep from dying, the land would keep all right.

Yes his counsel was good and his humour was droll. Donald Stewart was condemning the habit of cigarette smoking. Lynch was being a bit philosophical. As he waved the broken fork-handle which he usually carried in latter years, he said it wasn't the smoke that he minded as much as the loss of time which it meant. He said the man he would never hire was the man who smoked cigarettes and wore a straw hat, because if the man wasn't wasting time making a cigarette, he would probably be chasing his hat.

Neighbours wanted Lynch to go into politics but he always declined. However, his nephew, Edwin D. Lynch, (son of William Lynch) who came with the family in 1871 was occasionally in politics and was elected to the Legislature for the home constituency of Lakeside in 1903 and again in 1907.

But other well earned honours came to Walter Lynch. Hill, the Portage smithy who wrote the History of Manitoba, conferred with Walter Lynch and Donald Stewart on many and many a week-end when the big book was in preparation. And Walter Lynch was the first president of the Manitoba Agricultural College. As things were constituted then, a man could be president of the Board without residing at the college. In any case it was a fine tribute to the pioneer farmer at Westbourne.

Walter Lynch never married. He explained once that he liked the ladies too well to ever marry one. And as a bachelor, I fancy he was like the majority; he didn't always wash on Monday and iron on Tuesday. In winter, he often wore two or three pairs of trousers; said he did it so the holes in each pair wouldn't match up.

He died in 1908, at the age of 73 years. His last years were spent on the old home farm at Westbourne. By that time the farm was being operated by his nephew Edwin Lynch. It was a good farm. When Walter Lynch had all the country west of Red River to select from, he chose that Westbourne farm, because he liked it. And he never changed his mind about liking it. He considered it the best place to live and the best place to die.

Charlie Rear

Horseman Extraordinary

If men are born equal, it doesn't apply to horsemen. That there was or was not a separate Act of Creation for horsemen need not be debated now, but here was one horseman whose individuality stood out like Mount Robson. He was one of the remarkable characters, my friend Charlie Rear, horseman extraordinary.

The Charlie Rear which Canadian stockmen will remember was a man who lived horses, thought and talked little else. And when he was talking about them or holding a halter shank, he was as one transported to a better world. When he came back from the Royal Winter Fair one year, he told us he had received an Honorary Degree, from the National Breweries. He was now Charlie Rear, H.C. Asked what the letters of his new degree stood for, he said "Horse Crazy". But horse crazy or no, Charlie Rear was one of the best judges and one of the best known horsemen of his generation.

It is not long since he went to his reward. Will Rogers said for himself that he was sure a good horse and saddle would be waiting for him in Heaven and if Charlie Rear's reward is of his own choosing, I'm sure it will be one continuous Horse Show with his favourite Percherons winning all the Inter-Breed Specials.

Charles Rear was born at Barrie, Ontario. When he was 11 years of age, his family came west and settled south of Minnedosa. There young Charles grew up with horses. By 1910 he was dealing in horses at Minnedosa and shipping stock westward to the agricultural frontier, mainly South Western Saskatchewan, where agriculture was expanding and there was a big need for horsepower.

In 1912, Rear adopted Vanguard as a distributing centre and operated a sales barn. Six years later, he went to Kincaid and began dealing in stallions. That was the "golden age" in the stallion business and Rear handled thousands of them, some Canadian bred and many imported from countries of origin. Exactly how many he had bought and sold, he couldn't tell; bookkeeping to him was neither decent nor essential. He observed that when horsemen hired bookkeepers, they always discovered that they were losing money and on the way to bankruptcy. Without a set of books, a horseman might be "broke" and not know it, in which case it wouldn't matter. So, no bookkeeper for him.

Nor did his system of keeping books improve with the years. In later years, his records, correspondence, accounts, pedigree certificates, pictures of horses, etc., with no two pages attached, were kept in a suitcase under his bed. To locate a statement or other object of search, might be an all-afternoon job. But in the course of such a search, some missing cheques or some paper money would probably be discovered.

Actually, however, he rarely took a note during those years at Vanguard and Kincaid. When he sold a horse "on time", he would mark the transaction and the amount owing, on the barn door and scratch it out when payment was made. Every now and again they had to replace a few boards in the door. That was probably where somebody got the idea of the "loose leaf" system of keeping records.

In 1925 Charlie Rear transferred his headquarters from Kincaid to Regina and in 1931, he moved to Saskatoon. It could be assumed that wherever Charlie Rear was living, Saskatoon, Regina, Melfort, Lacombe or elsewhere, he would have a barn and a string of stallions and other horses. No matter what the state of the horse market or the state of his finances, he was ever ready to buy or sell a horse or hire a stallion.

The state of those finances did fluctuate in an amazing way. A Saskatoon bank was threatening foreclosure at one period in the '30's, and when Charlie Rear realized that the bank was in earnest, he went out and collected a lot of service fees. Returning to the city, he paid his indebtedness and announced to his banker that he was depositing some surplus cash in another bank. Then he added, "I'm taking a suite at the Bessborough Hotel where you can find me if I'm wanted". "Yes sir," he said one time, "I was broke yesterday, but this is another day and if any of you fellows need money, let me know."

Trouble was that when C. M. Rear saw a horse he wanted, he didn't always stop to count his money and sometimes he overspent. He bought a lot of stallions in Iowa and neighbouring States. He returned to Saskatoon on one occasion with a carload of American stallions but with insufficient cash to pay the freight charges. The railroad company refused to release the horses and delegated a man to watch them. A representative of the railroad went to see Mr. Rear, said, "I'm here to collect $275 freight on your car of horses". Rear was honest. His reply was, "I haven't got it; if I had that much cash, I would have bought another stallion".

Charlie Rear's influence in the Percheron and Belgian breeds was not unlike that of Ben Finlayson's in Clydesdales. Both brought numerous horses to Western Canada. Rear had a notable record of wins at Canadian shows, especially the Royal Winter Fair at Toronto. At the Royal Winter Fair in 1928, Rear won the grand championship for Percheron stallions with Cadeau and also the grand championship for Belgian stallions with Goliath. In 1930 he had the grand champion Belgian mare at the Royal. Then there were those noted Percheron show mares, Crocadon Katisha and Blanche Kesako. The former which won the Royal grand championship in 1936 for George Fraser, had been a Rear mare, and about Blanche Kesako, twice grand champion at the Royal Winter Fair for Mr. Rear, more will be recorded.

The grey Percheron stallion Dean, was considered by Mr. Rear to be the greatest of them all. This horse did not have opportunity to mate with many pure bred mares, unfortunately, but he had a notable showing performance and a good breeding record. The story about the purchase of Dean is rather typical. Rear was touring the State of Iowa, looking for stallions. His travelling companion was E. L. Humbert of Corning, Iowa, who also wanted stallions. They arrived at an Iowa farm just before the lunch hour and as they walked through the barn, the Canadian's eye fell upon a good grey colt. The Rear heart began to beat fast, but instead of giving vocal expression to his emotions, he closed the door of the box stall quickly and passed on to avoid drawing any special attention to this colt.

The visiting horsemen were invited to dinner in the best Iowa custom, but Charlie Rear's appetite had failed, temporarily. He excused himself and returned to the barn, all alone, to see the grey colt. The young horse was living up to first impressions. "There," said Rear to himself, "is the horse to beat the Canadian Clydes." Rather than focus unnecessary attention upon Dean, the Canadian took an option on all the stallion colts on the farm. Then after the visitors were a "safe distance" away from the farm, Rear phoned back to say he was buying the grey colt, rising three years.

In Rear's ownership, this great grandson of Carnot, was undefeated over the Mid-Western Circuits, year after year. That was not all. In 1929 he was sent to the Toronto Royal where he was made reserve grand champion, being defeated for the supreme award by Carl Roberts' Monarch. But at the Toronto Royal in 1930 and again in 1931, Dean was awarded the grand championship. The mare Crocadon Katisha, grand champion at the Royal Winter Fair in 1936, was a daughter of Dean.

The story about that noted show mare Blanche Kesako is intriguing and I tell it as Charlie gave it to me. The mare was foaled in 1918 and had it not been for my friend who virtually discovered her in South Western Saskatchewan, her name would probably have escaped the record of famous horses. Rear was travelling a "back road" when he was obliged to take the ditch to let a team with a loaded wagon go by. Notwithstanding his precarious position in the ditch, Charlie Rear's eyes were on a grey mare rather than on the road. He stopped short, looked the mare over and tried to buy her. She was not for sale. But when the mare's owner was having a farm auction a short time later, Rear was on hand with money in his pockets. He bought the mare and her mate for $410 and then sold the mate for $200.

It was the fall season, just before the Royal Winter Fair. So determined was Rear that he would own Blanche Kesako and so confident of her show ring potentialities, that he made entry for her at the "Royal" and in his own name, weeks before the auction sale at which she became his property. It was too late to send her with the Provincial Exhibit but Rear sent her east by express. She was not well fitted however, and as it was her first time away from home she was homesick. Altogether, she was not able to win at Toronto, but at Ottawa Winter Fair the following week, she won the grand championship.

On three other occasions, Rear showed Blanche at the Toronto Royal. She was first in her class and reserve senior champion in 1929, grand champion in 1930 and grand champion in 1931. After winning numerous purple ribbons from Western Fairs and Exhibitions, Blanche was sold to Carl Roberts of Manitoba and at the age of 16 years and in foal to Monarch, she was sold again, this time to go to Australia.

It is not to be overlooked that Charlie Rear had both the grand champion Percheron stallion and the grand champion Percheron mare at Canada's major Winter Fair in each of two years, 1930 and 1931.

No wonder that the name of Charlie Rear was known wherever there was horsebreeding in Western Canada and even in Eastern Canada. We were told of a Federal Inspector calling at the home of a French-Canadian farmer in Old Quebec and being shown a stallion which, according to the owner, had been bought from a man

> "who lives away out on the prairies. I cannot remember his name but he has more stallions than any man in the world. I give him some cash and I promise to send him more but he not leave me his name or where he live and I cannot send money. I have $200 to send but my wife she will not let me send because I should know what that man's name. Maybe you tell me name."

Said the inspector, "Would it be Charlie Rear?" "That is the man," replied the Quebecker, "I will send him $200."

Obviously Rear wasn't too good in handling money. He was much more interested in horses than in money. With his mind so occupied with horses, it was difficult to do justice to the routine things in life. When he went to buy a rail ticket to Saskatoon, following the Calgary Spring Show in 1940, he left his club bag on a station seat and then remembered that he wanted to see a stallion in the country. Ignoring the time of the train's departure, he beckoned a taxi and drove out to see the horse. After an absence of four hours, he returned to find his club bag where he left it in the depot and the cheques and $800 in cash which "happened to be in the bag", quite undisturbed.

A little absent minded, that's true. But so are most great men. Rear wasn't one to observe regular hours. The necessity of eating and sleeping regularly was just a nuisance. After travelling a good deal at nights, on one occasion, he arrived in Saskatoon at an early morning hour and observed to one of those associated with him, that he must drive to Turtleford, 150 miles or so away, immediately. He was a bit tired and asked his co-worker to go with him. The car was filled with gasoline and while the younger man took the wheel without asking questions about the business reasons for the trip, Mr. Rear curled up on the back seat and went to sleep. Arriving at Turtleford at noon, the sleeping Charlie was awakened. He stretched and said, "Jim, what did we come here for?" Jim explained that he had not been told. He didn't know; Charlie Rear couldn't recall and so they had dinner and drove leisurely back to Saskatoon, talking horse all the way no doubt.

I recall saying "farewell" to him one evening as he was about to leave Saskatoon for Toronto. Four days later, I received a post-card from him, written in Vancouver.

He was regarded as one of the best judges of Percheron and Belgian horses in his time and his services were in demand at major shows, in all parts of Canada. He held offices in numerous horse breeders organizations, Dominion and Provincial. He was at home wherever good horses were bred and kept on the North American continent. A letter sent while he was visiting in Toronto one time carried this address, "Charlie Rear, Care of any Toronto Horseman, Toronto." Charlie Rear got the letter.

For awhile in 1944 and early 1945, he was a sick man and his friends were worried. He was not one to impose his grief on anyone. He was "better every day" according to himself. But he died in Saskatoon on March 12, 1945, age 64 years, and stockmen and showmen across Canada said, "We will miss Charlie".

Oh yes, Charlie Rear could enjoy a good horse of any type

or any breed. Good horses made life rich and worth while. Good horses could make him forget to go to dinner. He was kind to horses, fed them well, sometimes too well with over-fattness the result. It hurt him to see horses which were thin or showing the effect of abuse. When the Saskatchewan Percheron Club offered for perpetual showring competition, the C. M. Rear Memorial Shield, it was to commemorate the memory of an unusual gentleman, a great horseman.

Frank Collicutt

The One and Only

The name is Frank Collicutt, one of the best known names in the live stock fraternity. And didn't he start from "scratch"! His first job was that of "newsy" on the Calgary and Edmonton Railroad, just after it was completed in the autum of 1891 when the rails stopped at the south side of the river at the Edmonton end. But young Collicutt had no intention of railroading for very long. He was going to be a cattleman; and a great cattleman he did become.

He was born in New Brunswick (March 27, 1877) and in the spring of 1889, the family set out for Calgary. Great stories were told about opportunities out west. The Collicutts would farm. A place was bought three miles north of Calgary and there the family lived for two years with Frank getting a bit more education in Calgary schools. The first farm was sold and the family moved to a piece of land just south of the site on which the Alberta Stock Yards were located later.

Young Frank was 15 years old that year when the trains began to operate over the Calgary and Edmonton line and selling papers gave him the first dollars he could call his own. Mighty big dollars they were! Wasn't much of a job; papers aren't alive like grass and cattle but just the same the work gave him a chance to meet a lot of good people. He met Pat Burns, the chubby young Irishman, who was always in a hurry and whose cattle and meat business was growing bigger every day. He also met Frank Oliver, that dynamic publisher and statesman, who had ox-carted his way to Edmonton in 1876.

These two Franks met every time the train went north to Edmonton. Frank Oliver would come across the Saskatchewan River on Jock Walter's Ferry, carrying an armful of his papers, the Edmonton *Bulletin*, hot off the press for Frank Collicutt to sell on the train. Jock Walters, by the way, had dragged the cable for his ferry all the way from Winnipeg, using a pair of oxen, in 1884. Young Collicutt received more than papers from Oliver. Each time they met he received sound advice. Said the older gentleman, "Get yourself some good land laddie, and watch this country steam ahead".

Frank Collicutt was 18 years of age when he went to work for Pat Burns. Herding cattle on the Burns Ranch at Olds was his first job. After a year, he hired with Gordon, Ironside & Fares and three years later he began buying cattle and dealing on his own account. It gave him an opportunity to know every corner of the cattle country and Frank Collicutt was quietly deciding where he wanted to locate to raise cattle for himself.

By 1900, his mind was made up. He bought a section of land 25 miles north of Calgary. It looked like ideal cattle country with lots of grass and spring water. It was the nucleus of the famous Willow Springs Ranch and gradually the ranch was enlarged.

Settlers were flocking into Alberta and the supply of breeding cattle was short. Frank Collicutt sensed opportunity and in four years he shipped 14,000 head of Manitoba cows and heifers into Alberta territory. But, after the severe winter of 1906-07 which left dead cattle everywhere, the Manitoba cattle were no longer popular. The "dogies" from Manitoba farms didn't know how to look after themselves in a bad winter. And so, Collicutt went back to work for Pat Burns in the spring of 1908, and remained until 1914.

Travelling over the Alberta country in those days afforded lots of rich experience—and some not so rich. A chap by the name of Russell had a place on the Red Deer River about where Drumheller is now and had some cattle ready for market. Sure, Frank Collicutt would drive out to see the cattle. He drove into Russell's farm yard late one afternoon and learned that Mr. Russell had gone to Rosebud. But Mrs. Russell was there and Frank was invited to stable his horses and wait. "Feed up your team", she said, "and come on into the house because supper will soon be ready." The team was stabled and then Mrs. Russell came to her visitor and said, "I need help, can you operate a ferry?" The correct answer would have been "no", but the pioneer said he would try anything until it bucked him off. The problem was that the hired men were haying on the north side of the river and Mr. Russell was supposed to be home in time to bring the men and teams across at quitting time.

It was now quitting time. The men were waiting on the other side of the river and the ferry was on this side. Mrs. Russell confessed she knew nothing about the ferry but, anyway she and the willing Frank Collicutt got on and began to pull ropes and move things. Nothing happened, so they pulled some more ropes and, strange to say, the ferry leaned into the current and moved away from the shore. But in midstream, the ferry stopped and no amount of coaxing and no amount of selected adjectives would make it move. Minutes passed that seemed like hours. The Russell home and a hot supper were on one side. The hired help and teams were on the other and a man and a woman who had never met before were in the middle of the river. Mrs. Russell said: "What's your name?" The answer was, "Frank Collicutt, but I'm a cattleman and not a sailor, and all the things those hired men of yours are saying about me, aren't true". Well, it was getting dark and everybody felt helpless and mad. And then, for no apparent reason, something happened and the ferry began to move toward the north bank. The situation was saved but, after that, when Frank Collicutt had to cross a river, he usually chose to ride a good horse.

It was early in 1912 that Frank Collicutt made a start in pure bred Hereford cattle by purchasing 140 breeding cows and heifers from Baxter Reed Ranch Co. of Olds. The cows in that group were mostly bred in England and imported to the United States before being bought by Mr. Reed for his Alberta ranch. Frank Collicutt realized the importance of selecting superior sires for his herd of well bred cows. The first selections were bulls carrying the names Drumsticks and Governor Hadley, both of which were from the herd of Warren T. McCray of Kentland, Indiana. Then there was a succession of even more noted bulls at Willow Springs Ranch. There were Beau Perfection 11th and Fairfax Perfection, and in 1917 Collicutt astonished the Canadian cattlemen by going to the Harris & Sons' Sale in Missouri and buying the bull Gay Lad 40th for $11,900.00. The record does not end there because a year later, the noted Hereford bull Gay Lad 16th, which had come to Alberta at $20,000.00 became the property of Mr. Collicutt.

And those good bulls left their mark on the big herd at Willow Springs. It was a big herd. By 1916 it numbered 600 head of registered Herefords and by 1922, Mr. Collicutt's 800 registered cattle constituted the biggest herd of pure bred Herefords in the world.

Willow Springs cattle went out to the shows and won the highest honours; at Calgary, over the Western Exhibition circuit and at the Toronto Royal Winter Fair, it was the same. Frank Collicutt's son, George, became a master fitter and showman and helped to bring glory to the Willow Springs Ranch and to the Province of Alberta.

Some of the most exciting show ring battles staged on Western soil were at Calgary in 1917 and 1918, when the imported Herefords, cream of the American herds, were

THE ONE AND ONLY FRANK COLLICUTT

Courtesy of William Bradley

vieing for honours. In that notable year of 1918, one of the most exciting in Hereford history, the Calgary championship for males went to Collicutt's Gay Lad 16th, and the championship for females went to Collicutt's cow Sally. Collicutt had both champions and then sold the calf, yet unborn, from those two aristocrats, for the sum of $1000.00. Not a bad price for a calf nobody had ever seen, but at least it had a good chance of inheriting the stuff that makes champions.

And through the years Frank Collicutt continued to breed and show winners. At every one of the first eighteen Royal Winter Fairs at Toronto, Frank Collicutt was an exhibitor. At Kamloops in 1945, he said, "I'll bring you a Grand Champion for your sale next year". Sure enough, in March 1946, at one of the last bull sales to which he contributed, one of his bulls was made Grand Champion and then sold for $3,000.00.

But my friend, Frank Collicutt, was more than the businessman and the cattleman. He was the pioneer gentleman, resourceful, yes, but oh so kindly. If he had a string of bulls at Kamloops or Calgary and somebody was tagging for the Red Cross, Frank Collicut was likely to say, "take a bull". And the bull would be auctioned off with all the proceeds going to that charitable cause. When I stood with him at Kamloops one year, the Red Cross representative said, "Mr. Collicutt, which bull are you giving for the Red Cross this year?" And the answer was, "the best one, the one that fetches the most money". It always seemed marvellous that any one, who gave so freely to needy folk and needy institutions, could have anything left. But to Frank Collicutt, there was no better use for money than helping people.

And there were few better horsemen. The hours he spent in the saddle would add up to many years. There were times when speed was important, but still no means of transportation appealed so strongly as his saddle horse. When I talked with him in the spring of 1946, when he was considering going to Panama for a daughter's wedding he said, "I w'd like to fly down there, but I don't know how I w'd get along because I've never been on anything higher than a saddle horse in my life".

I told him once I was coming out to the ranch for a visit. He said, "it will take us a couple of days to get used to you, so you must stay at least a week". That was the brand of hospitality dispensed at Willow Springs, the brand for which the Alberta Foothills were famous. Mrs. Collicutt was Miss Murdock and she, too, was an Alberta pioneer, her father being George Murdock, Calgary's first mayor.

In October 1946, it was announced that the famous Willow Springs Ranch including 2700 acres of land, about 300 pure bred Herefords, some horses and machinery, was sold to Mr. Inwall Sundal of Picture Butte, who would take over on June 1st, 1947. But it was a stipulation, written into the agreement of sale that a bedroom in the old stone ranch house would be reserved for Frank Collicutt as long as he lived. The pioneer rancher was retiring, but he had no intention of living very far from his foothills and the grassland on which his beloved Herefords had grazed and grown fat through the years.

Kootenai Brown

When I visit lovely Waterton Lakes in Southern Alberta, I think I can see, with my mind's eye, a magnetic figure of a man dressed in leather. He is slender and wiry and he has a rare twinkle in his eye that betrays good humour and a life of adventure. He is John George Brown, but on account of trading and associating with Kootenai Indians, he is best known as Kootenai Brown.

Early Southern Alberta had other Browns, picturesque characters, all of them. There was Jeb Brown and "Diamond R" Brown and "7 U" Brown and "Poker" Brown and "Bull" Brown, known for his many work oxen. But most colourful of the Browns was "Kootenai". A man of amazing resources, was Kootenai Brown. He was scholar, sailor, army officer, prospector, cowpuncher and buffalo hunter, and ultimately he was park superintendent in the pay of the Dominion Government. On top of all that, he conducted some farming and did the first cultivation on the soil of what is now Southern Alberta.

But where did this soldier of fortune hail from? And what brought him to the Foothills? Kootenai Brown was an Englishman, born in 1839. He was educated at Eton and Oxford. Throughout his life on the Canadian frontier, he bore the mark of the scholar. His journals were written with clarity and accuracy and the rough bookshelves in his log cabin were lined with the works of Shakespeare, Tennyson, Byron, Goldsmith and others of their kind.

With school-days past, young Brown joined the Imperial Army and was gazetted an ensign in the Queen's Lifeguards. But according to story, he became too friendly with the ladies in Court and was sent away to India. In India, so the tale goes, somebody got into the path of a pistol bullet and John George Brown developed a strong urge to see South America, without delay. From South America he walked north across Panama and continued on foot until in '62 he reached San Francisco.

He was ready for any challenge. The first to present itself was the report about gold in the British Columbia Cariboo. He trekked north to Barkerville, but met with no particular luck in the hunt for the yellow metal. He heard about strikes on the North Saskatchewan River. In the spring of 1865, Brown and three or four other gold seekers made up their minds to cross the plains. They had several horses; they climbed mountains; they swam rivers; they packed through the South Kootenai Pass and came out on to the plains. From the last point of vantage before leaving the mountains, Brown looked down upon the blue water of a lake girdled with mountains. It was his first glimpse of Waterton Lakes. Back of it all, the prairie grassland was "black with buffalo". "This," he said to himself, "is what George Brown has dreamed about; this is better than gold."

But Brown didn't stop at that time. There was a good reason. He and his party were being pursued by a band of Indians on a scalp-hunt. Scalps are difficult to replace, so the white men, instead of stopping to enjoy the scenery, pressed on eastward. About where Medicine Hat is now situated they had a battle with Indians, but managed to come out of it without any major loss. Brown went on to Fort Garry, then to Duck Lake where he spent the winter and in the spring, back to Fort Garry.

But all the while, Brown was thinking about those blue waters up against the mountains and about a year and a half later, (1868) he returned to squat on land which surveyors of years later marked as section 31, township 1, range 29, West of 4th Meridian. He cut logs; he built a cabin and a stable and he began to cultivate some land. It was the first cultivation in what is now Alberta, outside of a little at Fort Edmonton.

He made excursions into the mountains. He travelled across prairie to Duck Lake and Fort Garry. He went deep into United States territory, but always he returned to his beloved Waterton Lakes. Nothing which he had seen on his travels on four continents had cast such a spell over him as Waterton. Perhaps it was the ghost of Sokumapi whose name is linked with the Indian legend explaining a miraculous creation for Waterton.

That region, according to the legend, was not always so beautiful and peaceful. On the contrary, it was flat and treeless and dry. Among the Indians living there was a young brave called Sokumapi who was whisked away by the Seven Devils who ruled the underworld. While in slavery to the devils, the young brave fell in love with a maiden who was captive like himself. They planned escape and while their captors slept, they slipped away, taking with them a bucket of water, a stick and a stone which turned out to possess magic properties. When the devils awakened, they pursued the fleeing lovers and were about to overtake them as they reached the area close to the present Waterton Lakes. Sokumapi threw down the stick and immediately it became a forest of trees, retarding the progress of the pursuing devils. The pursuers came again however, and were gaining when Sokumapi dropped the stone and saw it become a mountain, protecting the fugitives. The water, when spilled upon the ground, became a lake and the bucket became a canoe. In the canoe, the lovers crossed the lake. The Seven Devils never again found the residents who lived about the beautiful lake, enjoying safety and peace. Needless to say, the spirits of Sokumapi and his sweetheart linger peacefully in the Waterton Lakes region to this day.

Well Kootenai Brown was not the first white man to see Waterton Lakes, but he was the first to call that area his home. It seemed most logical that when the region of Waterton Lakes was declared a National Park, the frontiersman Brown was named the first warden and then Acting Superintendent.

Although Brown was the first to cultivate land in that south-west country, it must be understood that he had many other interests. He hunted buffalo and witnessed the destruction of the great herds; he traded with the Indians; he served as guide and interpreter and he was interested in cattle and oil. There are several stories, not quite alike, about the discovery of oil in the mountains. What is most common to all versions however, is that Brown asked the Stoney Indians to be on the alert for a fluid that looked and smelled like a mixture of kerosene and molasses. They did discover the stuff and drilling began in the mountains in 1901, but after a short-lived boom, the well gave out.

Kootenai Brown and his friend, Fred Kanouse, were the ones with whom Senator Cochrane of Quebec met up as he drove a buckboard and pair of bronchos in from Fort Benton, Montana, early in 1881. The Senator was there to determine for himself if range cattle would survive and prosper. Brown and Kanouse could speak with authority and later in that year the first Cochrane herd, numbering 3,000 cattle, was driven in from Fort Benton, Montana. It was the first of the big herds to move on to Alberta range. Brown had seen many winters in that country before the herds came in and he advised the cattlemen to put up some hay as a protection against a bad season. This advice was not accepted by many of the ranchers until some costly demonstrations showed that Brown was right.

This same Brown was of much assistance to the Mounted Police when they came to be his neighbours in 1874. He knew the country, the climate, the Indians and the law-breakers a lot better than the new policemen and they took his direction. And they tried to emulate his marksmanship. With a six-shooter. Kootenai Brown had a deadly aim. There were those who saw him shoot the heads off prairie chicken, one after another. The revolver holster was a standard part of his attire, and the weapons it carried were loaded and ready for use on short notice.

Kootenai Brown died in 1916 and was buried in a plot on the shore of Lower Waterton Lakes, quite close to the park highway. And buried beside him in the plot are his two wives, one on each side.

Brown's first wife was a half-breed woman from North Dakota and the second wife was a Cree whom he got in a trade. He had an eye for beauty, both in natural scenery and in women, and when a band of Saskatchewan Crees came to trade, Brown's wandering eye fell upon a very pretty young squaw. He wanted her for his wife. Two horses were offered but they were not enough to entice the Indian father into parting with his daughter. Three horses were offered and finally Kootenai secured his squaw at the extravagant price of five horses. But as time was to show, it was a good investment for him, because she proved to be devoted and faithful throughout his life. The worst thing about her was her name, which was Chee-Pay-Tha-Qua-Ka-Soon, meaning "Flash of Blue Lightning". Kootenai Brown shortened her name for his own use, called her Neech-e-mouse, meaning loved one; but he made very sure that others paid his wife proper respect and to them she was Mrs. Brown.

Once, Brown made the mistake of bringing a white girl home. The Flash of Blue Lightning flashed. She would have none of that. She left to return to her people. But Brown recognized his mistake and followed her, and promised that such an error of judgment would not be made again.

Brown died before his Cree wife. He told his faithful squaw that he would return as an eagle. When an aeroplane landed there some time after Brown's death, she became excited, called to her Kootenai and rushed to caress the machine.

In most respects Kootenai Brown depicted the spirit of the Western Frontier. Certainly he was more colourful and more daring than the average, but he was also loyal and friendly and generous. He was one for whom danger held no fears. He was loved by his friends and respected by all others.

Friends and acquaintances, wishing to commemorate his name, erected a stone cairn with tablet affixed, in the Waterton Park, in 1936. Those friends and acquaintances could never forget the inimitable Kootenai Brown, but they were anxious that future generations should know about him too.

Courtesy of R.C.M.P.

KOOTENAI BROWN

The Man Murray

I don't suppose anybody left a more vivid mark upon the youthful face of Western Canada than the late Walter C. Murray of Saskatchewan. It wasn't just what he did but it was the "Murray-way" he had of doing it that made him loved. He distinguished himself as a philosopher and he was a great educator but more than that, he was distinguished for his tremendous capacity for friendship. He was a great Canadian.

I was engaged by the University of Saskatchewan in the spring of 1928 but it was several weeks before I met the president. Then one day a man came into my new office and offered his hand and said, "My name is Murray". His kindly informality didn't somehow suggest a University President and I asked, "What department are you in?" He chuckled a typical Murray chuckle and said, "I Work in the President's office and if you get into trouble give me a call".

Walter Charles Murray was born at Studholm in King's County, New Brunswick, on May 12, 1866. He said that county had produced more good intentions than any area of similar size in the world, but that Pictou County over in Nova Scotia was still in the lead for foreign missionaries and college professors.

From the local schools, young Murray went to the University of New Brunswick and graduated in 1886, a distinguished gold medalist. He was awarded a scholarship which permitted him to pursue graduate studies overseas and he elected philosophy at the University of Edinburgh. Leaving Edinburgh he travelled in Europe and studied in Berlin and then returned to become Professor of Philosophy at his own University of New Brunswick. Dalhousie University wanted him and got him in 1892, and there he remained until 1908 when he accepted the challenge of the new North-West.

The Province of Saskatchewan was created in 1905 and two years later, under Premier Walter Scott, an act was passed establishing the University of Saskatchewan. A Board of

Governors was appointed in January 1908, and in August of that year, the Board persuaded Dalhousie's magnetic young Professor of Philosophy to become the first president. Momentous decisions had to be made. First there was the site of the provincial University. Battleford and Regina, as well as Saskatoon, were making strong bids for it. Saskatoon won. And then when the new president saw the site for the first time, an old she-coyote was emerging from her den just where College Building now stands. Incidently there is still an occasional wolf around there.

Then there was the relationship of the College of Agriculture to the University which had to be determined. Murray had a vision of a Provincial University dedicated to service, a vision of a peoples' University. It was to be the servant of an agricultural area, conducting useful research, and turning out able leaders, and raising cultural standards. An Agricultural college there must certainly be; but where?

Tradition said the college of Agriculture should be separated by a safe distance from the University but Murray had other ideas. As one of my friends observed, Murray "did not establish another University—he founded a new one". And after Minister of Agriculture Motherwell had been convinced that Murray was right, the decision was made to place the College of Agriculture along with the College of Arts & Science at the very heart of the new University. Murray started it and the other three Provincial Universities in Western Canada adopted it. That decision and the intimate relationship between the University and the agricultural community, gave the president his biggest pride in after years.

Well, President Murray had a Provincial University on his hands and no place to put it. Temporary quarters were secured in the Drinkle Building on 3rd Avenue in Saskatoon and 70 students registered in Arts & Science for the first term which began at the last of September, in 1909. The Arts faculty in addition to President Murray consisted of Professors G. W. Ling, E. H. Oliver, R. J. Bateman and Arthur Moxon. And President Murray's original Agricultural Faculty, also set up that year, consisted of Dean Rutherford and Professors Alexander Greig and John Bracken.

On July 29, 1910, Sir Wilfrid Laurier laid the corner stone

for the building now known as College Building and it was opened for use in October, 1912. It was the first of a series of beautiful Greystone buildings, Collegiate Gothic in style. It was a brilliant blue-print for a peoples' University, that was drawn by "Architect" Murray and gradually the plan took form to make the Saskatchewan campus one of the most lovely in Canada. The prehistoric glaciers which brought down those mighty limestone boulders from which the University buildings were constructed, received "Honorary Degrees in Absentia" quite regularly from Dr. Murray. Admittedly, he didn't realize when he picked New Brunswick field rocks in his youth, that stones could be so beautiful and so beneficial to education. Those limestone buildings will always be a memorial to the first president.

The faculty of Arts & Science and faculty of Agriculture were the two originals. Then came Engineering, Law, Pharmacy, Accounting, Summer School, Medicine, Education, Household Science, Music, and so on. It was a phenomenal expansion.

But nobody could accuse Walter Murray of being interested only in Saskatchewan. He also responded to the call for public service in many parts of Canada. In the course of time he was to go from one Royal Commission to another. Incidently the first commission upon which he was called to serve was in Nova Scotia when the railroad freight handlers went on strike. There he was associated with a lifelong friend, Clarence McKinnon, and a satisfactory settlement was secured. But what Mrs. Murray remembered and enjoyed was that before the freight handlers went back to work after the settlement, she and her daughters were leaving Halifax for a holiday and Commissioner Murray was obliged to carry the family trunks and load them on the rail cars single handed. Again in 1931 he was appointed to a Royal Commission investigating transportation in the Dominion.

For a time he was chairman of the Board of Trustees for the Carnegie Foundation. In his later years he was chairman of the Board of Governors of Saskatoon City Hospital and served in important posts in his church. In fact, he had his fingers in everything that was for good.

Dr. Murray's relationship to his students was extremely

happy. He got along well with them. He could call most of them by name and actually he knew a great deal about the individual problems confronting them. In student affairs, his policy showed how well he understood that students should be self-governing to a reasonable degree and his students didn't let him down. In those later years when they met to express their loyalty and love, he didn't use many words, but the tears which filled his eyes said a lot.

He loved clean sport and he followed the student teams with most enthusiastic interest. He loved it when Saskatchewan made a brilliant play and he loved it when a wee laddie met him at the door of Knox Church one Sunday morning and said, "You're the boss of the University aren't you; well you're going to lose the hockey game against Edmonton tomorrow night unless you get a different goalie".

No one enjoyed good humour more than Murray and there was no lack of originality in his own. The first two dormitories on his campus, Saskatchewan Hall and Qu'Appelle Hall, were called after two rivers in the province. He threatened to call the next one Carrot Hall. It was his observation that "the modern pastime known as necking had done more to discourage the habit of tobacco chewing than a thousand years of reform". In 1937, that unforgettable drought year, we were having trouble to get the stock to eat the only roughage we recovered, Russian thistle hay. Dr. Murray had a solution. Put a fence around the stack and he said the cattle would be sure to show a new appreciation. It worked according to Dr. Murray with buckwheat straw in New Brunswick.

In training, Walter Murray was a philosopher but all through the years, nothing gave him greater satisfaction than his associations with agriculture. In the formative years, he conferred with Dean Rutherford in the planning of the University barns and the laying out of the fields. And he watched the horses and cattle and sheep, and pigs. He loved growing things and enjoyed nothing more than strolling through the barns and talking to the horses.

Though he had that great interest in animals, he had a great and sympathetic love for people. I recall that when sugar rationing came into effect in 1942, a certain little girl remarked sadly that there would be no sugar now for her pony. The great and sympathetic gentleman meditated. That pony should have some sugar and from that day forward, three lumps of sugar were delivered every Tuesday afternoon following the weekly Kiwanis luncheon at the Bessborough Hotel. Yes, the man with Honorary Degrees from Queen's University, McMaster, McGill, Alberta, Manitoba, Saskatchewan and Wisconsin, was never too busy to do those kindly little things which endeared him to thousands. Nothing in his full and busy life was more important than helping somebody who needed his help, even to the little girl who was short of sugar for her pony. It just seemed that nearly all the little people of his acquaintance had bicycle funds, or toboggan funds, or pony funds, to which the great man with a passion for sharing, subscribed regularly.

I was riding with him in his car one day when we encountered an old sheep herder on the trail, 15 miles south of Saskatoon. We chatted with the old timer as he munched his evening meal on the roadside. We learned that he was out of tea and out of tobacco. That could be serious. We returned to Saskatoon in sufficient time for our evening meal, but Dr. Murray couldn't stop; he phoned home to say he wouldn't be there. Instead of going home for supper he got a bottle of tea at one restaurant and a supply of tobacco at another and started back on a 30 mile drive, to bring a bit of cheer to the old shepherd whom he had never seen before.

If there was a Santa Claus in Saskatoon, his other name was Murray, and in those years of depression, no one will ever know how much aid and assistance he gave, nearly always anonymously. That was the way he helped a good many poor student along and that was the reason he was obliged, usually, to give a post-dated cheque when he was canvassed for Red Cross or the Community Chest. Money was not for hoarding or storing, it was for helping people in need. When a mysteriously ordered load of coal was delivered anonymously at the manse or a box of apples at the School for the Deaf, it had all the marks of a Walter Murray trick.

And speaking of Santa Claus, no one who had the thrill of attending a Murray Christmas Party could ever forget it. It began as an annual when the University faculty was small and it was mainly for the children but every mother and every dad connected with the University was invited. In later years the big Murray residence could scarcely hold the crowd. Dozens of wee ones, laughing and crying would be lined up at the long table for the party and the more milk that spilled down baby dresses and onto the polished floor, the more Dr. Murray chuckled.

Not much wonder that those who knew that man with such distinguished gifts of leadership and character, wanted to build a splendid and useful memorial to him. Many of the letters which came carried the most earnest expressions of admiration.

In his last months, Dr. Murray was a sick man. In the autumn before he died, he paid me a fine compliment. He had a premonition that his time was short and he asked me one day to see that certain of his self-assigned jobs were not neglected. There was a soldier overseas whose mother in Saskatoon might need some special assistance; there was a certain tree to be planted on Memorial Avenue for "one of the boys"; there was a job in Knox Church which would require attention. He was far too busy to die; but he "broke camp" on March 23, 1945, age 79, and men and women in all provinces and in all walks of life, mourned his going. They mourned the passing of one of God's gentlemen, a noble Canadian, a man who loved his fellows and lived to make Canada a better place.

The Horticulturist of Dropmore

When the University of Manitoba, on May 16th, 1947, conferred an honorary degree upon a "man of the soil", it was something of an innovation, but folk said, "that's great; nothing could be more fitting". The little "man of the soil" was Frank Leith Skinner, M.B.E., and the honour recognized his outstanding contributions as a progressive pioneer farmer, an eminent plant breeder and a fine gentleman.

It seems a far cry from fish curing in Aberdeenshire to lily growing in Manitoba, but that is part of the story. The Skinner fish business was going well until a major disaster was encountered late in 1894. Frank Skinner's father had a boatload of cured fish on the way to Danzig. Prices slipped and then collapsed. Not only did the cargo of fish fail to meet the costs, but there was an additional loss-charge of half a crown per barrel. The Skinners were ruined. Everything they owned had to be sold and the elder Skinner, more than a little humiliated, went to work making barrels for some of those men who had previously been his employees.

The experiences of that year were heartbreaking. The family decision was to try something else, try anything, try Canada. Frank Skinner, the youngest member of the family, was 13 years old that spring of 1895 when the family set sail for Canada. A half-brother had gone to Manitoba in 1882, worked on the railroad grade and selected a homestead where the first C.P.R. survey gave prospect of a railroad running northwest from Winnipeg. His money helped to bring the Skinners to Canada and they went directly to Russell, Manitoba, and then to the homestead community where they had the shelter of the brother's log cabin.

The newcomers looked around, chose land which they fancied and squatted. Legal claim mattered little in those years when there was so much land and were so few settlers. A year later, the father filed on the homestead which, in after years, was part of Frank Skinner's farm and in due course, the youthful Frank filed on one also.

The homesteads were 30 miles from the nearest railroad, a fair distance to go for supplies or to post a letter. And, when there were urgent reasons for going to town, the distance was just as great. When young Frank developed a violent toothache and had endured it as long as he could, he rode horseback to Russell. At the end of the 30 mile ride, incidentally, the infected tooth wasn't the sorest part of his anatomy. The pioneer dentist's rough technique didn't make matters any better, and the lad concluded that he might have had some blacksmith nearer home do the job.

With so much good grass in that sparsely settled land, the Skinners decided to keep cattle. Frank and his brother together ran up to 400 head. Frank rode over hundreds of square miles of that country, following the roaming cattle. If he wasn't hunting or driving cattle, he was studying the native flowers and plants.

The life of a cowboy is not without hazard. When Frank Skinner and his helper went mounted on one occasion to recover a wild cow, which had left the herd, they managed to get two ropes on the angry beast, and were escorting her homeward. But a loop of rope got on her foot and Frank Skinner concluded that he must get off his horse to straighten it. Immediately he set foot upon the ground, the cow charged and upset him. The other cowboy's rope was too slack and the cow seized what she supposed was an opportunity to exterminate this human creature. Frank Skinner's position on his back on the ground was not a nice one, but he found that by fighting with his feet he could be fairly effective in holding off the attacking cow until his mounted partner tightened his rope and hauled the cow away. He was pretty lucky or he could not have said, in coming out of the combat, that his pride was the only part that was badly hurt.

Frank Skinner's operations grew steadily bigger until he was farming 700 acres, of which 70 acres were devoted to intensive horticulture and nursery work. As a commercial nurseryman, he ultimately grew more stock than any other in Western Canada, and he had customers all the way from Yukon to Colorado and from Newfoundland and New York to the Pacific. Yes, he was shipping bulbs to Europe and lilies to Holland, if you please.

The nursery business began as a hobby. Actually, Frank Skinner had an insatiable fondness for plants from boyhood days in Scotland. According to his mother, he was transplanting things at the age of five, and "pulling the plants up daily to see if they were taking root". In the early years in Manitoba, Frank Skinner's spare time was spent studying the native plants and working in his most ambitiously planned garden. By 1912 he was breeding roses. Breeding ornamentals in the homestead districts did seem preposterous, but there he was, quietly laying the foundation for unusual service to his new land.

A series of circumstances caused Mr. Skinner to launch into the nursery business. For years, the surplus ornamentals and fruit plants from the Skinner farm were distributed to friends and others without charge. But farming operations, which were profitable up to 1919, took a sudden change for the worse. The farm was a source of loss in 1920 and '21, and it became necessary to obtain other revenue.

Then, by some coincidence, Mr. Skinner's place was visited by a high-powered deputation of Horticulturists. It was 1921. As the touring party, including some visitors from the United States, reached Winnipeg, some of the members concluded they had gone far enough. The idea of going to Dropmore to see what some remote farmer-plant breeder was doing didn't seem awfully exciting. Professor William Alderman of the University of Minnesota made the trip, however, and he was accompanied by M. B. Davis, at that time Assistant to the Dominion Horticulturist, and George Chipman of Winnipeg. Professor Alderman may have considered the possibility of encountering polar bears and Eskimos, but he was due for a pleasant surprise. What he saw in the way of horticultural achievement opened his eyes. He saw the first hardy pear (Pyrus ussuriansis) in Western Canada, a Siberian pear, which Mr. Skinner secured through the Arnold Arboretum in 1918, and he saw flowers and shrubs and horticultural treasures which astonished and thrilled him.

The visitors filled Frank Skinner with encouragement. They convinced him that this had been a hobby long enough and that he should share what he had with more people in Western Canada and elsewhere. The result was that Skinner's

Dropmore Nursery Stock went on the market late in 1921. He continued with his farming operations, raised cattle and grew grain. But the nursery business expanded at a notable rate and was ultimately keeping fifteen or more men busy for most of each year.

Through the years, Mr. Skinner's constant search for new plants took him to many parts of the continent. In 1910 he made his first trip to the Pacific Coast and after that he spent a great deal of time in Northern British Columbia, Northern Ontario and as far south as Colorado. In his later years, his correspondents included horticulturists in many parts of the world, including Europe and Asia.

The tangible evidences of his achievements were many. Somehow, between one day's work and another, he found time to write many articles for popular and scientific journals. He gave to the West and to the world an imposing list of new varieties of plants. Betty Bland Rose was one of his contributions and the Mandarin Plum was another. Many of the one hundred or so new plant varieties which he produced or introduced were the result of his contacts with North Asia and other far distant parts of the world.

Horticultural workers elsewhere may have been late in learning of Skinner, but they recognized enthusiastically the merit of his work. He was the first recipient of the Stevenson Memorial Medal (1932), given for outstanding contributions to Prairie Horticulture, on either side of the International Boundary. In 1937, he received the Minnesota Horticultural Society Bronze Medal for "the most meritorious contribution to horticulture in the North-West". He was named a Fellow of the Royal Horticultural Society of England. He was awarded the Cory Cup by the Royal Horticultural Society of England for his Maxwell Lily, which he produced and displayed in London in 1933. He received the Award of the Alpine Garden Show in London, England, and he became a Member of the British Empire, in the George VI Royal Birthday Honours List 1943.

It was a distinguished record but, best of all, he was still a Manitoba farmer and very proud of it. When The University of Manitoba conferred upon him the Honorary Degree of LL.D. it was to a farmer, horticultural explorer, plant breeder and a great Canadian citizen. And, by the way, he was a bachelor.

I think of those lines from Whittier:

Give fools their gold,
And knaves their power;
Let fortune's bubbles
Rise and fall;
Who sows a field,
Or plants a flower,
Or trains a tree
Is more than all.

Manitoba Cattle Barron

There was nothing very dramatic about this sodbuster, John Barron. He didn't hang loaded guns on his belt, he didn't fight Indians and he didn't even go about making high-powered political speeches, at least not often. But he was one of the solid pioneers who started with nothing more than a ten-dollar farm and remained to become one of the leading agriculturists of the West.

He was born at Elora, Ontario, in 1850, and grew up close to the limestone rocks of the Grand River and close to the famous Shorthorn breeding establishment founded by Alexander Watt. The Watt cattle were broad-backed, thickly fleshed and royally bred. They filled young Barron with admiration and they fired him with determination. "Yes sir," said the lad to himself, "breeding better cattle is a high calling and some day I must have my own Shorthorns."

His first job near home was burning lime at fifty cents a day. But it would take too long to save the money he needed for a farm that way so he was tempted to face the hazards of the new North-West. It was a terrific decision, but he decided in favour of the frontier. He arrived at Winnipeg after a three weeks' journey. It was 1878 and he was one year ahead of the rails to Winnipeg. He continued west, and didn't stop until he sunk his heels into the good mud of Carberry Plains. The particular piece of land which caught his fancy and on which he settled was three miles north of where Carberry is now situated. That was the beginning of Fairview Farm.

John Barron was homesteading in a land still filled with uncertainty. Before many seasons he was to taste numerous varieties of hardship. He was to know the terrifying isolation produced by a three-day prairie blizzard; he was to feel the moral let-down of an August frost which left a ruined crop behind it; he learned what it was to harvest the hard way and thresh in the snow; they threshed until Christmas in 1890. And he experienced the horror of a crimson glow on the horizon which told that a prairie fire was advancing.

Isolation produced various problems. The nearest medical doctor was at Winnipeg and if plough shares had to be sharpened, there was nobody nearer than Portage la Prairie, who could do the job. One couldn't even get married without importing a minister. But "love will find a way" and on December 22nd, 1879, Rev. George Roddick, the beloved pioneer minister at Brandon drove down to Carberry and married John Barron and Miss Helen Hope.

John Barron was here to stay. His sharp eyes were fixed upon the goal of balanced farming, productive fields and better livestock. Four years after his arrival, he bought his first pure bred heifer. Her name was Lady Fairview. Of course, she was a Shorthorn, and she was one of a very few pedigreed cattle in all the West at that time. Lady Fairview couldn't have attracted more attention in that homestead community, if she had been a halter-broken buffalo. She was a bovine queen in a vast new cattle kingdom and John Barron treated her with attention befitting royalty.

Herd building was slow when one had but a single pedigreed cow to begin with. But by saving nickles and dimes and foregoing everything that savoured of luxury, Barron was able to buy four select heifers from J. and W. Russell of Richmond, Ontario, in 1888. Then for a period of years he had the fortune to have a series of superior sires. In 1889, he bought the bull, Barrington Waterloo, and in '97 he bought Topsman, from the Russells of Ontario.

Old timers still talk about Topsman. He was about the greatest Shorthorn bull Western Canada had seen up to that time. He was built like a box-car but he had a cantankerous disposition, which seems to be a bull's perogative. When showing Topsman on one occasion, John Barron's new hat fell to the ground. "Christie Stiffs" didn't grow on willow bushes in those days and the frugal John paused to recover his prized new head-piece. But it was the wrong thing to do because it gave Topsman a chance to get his head down and launch an offensive. The bull seized the opportunity for which he had evidently waited and John Barron was rolled over and over before he managed to escape. Never again did he forget that handling a bull is a full time job and that "new hats are a lot cheaper than doctor bills and caskets".

John Barron took Topsman to the Winnipeg Exhibition in 1899 and there won the Grand Championship. A little later Topsman was sold to go back to Ontario where he added to his show-ring triumphs by winning the Grand Championship at Toronto Exhibition.

Year after year, John Barron's cattle went over the Western Exhibition circuit and accumulated innumerable prizes and Championships. He could have papered the inside of his house with prize ribbons. Probably the most famous of his show animals was the white heifer, Lavender 47th. He considered her to be the crowning achievement in a life-long undertaking. Best of all, she was bred and reared right there at Fairview. She won all around the Western circuit as a yearling in 1918; at Toronto that fall, she was reserve champion Shorthorn female, while Barron's bull, Lancaster Lad, was grand champion male.

In the next year, the white heifer was grand champion at Toronto and then she sold in November to G. C. Beaching, of De Winton, Alberta, for the record figure of $5,000. The man who fitted the famous heifer was George Morrison, another quiet Scotsman, who was Barron's herdsman in the later years. I've wondered whose heart was more nearly broken, John Barron's or George Morrison's when it was ultimately established that Lavender 47th was not a satisfactory breeder.

The farming people who secured foundation stock from John Barron were very numerous and his influence in livestock improvement was immeasurable. In 1919, when J. H. McCulloch and F. W. Crawford conducted an intensive study of Shorthorn Breeding in Western Canada, they drew certain pointed conclusions, among them that: "John Barron of Carberry, Manitoba, has won more prizes at Western Canada shows during the past five years than any other exhibitor." Further, that: "John Barron owned and developed four out of the eight bulls that led all others as sires of prize-winners at Western Canadian shows held during the past five years."

They were unique tributes. John Barron's triumphs were the fruits of perseverance. His herd was one of the great achievements in the history of Western Canadian agriculture. It was a herd built the hard way, not a herd put together with profits made from mining or speculating. His show herds were composed nearly always of home bred cattle. Often too, they were fitted by the master, himself. And he could show a beast the correct way. I remember watching him show Augusta Star in 1918. It was a serious business with the old gentleman, but it was well done. His erect posture, his sharp eyes and his little chin whisker which could scarcely substitute for a necktie, were all part of the show.

Western agriculture reaped much benefit from the constructive toil of John Barron. And as a token of appreciation, fellow cattlemen honoured Mr. and Mrs. Barron at a big banquet at Brandon, on April 3rd, 1919, and presented them with gold watches and sincere tributes.

John Barron was president of the Dominion Shorthorn Breeders' Association in 1920 and 1921. He gave good leadership. He took a fling at politics and contested his constituency of Norfolk in 1899 and lost by a small margin. But in his Municipality of Cypress, he was reeve or councillor, off and on for nearly thirty years. That showed what the local people thought of his judgment.

John Barron was a quiet man who minded his own affairs. One didn't get to know him over quickly. Duncan Marshall said he "played a lone hand". Indeed he was rather abrupt and it didn't do to leave his gate down after going through it or forget to return the hay rake borrowed for a day. He could explain his displeasure in very few words.

John Barron was all farmer. He was a big farmer, a broad minded and practical minded farmer. His cattle were healthy and fat and his soil was maintained in a good state of fertility. He hated weeds; he hated scrub bulls; he disliked salesmen and he didn't think much of those who broke the Sabbath. There was no more honest man in all the West. And as for his nature, I would contend that nobody is better able to judge than the hired men. And they were for the boss; they liked working for John Barron.

Ill health made it necessary for John Barron to disperse his herd in October, 1921. Cattle values were tobogganing and it was a bad time to sell. Prices were disappointing, but the pioneer said there was satisfaction in knowing that others were benefiting by his life-long efforts to produce better cattle. John Barron died on February 12, 1926.

